What Everyone Is Saying About Start Up

"Bill Stolze has an outstanding track record as an entrepreneur and as a business school teacher, and *Start Up* combines the best of both worlds. Start Up is well researched, clearly written and very logical—a perfect guide for anyone who wants to learn how to start and grow a business."
— Peter S. Prichard, author of *The Making of McPaper*,
president of the Freedom Forum,
and former editor of *USA Today*

"In my opinion this book contains important, fundamental reading for any person considering entering the world of entrepreneurism. Bill Stolze has 'been there' and he knows how to help others achieve."
— Tom Golisano, founder and chairman,
Paychex, Inc.

"The health of the American economy—and its competitiveness in world markets—is increasingly dependent upon the work of the American entrepreneur. Bill Stolze's book—*Start Up*—provides an invaluable tool to anyone thinking of starting his or her own business. For those of us in Washington, it provides great insight regarding how public policy can best help the most dynamic sector of American business."
— Congressman John J. LaFalce, N.Y., chairman of House Committee
On Small Business for eight years (1987-1994),
and now ranking minority member

"The merit of this offering is not in its science—it is in Stolze's opinions, points of view, experiences. The man is a sage. Reading and heeding his book will save any first time entrepreneur a lot of heartache. *Start Up* is no Victor Kiam/ Donald Trump ego trip. It is an unabashedly humble attempt on the part of a very bright, accomplished man to share his experiences and knowledge with others, to their hopeful benefit."
—Fred Beste, managing partner, Mid-Atlantic Venture Fund

"The fact that this is the Fifth Edition of *Start Up* tells the story. *Start Up* is one of the most thorough and powerful presentations I've ever read on the do's and don'ts of starting a business. It's a must read for anyone who has the daring to 'go it alone.'"
—Louise Woerner, founder and CEO, HCR, Rochester, N.Y.

"I should tell you again what a hit your book has made in my classes. It is brief and easy reading, yet goes straight to the point in a way that more 'academic' textbooks can't seem to match. It has become a mainstay in my teaching 'arsenal,' and I am happy to recommend it to my colleagues."
—Prof. Lanny Herron, Department of Management, University of Baltimore

"Only a founding entrepreneur could possess the wealth of knowledge that Bill Stolze shares with his audience in *Start Up*. It is a 'must read' book for all who are about to embark on an entrepreneurial endeavor. I highly recommend it to all about-to-be entrepreneurs, those entrepreneurs who currently are struggling with day-to-day business decisions, and anybody else who just wants a 'good read.'"
—Mary Graff, asst. director, Nebraska Business Development Center

"I just finished your excellent book, *Start Up*, and wanted to write to congratulate you. Most books on entrepreneurship are too polite and abstract. Yours is down-to-earth and practical and will fill a gap in the literature. New chapters and additions make the fifth edition even more valuable than the fourth was."
—Peter Faber, partner, the law firm of McDermott, Will & Emory, New York, N.Y.

"In this period when business start ups require unusual devotion and talent, guidance based upon real world experience is invaluable. Bill Stolze provides this kind of guidance, and does so with clarity, verve, and style."
—Paul S. Brentlinger, general partner, Morgenthaler Ventures

"A tour de force! Bill Stolze has written the best guide available on how to launch and manage a new venture. He tells it like it is. It is packed with invaluable advice, experience, and insights from how to deal with venture investors to how to cash in your chips. If you are involved in a startup or thinking about a start up this book is a must read."
—Dr. Warren Keegan, director of the Institute For Global Business Strategy, Pace University, and author of *Global Marketing Management*

"Anyone who has been involved in forming a new business undertaking will recognize the importance of this book. *Start Up* is a hardheaded and practical guide to starting a new business, whether inside an existing company or as an independent new venture."
—Charles E. Exley, Jr., retired chairman and CEO, NCR Corporation

"Bill Stolze's approach to venture start-up issues is elegant! It grasps both the problems, and in my opinion, the solutions in a very straightforward way. The section on women entrepreneurs is a real bonus, opening up new dimensions on the traditional view of new business founders."
—Richard G. Schiavo, director, Academy of Learning Centers, U.S., and former dean, College of Business and Technology, Franklin University

"I was given your book *Start Up* for Christmas and read it before returning to work on January 2. It was the most encouraging book I have ever read."
—Jeffrey Medler, founder and president, Exhibit Alternatives

"*Start Up* is an invaluable guide for the entrepreneur who is starting a business. It doesn't stop there. It also offers excellent guidance for decisions which need to be made when one's business becomes successful. It is full of advice and Bill Stolze's style makes the reader feel he or she can pick up the phone and call a friend."
—Joanne Bauman, regional director of the Small Business Development Center at Binghamton University

"Bill Stolze has been able to put into one book all of the essential elements to be a successful entrepreneur and small business owner. I find my students find it a useful reference and a book to use well after graduation. *Start Up* is an essential text for any class that teaches invention, innovation, or entrepreneurship."
—Prof. John Kleppe, Electrical Engineering Department, University of Nevada-Reno

"Bill Stolze achieves a goal that is unique: His book *Start Up* contains enough theory about entrepreneurship that should satisfy those interested in this topic. However, the book's main strength is the practical knowledge it imparts to those who want to start and develop a business. *Start Up* is also a natural for the classroom and I have used it for seven years as the principal textbook in teaching the subject at colleges and universities in the United States and England. I have read all of the well known books on entrepreneurship and this is the best."
—James N. Doyle, lecturer in entrepreneurship,
Simon Graduate School of Business, University of Rochester
and former president of Sarah Coventry, Intl.

"Enclosed is the check I promised to send you for 10 more copies of your great book *Start Up*. Great title; great book; important and useful; straight forward advice and guidance clearly articulated. A winner from a winner."
—Francis X. Driscoll, former venture capital consultant
and past president, The New York Venture Capital Forum

"Most valuable book I have had in my college career."
—M.B.A. student, Simon Graduate School of Business,
University of Rochester

"We recently read your new book *Start Up*, and we like it. In fact, we like it so much that we now hand a copy to every new client who comes to us for help in launching a new business and we insist that they read it."
—Joseph Hurley, partner, Bonadio & Co., L.L.P., CPAs

START UP

An Entrepreneur's Guide
To Launching and
Managing a New Business

5th Edition

By
William J. Stolze

CAREER PRESS

Franklin Lakes, NJ

Copyright © 1999 by William J. Stolze

All rights reserved under the Pan-American and International Copyright Conventions. This book may not be reproduced, in whole or in part, in any form or by any means electronic or mechanical, including photocopying, recording, or by any information storage and retrieval system now known or hereafter invented, without written permission from the publisher, The Career Press.

The author and publisher shall have neither liability nor responsibility to any person or entity with respect to any loss or damage caused, or alleged to be caused, directly or indirectly by any information contained in this book.

This book is designed to provide accurate information in regard to the subject matter covered. It is sold with the specific understanding that neither the author, nor the publisher, are rendering legal, accounting, or other professional services. If legal, accounting, or other professional counsel, assistance, or advice is required, a competent professional person should be consulted.

The interviewing, hiring, employment, promotion, and termination of minorities, women, and the handicapped are complex issues. They are all covered by federal, state, and local laws and regulations subject to change and interpretation. This book is sold with the specific understanding that neither the author nor publisher are rendering legal advice on these matters.

The business plans in Appendix 1 and Appendix 2 are copyrighted by the authors and reproduced by permission.

START UP, 5ᵗʰ EDITION
Cover design by Foster & Foster
Printed in the U.S.A. by Book-mart Press

To order this title, please call toll-free 1-800-CAREER-1 (NJ and Canada: 201-848-0310) to order using VISA or MasterCard, or for further information on books from Career Press. The Career Press, Inc., 3 Tice Road, PO Box 687, Franklin Lakes, NJ 07417

Library of Congress Cataloging-in-Publication Data

Stolze, William J.
    Start up : an entrepreneur's guide to launching and managing a new
  business / by William J. Stolze.—5ᵗʰ ed.
      p.   cm.
    Includes index.
    ISBN 1-56414-432-1 (pbk.)
     1. New business enterprises—Management. 2. Entrepreneurship.
  I. Title.
  HD62.5.S755   1999
  658.02'2—dc21
                                                                                99-32693
                                                                                       CIP

Contents

Introduction	Entrepreneurship and the Road to Success	11
Chapter 1	Decisions, Decisions!!	13
Chapter 2	Which Comes First: Whether or How?	15
Chapter 3	Why People Start Companies	16
Chapter 4	What Makes an Entrepreneur?	19
Chapter 5	Upside/Downside: Reward and Risk	23
Chapter 6	5 Ways to Get Rich	25
Chapter 7	Entrepreneurship for the Retiree	27
Chapter 8	When Is the Right Time to Start a Business?	30
Chapter 9	To Team or Not to Team	32
Chapter 10	Stolze's Law: The Peter Principle in Reverse	35
Chapter 11	The Theory of Distinctive Competence	37
Chapter 12	Why Small Companies Are Better	40
Chapter 13	Startup Strategies That Work: Picking Your Product and Market	43
Chapter 14	Product/Market Matrix	53
Chapter 15	Supply-Side Strategy	56
Chapter 16	Fads vs. Trends	59
Chapter 17	Product/Market Zig-Zag	62
Chapter 18	Buying a Franchise: Another Way to Own a Business	64
Chapter 19	Why People Buy: Value, Benefits, and Price	66
Chapter 20	Marketing Means Selling	68

Chapter 21	Using the Internet for an Entrepreneur	76
Chapter 22	Other Ways to Market: Franchising and Multilevel Marketing	80
Chapter 23	Forms of Business	83
Chapter 24	Setting Goals	86
Chapter 25	What! Me Write a Business Plan?	88
Chapter 26	Homemaker's Theory of Cash Flow: Forecasting Capital Needs	96
Chapter 27	How Much Money Is Enough?	100
Chapter 28	Where and How to Look for Financing	103
Chapter 29	How to Obtain a Loan: Improving the Odds	108
Chapter 30	Taking on Investors	113
Chapter 31	The Importance of Control: Who Needs It?	115
Chapter 32	Watch Out for the Sharks: And Other Advice for Dealing With Venture Investors	117
Chapter 33	How to Get a Venture Investment: Improving the Odds	128
Chapter 34	Staying Private/Going Public	132
Chapter 35	Will the Government Really Give Me Money?	137
Chapter 36	Working With Public Accountants, Bankers, and Lawyers	142
Chapter 37	Staffing Up, Staffing Down	147
Chapter 38	Reviewing Performance and Setting Standards	152
Chapter 39	Who Needs a Mentor?	158
Chapter 40	What Is Really Important? Operating Lean and Mean	160
Chapter 41	Patents, Copyrights, Trademarks, and Trade Secrets	162

Chapter 42	Two Plus Two Equals Five—No, Two Plus Two Equals Three: The Theory of Acquisitions	166
Chapter 43	Making an Acquisition Work	169
Chapter 44	Selling the Rest of the World: Exporting as an Opportunity	172
Chapter 45	Help! Help! Where Do I Go for Help?	178
Chapter 46	Entrepreneurship for Women! Is It Different Than for Men?	184
Chapter 47	This Is How It Should Be Done! Valerie Mannix and Mercury Print Productions, Inc.	190
Chapter 48	Managing a Turnaround	196
Chapter 49	When Should the Entrepreneur Step Aside?	200
Chapter 50	Cashing Some Chips or Getting Out	202
Chapter 51	This Is How It Should Be Done! Tom Golisano and Paychex, Inc.	205
Chapter 52	This Is How It Should Be Done! Paul Orfalea and Kinko's, Inc.	210
Chapter 53	25 Entrepreneurial Death Traps	216
Chapter 54	The Personal Computer and the Entrepreneur	220
Chapter 55	In Search of Excellence and the New Venture	225
Epilogue		226
Appendix 1: Sample Business Plan: LawTech		227
Appendix 2: Sample Business Plan: Easy Shopper		251
About the Author		281
Index		283

Introduction

Entrepreneurship And the Road to Success

This is a book about entrepreneurship and the problems associated with launching and managing a new business. I hope to reach the reader who is either considering embarking on a new venture or who started a business within the past few years and wants to make that business grow.

In writing the first edition 10 years ago, I thought I could transcribe lecture notes used in an entrepreneurship course I was teaching into chapters of a book. It soon became apparent that to be of any value, a book must include much more than can be packed into a 12-week course. The final product had about three times the number of chapters than first planned and was a much more difficult project than I ever imagined. Subsequent editions had more chapters and included a great deal of additional information. It should not have been a surprise, but I learned that writing a book is very hard work.

This fifth edition includes a number of chapters written by others. I did this for two reasons. First, some of this material covers issues on which I do not have much personal experience. The people who contributed are all more expert than I and their comments more valuable. The second reason is to present the other side of certain issues where I have a bias that is sometimes in conflict with conventional wisdom. This, I believe, makes *Start Up* a better book.

This book contains many examples of companies and how they got started. Included are a variety of different types of businesses, each of which seemed to have had some kind of unique problem that should be of interest to the reader. Several of the examples are companies that now have sales of several hundred million dollars, while some are much smaller. Each of the entrepreneurs overcame many problems in selecting products and markets and in raising capital. To me this says that persistence, imagination, and selling skills are important qualities to have in order to succeed in starting a business.

Another section of great interest is Chapter 53, titled "Twenty-Five Entrepreneurial Death Traps." It was written by Fred Beste, who has many years experience investing in and working with start-up companies. His comments are extremely perceptive.

Much of the new material in this fifth edition was added at the suggestion of readers who contacted me with their ideas for additions and changes. Without exception this advice was constructive, of great value, and much appreciated.

Even today, when entrepreneurship is in the curriculum at about 1,400 colleges and universities throughout the world, there is still disagreement in many business and academic circles as to whether this is a subject that can be taught.

Compare teaching the entrepreneur to teaching someone how to compose music. You can teach a person musical theory, composition, counterpoint, and orchestration but there is only one Mozart. Similarly with entrepreneurship, you can teach a person how to select products, how to identify market opportunities, and how to raise capital, but few will be a Bill Gates, Lillian Vernon, Ross Perot, Mary Kay Ash, or Steve Jobs.

In selecting examples of companies to include I draw heavily on my own experience as a founder of a successful high-tech business, as an investor, director, and active participant in a number of recent start-up companies, as a teacher of entrepreneurship, and as an adviser and consultant to several hundred entrepreneurs in various stages of planning for, beginning, and running a business.

In teaching this subject, I made extensive use of entrepreneurs as guest lecturers. They told the stories of the founding of their companies with particular emphasis on the unusual problems they encountered. Over the years, almost 100 have spoken to my classes. Their tales of elation and woe have influenced much of this book.

This is neither a "how to" manual nor an academic treatise. The subjects covered are those I consider essential in determining whether a new company succeeds or fails. My intention is to identify and discuss key issues only. This means that there are some aspects of starting and running a business that are not covered at all. You should seek guidance on these from others.

Even the subjects I identified as key issues also presented a problem, however, in that some are complex and impossible to cover with any degree of thoroughness in a single short chapter. Specialized areas such as selling, franchising, raising venture capital, export marketing, writing a business plan, etc., should be and are the subjects of entire books. On these, my goal was to alert the reader to their importance and cover some of the fundamental issues involved.

I spend a lot of time telling about my experience at RF Communications, a company I founded with three associates. My partners were Elmer W. Schwittek, Roger R. Bettin, and Herbert W. Vanden Brul. Both Elmer and Roger are extremely creative and very customer-oriented engineers and astute business managers. Herb is also a very able businessman and one of the few entrepreneurial lawyers I ever met. The chemistry between the founders of RF Communications was especially good; we worked closely together through the entire history of the company and share equally in the success we achieved.

Suggestions, comments, or questions from readers about this book or any aspect of entrepreneurship and starting a business would be much appreciated. I can be reached by e-mail at wjs896@aol.com or through the publisher.

Start Up is dedicated to all of you readers who actually start a business. I hope it helps you along the road to becoming a successful entrepreneur. Good luck.

Chapter 1

Decisions, Decisions!!

One thing that always seems to come as a surprise to a new entrepreneur is the number of decisions that must be made and the questions that must be answered before the business even gets underway. Among these are: *Should I start the business alone or with partners? What product or service should be the basis of the business? What is my market? Is the potential of the business enough to provide an honest living? How can I raise initial capital?* The questions go on and on.

This situation is especially difficult because there is rarely any scientific basis for making these decisions. There are no formulas that will help. There are no equations you can apply.

Eventually, you will conclude that there are really no right or wrong answers to these questions. The best you can hope for is an answer that works. You will never know whether a different decision or answer would have been better or worse. Almost every important decision is subjective. In the final analysis, almost every important decision is based upon the entrepreneur's personal experience and intuitive judgment.

I lecture to groups of entrepreneurs and small business owners at many seminars and meetings. People in the audience ask questions about every possible aspect of starting or managing a business. My response almost always begins with, "Well, it depends..." and then I go on to answer as best I can. Comments like, "on the other hand," "in another situation," "but then again," and similar qualifying phrases are also generously sprinkled in my responses. Sometimes I have the feeling that the answer to every question about starting a business is, "It depends."

Long ago, I read one author's comment that, "Entrepreneurship is a profession for which there is no apprenticeship." No matter how many books you read, no matter how many courses or seminars you attend, no matter how much advice you get from "experts," no matter how many small companies you work for, there is no substitute for the actual experience of doing it yourself.

In the words of a great philosopher, "You ain't done it until you've done it." The crucial decisions you make in developing a plan for the business and getting the business underway are yours and yours alone.

Get all the help you can from every source you can identify as having potential value. Much of the advice and many of the suggestions you receive will be contradictory, but doing this still can help in many ways. It will give you more self confidence and help you avoid some of the mistakes others made.

You hear horror stories about the high percentage of new businesses that fail—these statistics are undoubtedly true. However, there are steps you can take that will greatly improve the odds. I try to describe many of them in this book.

But when the chips are on the table and the go-ahead decisions must be made, you will be on your own. Many entrepreneurs describe this as the loneliest experience of their entire lives and the most difficult decision they ever had to make.

If you do decide to go ahead, give it everything you have. Years later many people will ask whether you regret taking this step into the world of entrepreneurship. Almost all entrepreneurs will tell how hard it was. Some will regret the move, but many will say it was gratifying beyond belief.

In some cases the entrepreneurs become rich, in some they barely eke out a living. Some businesses fail or are abandoned. But in almost every case the process of starting your own business, of being your own boss, of seeing whether you have what it takes, can be the most exciting experience of a lifetime.

Chapter 2

Which Comes First: Whether or How?

Several years ago, I led a seminar on how to start and manage a new business. Five successful entrepreneurs came in and told the stories of the founding and early years of their companies.

During the discussion, a young man in the audience asked a simple yet searching question to which I immediately responded with the wrong answer. His question was, "Which comes first, the decision to have a company or the idea for the product or service upon which the new company will be based?" My quick answer was that the idea for the product or service comes first.

After thinking about my own experience for a few moments and asking the other speakers about theirs, it became apparent that in all five cases the opposite was true. Since then I discussed this issue with many company founders. Now I believe that in the majority of ventures, the founder first decides to start a company and then struggles (sometimes for years) to find a product or service to use as the basis for the company.

Is this good or bad? On balance, I think it is good. There are many reasons why people start companies. These include the desire to prove they can do it, the possibility of large financial rewards, and dissatisfaction with their present job. One thing seems to be clear: The reasons why people start companies are largely unrelated to what the company might do.

I suggest that potential entrepreneurs should first struggle with the question of whether to start a company. Decide if you have the personal qualities needed, the support of your family and friends, the willingness to put in the long hours that will be required, and the ability to make the sacrifices and take the risks.

Only after you have decided to start a company is it possible to address the question of *how*. This is a complex issue and might include developing or inventing a product, associating with a partner (or partners) who has an idea for a product or service but no knowledge of how to proceed, buying an existing company, buying a franchise, or identifying an unserved market niche that offers an opportunity. This may take a long time and involve one or more false starts.

If you think you want to start a company, don't worry about the fact that you have not invented "a better mouse trap." First, decide that you really have the desire to go ahead and then take on the question of how to do it.

The questions of whether to start a company and how to start a company are, of course, what this book is all about.

Chapter 3

Why People Start Companies

What drives people to become entrepreneurs? It's a question with many answers. Often, these individuals are not entirely sure themselves, and the answers are apt to change over time as their perceptions change.

I divide these reasons into two broad categories: the **reactive** reasons and the **active** reasons. Reactive reasons are those things that are objectionable about working for others. They are the negatives that push you out. Active reasons are those things that are attractive about having your own business. They are the positives that pull you out.

The following list was compiled from many sources over a period of years. I do not necessarily agree with all of them, but they are the reasons most often heard.

Reactive reasons

1. Inequity between contribution and reward

People who are by nature high achievers tend not to get along well in large organizations. They want rewards based upon accomplishment—not on seniority, conforming to the corporate culture, or political clout. The person who just made a major contribution does not want to be told, "Be patient—your turn will come."

2. Promotion and salary policy

Have you heard the comment, "You're too young to make so much money?" When I was 26 years old I had a very good engineering management position at RCA Laboratories designing FM radio and television receivers. The lab was in midtown Manhattan and our family lived in the outskirts of Queens—about a 1 1/2 hour commute. We decided to leave New York City, which required my changing jobs.

My position at the time involved working with other TV manufacturers and I had exceptionally good contacts for a person my age. I interviewed at Stromberg-Carlson, a long-defunct TV manufacturer in Rochester, N.Y., and General Electric in Syracuse. Almost immediately, Stromberg-Carlson offered me a job at a 50 percent increase in salary.

During my interview with GE, I was asked what kind of salary I expected, so I told the interviewer about my other offer. The man interviewing me was the chief engineer. He gulped, reached into his drawer, and pulled out a sheet of paper with a curve on it. He said that if they paid me the money I was asking I would be the highest paid person my age at GE. Yet he made me an offer at that salary.

In my evaluation of the two offers I decided that the GE deal was good news and bad news. The good news was that nothing would make me happier than being the highest paid 26-year-old at General Electric. The bad news was that my new boss would work very hard to get me back on the curve.

I took the job at Stromberg-Carlson.

3. Adversity

This is one of the most common reasons why people start companies. Your job might be in jeopardy or you might be concerned that cutbacks in the organization will limit your future prospects and opportunity. The fear of losing a job causes many people to think about starting a business.

Before I started RF Communications, I was employed in a senior marketing position at General Dynamics' Electronics Division. The company was having serious business problems and was beginning to make major cutbacks and organizational changes. My boss and I did not work well together and I was convinced I was in danger of being fired. This was an important factor in my decision to start a company.

Since then, I have thought a lot about the subject of job security and I get very upset when a young college graduate seems unduly concerned about a retirement plan, fringe benefits, and so forth. Long ago, I concluded that there is only one kind of job security that means anything—your ability to get another job fast. Keep your skills and your contacts up and keep your resume current.

During the 1970s getting a job at IBM was considered the next best thing to heaven. Many employees began planning their retirement the day they started. Back then, IBM employed about 400,000 people. Today they employ about half that number. Working for IBM no longer looks like heaven.

Many other major corporations have had large staff reductions, and will continue do so in the future. However, in making these reductions, large companies often provide generous termination pay—sometimes as long as nine months to a year. Several friends have recently started businesses after receiving such severance packages. This provided them with income for many months while they were getting the new business underway.

4. Red tape and politics

These do not require much discussion. They are shortcomings of all large organizations that drive the entrepreneurial type bananas. Politicians and bureaucrats are rarely entrepreneurs.

5. Champion of orphan products

It's a lonely feeling to try to promote a product that is outside the mainstream business of a large company. In many cases it is more difficult than starting a company from scratch. Even if you succeed there are probably no significant rewards. Belief in an "orphan product" can strongly encourage the step into entrepreneurship.

Active reasons

1. To be your own boss

Many entrepreneurs have personality traits that make it difficult (if not impossible) for them to work for others. The only sure way to avoid this is to have your own company. Running a company gives you the opportunity to get out of a professional rut, to see a job through from beginning to end, and to control your own destiny.

Another great aspect of being your own boss is that you will have much more time flexibility. You can schedule business activities to be more consistent with the demands of home and children, along with other interests.

2. Fame and recognition

It is the opinion of some that this is an important reason why people start companies. (I do not agree.) Most entrepreneurs I know are fairly conservative individuals who do not seek the limelight. Ken Olsen, founder of Digital Equipment Corporation (DEC) and a multimillionaire lived in the same house for many years he bought shortly after starting DEC. An article in *Fortune* suggested that "Olsen's unostentatious style has kept him from becoming a business celebrity."

While there are surely many exceptions, my conclusion is that the extrovert egotist is much more common in the large well-established company than the startup. The worst thing that can happen to large companies is when their presidents begin to believe what they read about themselves in *Business Week* or *Forbes*. The struggle to bring a new company into existence is a great lesson in humility.

3. Participation in all aspects of a business

Nothing is more exciting than to be totally involved in the operation of a business. The entrepreneur helps conceive the product or service, helps design it, goes out and gets orders, makes sure the factory runs well, helps the customer put it in operation, and finally sees the effect that all of this has on the profits of the firm. What a thrill!

4. Personal financial gain

For some people this is very important. Gains can come more quickly and can be much greater than when working for someone else. This is not a negligible consideration. This issue is discussed in another chapter.

5. Joy of winning

Entrepreneurs are the ultimate achievers. Starting a company is a good way to satisfy the achievement instinct. Starting a new company, working for a new company, or just being involved in any way with a new company is just plain fun. It is satisfying and it is exciting. We spend more hours at our job than at anything else we do. Why shouldn't we enjoy it?

I am often asked why I started a company. Here are the reasons that I think were most important:

- The company I worked for was clearly on a downhill slide. I was convinced at the time that my job was in jeopardy. And, even if it were not, future opportunity was surely poor.

- I wanted very much to stay in Rochester, but for a person with my experience, there was nowhere else to work at the time.

- I am an engineer and, in the normal course of my work, was heavily involved in both the conception and creation of new products. I met and read about many engineers who had started some very successful companies. Inside of me I had a deep urge and desire to prove whether I had the skills to do it on my own.

- I had six children, the oldest of whom just entered high school. Providing each of them a good college education on an engineer's salary would be difficult at best. I thought that if the new company were successful it might be easier. In a sense it was a "now-or-never" decision.

My reasons, and the others listed, are not the only reasons to start a business. There are many quite powerful reasons. Starting a new company is a great challenge. To those with entrepreneurial instincts, it is very appealing.

Chapter 4

What Makes an Entrepreneur?

What makes an entrepreneur is a complex question. It includes factors from the environment in which an individual was raised, his or her family situation, and his or her personality traits. This question has been the subject of a great deal of both study and research. The following discussion is a summary of my own observations plus some of the conclusions of others.

About 20 or 25 years ago if you asked almost any expert to describe a successful entrepreneur, you would probably have been given a list similar to this:

- Male.
- Only child.
- About 35 to 45 years old.
- Bachelors or masters degree in engineering.
- Protestant.
- Born in the Midwest.
- Father owns a hardware store.
- Delivered newspapers and sold lemonade as a youth.

Should you be concerned if you do not fit this stereotype? Absolutely not! Very few of these are factors that determine whether an entrepreneur succeeds or fails.

However, much recent research and many of my own observations seem to indicate that there are qualities commonly found in successful entrepreneurs, and there are things that you can do if you are concerned about any you may lack.

Many writers on this subject seem to be primarily concerned with the qualities found in successful entrepreneurs. I look at the question a little differently and believe it is equally as important to consider those traits that successful entrepreneurs usually do not have and those traits that simply do not matter.

Personal qualities common in successful entrepreneurs

Motivation to achieve

In almost every case, successful entrepreneurs are individuals who are highly motivated to achieve. Often, they tend to be people who make things happen. They are often very competitive. Many researchers have concluded that the most consistent trait found in successful entrepreneurs is the sheer will to win, the need to achieve in everything they do. They don't want to come in third, they don't want to come in second, they want to come in first.

In addition, they're very anxious to know how they're doing. They want feedback. Several years ago, after a long business career primarily in marketing, I took a regular faculty position at a graduate business school. One of the things I found most difficult to adjust to was that I never knew how I was doing.

Teaching is hard work. You spend 16 weeks preparing, lecturing, grading, counseling, and so forth—and at the end the class just disappears. Over the years students will occasionally call or write, commenting about the value of the course, but that is the exception. It is poor feedback at best.

In marketing, on the other hand, you know exactly how you are doing, quickly and with certainty—either you are getting orders or you are not. It's a clear and simple test of performance. This may explain why successful entrepreneurs almost always have strong marketing skills.

The habit of hard work

Starting a company is hard work. Let no one kid you about that. Some time ago a student reported that one of his other professors said that unless you are prepared to work hard you should not start a company. He asked my opinion. I said the statement was nonsense.

I think the correct way to say it is that unless you already work hard you should not start a company. There is a big difference. Starting a company is unlikely to turn a lazy oaf into a raging bull.

I worked very hard when starting a company. But I also worked about as hard for the two large companies that employed me before that. Today, when I don't have to work at all, I work almost as hard as ever. I tell my family that I expect to go to the cemetery directly from my office.

An interesting example of a compulsively hardworking entrepreneur was Bill McGowan, the founder of MCI Communications. In 1986, at age 59, he suffered a heart attack that was followed several months later by a heart transplant.

Two weeks after leaving the hospital, he visited the office, one month later he began regularly attending board meetings. Within a year of the operation, he was back as full time chairman. Some people surely considered Bill McGowan to have been nuts, but I considered him a perfect example of the hardworking entrepreneur.

One motivational speaker said, "It's a dog-eat-dog world out there—for 40 hours a week. But when you get to 50 hours, suddenly there aren't as many dogs. When you get to 60 hours or more, it's downright lonely."

In his excellent book, *Winners*, published by Holt, Rinehart, and Wilson, Carter Henderson quotes Nolan Bushnell, founder of Atari game company and Pizza Time Theater, as saying it all comes down to one critical ingredient, "Getting off your ass and doing something." In summary, entrepreneurs are almost always very hard workers.

Nonconformity

Entrepreneurs tend to be independent souls, unhappy when forced to conform or toe the line. They're people who find it difficult to work for others, who want to set their own goals. It is hard to imagine anyone who is more nonconformist than Steve Jobs and Steve Wozniak, the founders of Apple Computer, or Bill Gates, founder of Microsoft.

Strong leadership

Starting a new company can be a harrowing experience full of uncertainty and risk. Successfully bringing a small organization through these trying periods requires a lot of leadership skills.

Street smarts

I do not know quite how to put this. Shrewd or sharp might be better words. Paul

Hawken describes it as "trade skill" in his excellent book *Growing a Business*, published by Simon and Schuster. We all know owners of some very successful businesses who were lucky to finish high school and never even considered college. Yet they always seem to make the right moves. Call it common sense, instinct, whatever you want. Successful entrepreneurs seem to have intuitive good judgment when making complex business decisions.

Personal qualities not found in successful entrepreneurs

Compulsive gambling

Almost without exception people who start companies are not gamblers. They are attracted to situations where success is determined by personal skill rather than chance. They strongly prefer that their destiny be determined by hard work and conscious decisions, rather than by the roll of the dice.

High risk-taking

Contrary to popular opinion, entrepreneurs do not take excessive risks. Through careful product and market selection, creative financing, building a good team, and thorough planning, the real risk of starting a new business can be quite low. In the world of small business, optimism is truly cheap and high risk takers die an early death.

Compulsive hip shooting

Snap decision making is not a common entrepreneurial quality. In fact, excessive caution is more apt to be a problem. Entrepreneurs tend to be careful planners.

Irrelevant factors

Age

This simply does not matter any more. During the 1950s, 60s, and 70s the large majority of people starting companies were in their 30s and 40s. Not true during the 1980s or today. Several years ago I invested substantial personal funds in a company headed by two 26-year-old entrepreneurs, both younger than my youngest child. Shortly after that, I helped two 19-year-olds plan a business and secure financing.

Steve Jobs and Steve Wozniak were both in their early 20s when they started Apple Computer. At the other extreme Ray Kroc was 59 when he started the McDonald's restaurant chain.

A recent national survey indicated that a greater percentages of teenagers than adults were interested in someday launching their own businesses. This may be the result of high visibility role models or the result of hearing their parents discussing whether or not they will be able to survive the next major layoff at their company.

Gender

Here again, it just does not matter. Until recently, entrepreneurship was considered by many to be the last bastion of male dominance in the business world. This is no longer true.

More businesses are now being started by women than are being started by men. I know many women who have started successful companies in recent years in such fields as building contracting, bicycle manufacturing, printing, software, real estate agencies, newspaper publishing, market research, law firms, accounting firms, and on and on. Later chapters discuss in more detail some of the unique problems still faced by women entrepreneurs.

Marital status

This is almost irrelevant (but not quite). For a woman, being pregnant or having several preschool children may not be the best time to take the step into entrepreneurship.

For a man who is the sole support of the family, having two or three children in college may not be the best time.

But this in no way means they should not start a business. It means that perhaps they should have done it several years earlier or wait a few years longer. When I started RF Communications I had six children ages four to 14. I figured this gave me four years to prove whether or not I had the skills to run a business before I had the problem of sending them to college. The question is when to start a business—not whether.

Educational level

Knowledge and skill are very important. How you acquire them is less important. Too many college degrees may be a handicap rather than an asset. One researcher suggested recently that one of the biggest handicaps you can have when you start a business is a Ph.D.

Bill Gates, founder of Microsoft, the country's largest software company, quit Harvard after his sophomore year. Interestingly, the information I have shows the educational level among women entrepreneurs to be significantly higher than among men.

Other

After writing this section of the book, something gnawed at me. Somehow I felt that I had overlooked an important personal quality. It occurred to me that intelligence is not on my list. People with below average intelligence should probably not start businesses, but it is not necessary to be a genius.

Somehow or other, being smart—whatever that means—ought to be better than being dumb, but I do know quite a few very average people who have started some very successful companies.

I watched a television program recently on which the founder of a major company with sales in hundreds of million of dollars was interviewed. He said he had graduated last in his high school class of 230 students. Then he added that he did not think he graduated at all, but they just wanted to be rid of him.

As I said at the start, if you do not fit the mold, don't panic. Every entrepreneur is an individual with different skills, different strengths and weaknesses, and different personality traits. Your smartest strategy as you start or develop your business is to be aware of your own special set of skills, strengths, and weaknesses, and build on these.

Chapter 5

Upside/Downside: Reward and Risk

Conventional wisdom is that starting a company is an extremely risky proposition. Data from many sources show that a high percentage of new businesses in the United States fail within the first few years. These statistics put fear in the heart of anyone thinking about launching an enterprise. I urge you not to be too concerned; it's not as bad as many people seem to think. In fact, the odds can really be quite good.

First of all, the above quoted data includes all start ups, such as corner grocery stores, gasoline stations, trendy restaurants, and similar businesses that have a notoriously high attrition rate. Conclusion: Avoid these businesses entirely and your chances of surviving will increase dramatically.

Secondly, many people starting businesses are doomed almost before they begin because of poor initial strategy. The most frequent error, in my view, is to select an offering (either product or service) that is distinguished from competitors only by price. If you heed the advice later in this book on "Start Up Strategies That Work" and find ways to concentrate, differentiate, and innovate in every aspect of the business rather than selling price alone, the odds of success will be better.

Finally, I suggest that instead of thinking only about the risks of starting a business, consider the potential rewards at the same time. After all, the relationship between reward and risk is much more important than either alone. If the potential rewards are very great, it may be worth taking a higher level of risk than you would otherwise consider.

Risks and rewards come in many forms. The most obvious are financial, but for many entrepreneurs the financial issues are of less importance than others. The two I want to discuss first are professional and emotional. What different people consider acceptable risk will vary substantially. More things than money must be considered.

The professional rewards of starting a company and succeeding are obviously very great and do not need further discussion.

The most important professional risk of starting a business and failing is the possibility of suddenly becoming unemployed. The question to ask is how two or three years of managing an unsuccessful start-up company would compare to the same two or three years with your former employer when it comes to reentering the job market. My belief is that the broad experience and extensive contacts that come with being the head of a company (even if it fails) would make it easier to find a job. If this is true, or even almost true, it means that the professional risks of starting a company are low.

Emotional risks and rewards are another matter—the rewards can be very great, but the risks may also be great both for you and your family. Let us look first at the reward side. I started a company from scratch. We had two employees in addition to the four founders. Eight years later, at the time of our merger with Harris Corp., RF employed about 800 people—today it is closer to 1,600. These were jobs that would not have existed otherwise. Most of these employees have a spouse and children. There is a multiplier on top of these when you consider the company's suppliers and merchants in the community where our employees spend their income. All-in-all I estimate that the company I started in a basement supports 10,000 to 12,000 people in the Rochester area. Is this an emotional reward? You better believe it is!

Starting RF Communications was financially rewarding to the founders. My living standard and lifestyle moved upward considerably but not nearly as far as my income, so suddenly I had resources available for other purposes. I often tell my friends that I increased my skill at earning money faster than my wife increased her skill at spending it.

Important to me in my life were the educations my three daughters and three sons received in private Catholic high schools. It was during the 1960s and early 1970s, which were very hard times for young people. As a result of the success of RF Communications I was able to donate an athletic field to each of the two high schools my children attended plus a dozen or so scholarships that will help other young people get a similar education.

On the down side, the emotional risks associated with starting a business can be great whether the business succeeds or fails. Consider how your complete dedication to and immersion in the new venture will affect your marriage and family. When you spend every waking hour dealing with business problems it may not leave much emotional energy to deal with family problems. Are your spouse and children prepared and able to make the emotional investment needed for you to start a business. If your venture goes down, will you be able to prevent your marriage and family from going down as well?

These are scary questions that deserve a lot of attention. While the emotional rewards of entrepreneurship can be very great, so can the risks. Each person must assess whether and how they can handle these.

In addition to these two areas, where the risks and rewards must be carefully balanced, there is a long list of others where only reward is possible and the risk is zero. These include things such as the wish to be your own boss, the desire to be involved in all aspects of the business, getting away from the politics, red tape, and bureaucracy of the large company, among others. If these things are important to you, and they usually are, there is only an upside.

Chapter 6

5 Ways To Get Rich

It is widely believed that the most important reason to start a business is to make a lot of money. My personal feeling is that the possibility of financial gain is one reason to start a company, but not necessarily the most important.

A survey of 500 successful male entrepreneurs showed that making a lot of money ranked sixth in importance in a list of 10 reasons for starting a business. A similar survey of 113 women entrepreneurs showed the prospects for large financial rewards ranked 11th in a list of 16 reasons.

Each October, *Forbes* magazine devotes almost an entire issue to listing the 400 wealthiest people in the United States, along with their estimates of each person's net worth at that time. Rush to your nearest library to get a copy—it is fascinating. About half of the top 100 people on the Forbes lists made their fortune by starting their own businesses.

In July of 1998, *Forbes* published a list of the "World's 200 Working Rich," which was also a fascinating article. One the bottom of the page are a few names that you may recognize:

Even though these are mind boggling numbers it must be kept in mind that the net worth of many people on this list is mostly based on the market value of stock in their own companies. There are restrictions on the sale of stock by officers, directors, and major share holders in a publicly traded company. Therefore, in some cases it may be hard for them to convert the stock into cash. Even considering this restriction this is a group of very wealthy people.

It is estimated that at least 2 million U.S. men and women are millionaires. Nearly

Name & Company	Est. Net Worth	Name & Company	Est. Net Worth
Bill Gates, Microsoft Corp.	$ 51 Billion	Ted Turner, Turner Broadcasting	$ 4.8 Billion
Walton Family, Wal-Mart	$ 48 Billion	Philip Knight, Nike, Inc.	$ 4.7 Billion
Warren Buffett, Berkshire-Hathaway	$ 33 Billion	Micky Anson, Carnival Cruise Line	$ 4.3 Billion
Paul Allen, Microsoft Corp.	$ 21 Billion	Ted Waitt, Gateway Computer Corp.	$ 4.3 Billion
Michael Dell, Dell Computer Corp.	$ 10 Billion		
Sumner Redstone, Viacom, Inc.	$ 5.8 Billion	Ross Perot, Electronic Data Mgt.	$ 3.3 Billion
Lawrence Ellison, Oracle Corp.	$ 5.8 Billion	Leslie Wexner, The Limited	$ 2.3 Billion
Ted & Abigail Johson, Fidelity Inv.	$ 5.1 Billion		

90 percent made their fortunes by starting their own companies. The point here is to emphasize the unarguable fact that by starting a company it is possible to make an amount of money that staggers the imagination. The potential financial rewards of entrepreneurship are huge.

How about the downside? At RF Communications, each of the four founders invested $5,000. That does not sound like much now, but in 1961 it was about one-third of a year's salary. And, worse yet, none of us had $5,000. We borrowed, put the touch on relatives, cashed insurance policies, and so forth. As difficult as it was to scrape up the money and as uncomfortable as it felt at the time, the situation was not all bad.

We knew exactly what our downside financial risk was— $5,000. Since this represented about two or three years of savings we concluded that it was an acceptable risk. Most important the ratio of potential financial reward to known financial risk was high.

As it turned out, eight years later RF Communications merged with Harris Corp. and the four of us made a great deal of money, far more than we would have dared dream when we started the company. We did not become as rich as Bill Gates or any of the others on the above list, understand, but we became very comfortable.

I emphasize this point to my entrepreneurship classes by giving a short exam. I ask the class to list the five best ways to get rich. Try it. These are my answers:

- The best way to be rich is to be born rich. No close second. On the Forbes list most people who did not start companies became rich by inheritance.
- The second best way, also by a wide margin, is to marry rich. This is a problem since many people are quite young when they marry and aren't smart enough to recognize the importance of picking a wealthy mate.
- Third place is to win a state lottery. Unfortunately, the probability of winning a state lottery is far lower than the probability of being born rich.
- Fourth place, in a close finish, is to be in show business. Be an Elizabeth Taylor, a Michael Jordan, a Johnny Carson or a Michael Jackson. Show business, unfortunately, also requires that you have some talent. Incidentally, both Elizabeth Taylor and Johnny Carson seem determined to do the best they can to help a number of people marry rich.
- The fifth way is to start a company. This is the only way available to most of us, and clearly has the best odds.

A number of years ago I decided to do a bit of rigorous scientific research on this subject in an attempt to confirm the above premise. The research was conducted at the Rochester Yacht Club where I am a member and where I docked my 44-foot sailboat. Using the boat population of the club as my sample I first ascertained that the crossover between a "small" boat and a "big" boat occurred at about 34 feet. Almost without exception the "big" boats were owned by people who had started their own companies. The "small" boats were owned by Ph.D. chemists from Kodak.

There is no doubt in my mind that the only opportunity available to most people to make a lot of money is to start a company. The prospect for large financial reward may not be your primary motivation for starting a company but it certainly has a lot of appeal. Be aware that the potential for huge returns is there and the downside, in comparison, can be acceptably low.

Chapter 7

Entrepreneurship for the Retiree

A strange change has taken place in U.S. industry over the past 10 years or so. Many large and prestigious companies have had major staff reductions with more still to come. The change that I refer to is that no longer do they give their terminated employees two weeks notice, accrued vacation pay, a pat on the back, and send them on their way. Recently, it has become far more common to pay them anywhere from three months to a year or more of continuing salary (usually depending on years of service), continuation of health benefits for an extended period, and a considerable amount of assistance in retraining and in finding a new job.

A few years ago, one of my sons took what I refer to as involuntary/voluntary termination from a major computer company after working there as a salesman for about 11 years. I strongly encouraged him to do this because 11 years of direct selling was enough, even though he had moved up through progressively more responsible positions. It was time for a career change for him into a job with broader marketing responsibilities.

His termination package included about 50 weeks of pay along with other benefits. He called me at the end of his last day on the job and said he had not been as happy and excited in as long as he could remember. Immediately he took off for several months to participate in all the long distance sailboat races on Lake Michigan, Lake Huron, and Lake Ontario, as well as in Key West, Florida.

After about seven months, he accepted a position as director of marketing for a nonprofit organization at a significant reduction in pay. Here he got much more diverse experience. Recently he accepted a far better position with a market research company.

Obviously my son is not a retiree, but the benefits he received are an example of how generously laid off professionals may be treated by big companies these days.

In early 1991, the Eastman Kodak Company embarked on a planned cutback of 3,000 people on a voluntary basis. Their eligibility requirement was that age plus years of service had to equal 75. Guess what? By the end of the year more than 8,000 people accepted the offer. Interestingly, I understand that most people who left Kodak during this staff reduction were in their early 50s, much younger than I would have expected.

In late 1993, Xerox announced a planned reduction of 10,000 employees over the following two or three years. Recently, AT&T split the company into several semi-independent units which included staff reductions in the tens of thousands. These reductions undoubtedly included many layoffs as well as voluntary retirements.

In my opinion, many of these people are too young to retire. You may have heard the story about the recent retiree's spouse saying, "I married you for better or for worse, but not for lunch." Sitting in the sun in Florida is not part of my life nor is a rocking chair on the back porch in Rochester. By and large many of these retirees have immensely valuable business skills and a large number are seriously considering starting a business of their own. This chapter is devoted to some of the issues involved in a decision of this sort.

My first reaction when thinking about a 50-year-old retiree starting a business was that the problems were about the same as for anyone starting a business. But I soon decided they were different in a number of ways.

As I mentioned, in the Kodak case the company was extremely generous in the termination benefits it provided. I was told it included a year's pay and health benefits for life. In addition, a senior manager in his or her early 50s, for example, had the choice between a monthly-payment lifetime annuity, or a lump sum payment. The annuity would be in the range of 60 percent of his or her base pay before retirement and the lump sum payment could be well into six figures. Most people starting a business have neither the financial security of an annuity nor access to personal financial resources in the six figure range.

Another difference is that most employed adults in their 50s or older have reached a stage in their lives when financial demands have decreased. Their children are probably through college, they probably have little or no remaining mortgage on their homes and, since their salary was in many cases substantial, they may also have additional financial resources from savings and investments.

In comparison, when I started a company I had a wife and six young children, a large mortgage on my home, a car loan, no outside income, and a sizable debt as a result of the money I borrowed to get the business going.

It seems to me that the retirees from these big companies have the opportunity to start a business with minimal financial risk. They can take as much time as needed to analyze market opportunities, build prototypes of products, test a new service on an experimental basis, and do a top notch job preparing a business plan. And they probably know dozens of others in the same boat with whom they can form teams that bring together complementary skills. Raising outside capital may be harder because of their age but borrowing from a bank may be easier.

In talking to a number of personal friends who took early retirement from Kodak in recent years, I learned two other things that came somewhat as a surprise. First, many were completely unprepared emotionally to retire so suddenly and quite a few were extremely upset, almost devastated, when they learned their former employer, to whom they had given their entire professional life, suddenly considered them dispensable.

The second thing I learned was that many of them had been "unfulfilled" in their professional career. Even though they had done well and held responsible positions they had always worked under conditions where team performance was emphasized rather then individual performance. Many believe they still have what it takes and are highly motivated to reach the top of their profession and succeed on their own.

And, they have some very high-visibility role models. Ray Kroc started the McDonald's Restaurant chain at the age of 59. Colonel Sanders started Kentucky Fried Chicken at age 65. All of these things say "go ahead."

But there is a down side too. If these people had the personal qualities needed and the inclination to be an entrepreneur, why didn't it surface 20 or 30 years sooner? Some questions you should consider are whether you are really ready to work the long hours that will probably be required, is your spouse ready to support such a decision, and do you really understand the non-financial risks of starting a business? Health can also be an issue because it is in the early 50s that the old body begins to show wear and tear.

Finally, many professionals who spent his or her entire career in a large organization may have led fairly sheltered business lives. They may have never read a financial statement, surely never had to meet a payroll, and may or may not have developed management skills to complement their other professional skills. Is it reasonable to expect to teach such an old dog so many new tricks?

Another point worth mentioning is that it almost always makes sense to start a new business in an area related in some way with your previous job. By doing this it is possible to take maximum advantage of knowledge and experience that took years to acquire. However, care is needed to avoid violating the restrictions in any employment agreements with former employers. One way to minimize this particular risk may be to discuss your plans with your former employer before you actually start the business. Hopefully, you can get their active support and perhaps even an investment.

So the problems of starting a new business and becoming an entrepreneur are not the same for a recent retiree as they are for the younger entrepreneur. I do not suggest that you should not try. But I do suggest that you recognize very clearly what you are getting into before you decide it is a path you really want to travel.

Chapter 8

When Is the Right Time to Start a Business?

When RF Communications was about three years old I spoke to a local business group describing our early experiences. By then we had reached several million dollars in sales and had achieved a good level of profits. The start-up days were behind us. It seemed almost certain that we would survive and, in all likelihood, continue to do well.

At the end of the presentation someone in the audience raised his hand. His comment was, "Boy, you guys were really lucky, you started your business at just the right time."

I had never thought about the question before and had to stop a few moments before responding, "Boy, when we started our business it sure didn't feel like the right time," I answered. Three of the founders had quit their jobs, we had not raised any outside capital, we had invested all of our meager savings and personal borrowings in the company, we were operating out of a vacant beauty parlor, we had only a half-finished product and we had no orders.

Were we really lucky? Did we really start the business at the right time? Who knows?

In retrospect I now believe it is either always the right time to start a business or never the right time. If you need an acceptable reason to put the decision off forever, "It's a bad time," is as good a reason as any.

The company that I always considered as a role model early in my professional career was Hewlett-Packard. That company was started in a garage by two Stanford University graduate students in 1939—in the middle of the Great Depression. If there was ever a wrong time in the history of the world to start a company I would say that David Packard and William Hewlett did very well in finding it.

I do not suggest for a minute that you should rush out and quit your job before you are ready. Carefully evaluate the market opportunity, get as far along as you can in developing your product or service, prepare a good business plan, try to make arrangements for the capital you think you need, and then get on with it.

If all the pieces do not fit, perhaps it may be prudent to go back over the planning process. Perhaps you should delay if you decide it is necessary to revise your fundamental strategy to match changes in the economic conditions or the availability of capital. Consider as best you can the circumstances and difficulties you are likely to face.

Remember most of all, though, that it is always difficult to start a company. It is never easy. The issue is not whether it is the right time or the wrong time. The issue is that you must adjust your strategy and your plan for the business so that they match the times. And, when you look at others who built successful businesses, do not think that those entrepreneurs were fortunate enough to have found an easy road. In all probability they were just as scared and just as apprehensive as you, regardless of the times.

Chapter 9

To Team or Not to Team

There are two ways to start a company—alone or as a team. Whether to team with one or more other entrepreneurs rather than going it alone is a complex decision that depends mostly upon the personal qualities and skills of the individuals and the nature of the business you are considering. My opinion is that starting a company with a team of associates rather than alone is usually desirable and greatly improves your chances of success. However, teams are not without problems. Below is a discussion of some of the pros and cons of teaming.

Factors in favor of teaming

Complementary skills

The most important benefit of starting a company with others is that it brings together many complementary skills. Most people starting a company have never run a business before, and it would be quite unusual for them to have all of the skills needed. Teaming, for example, can bring an engineering/operating type together with a marketing/promoter type. I describe this as an inside/outside combination.

In a high-tech start up, the inside person would help conceive the product and be responsible for its design and manufacture. The outside person would be responsible for raising money and selling the product. In a service business, such as an investment advisory firm, the inside person would carry out the necessary research and make the investment decisions, while the outside person would concentrate on finding clients, managing relations with customers, and generally promoting the business. There is obviously much overlap.

Be sure each team member brings a key skill to the situation. More than three or four people are unlikely to be needed since in most start-up situations there are only a few key skills required. For instance, in my experience, a controller or financial manager need not be part of the founding group. Financial management is a skill that is easy to hire on a part-time basis.

On the other hand, many entrepreneurs, especially those with a technical background, often do not recognize the importance of having a marketing or sales person as a key member of the team.

Risk reduction

Companies formed by teams of three or four people have lower risk than companies formed by one person. If the founder should be unable to perform his or her duties for any reason, one of the other team members could step in and perhaps save the day. The chances for survival are better with a team.

Emotional support

Starting a new company can be a very lonely job. It seems that every decision you make, if wrong, might mean failure. I describe managing a start up as being equivalent to walking down a road that is covered with banana peels. If you step on one, the game is over. A team of equal or near equal partners makes it possible to share the emotional burden. For me this was very important. I do not think I could have started a business alone.

Investors like teams

The importance of this depends on how you go about raising capital and how much capital you need. Investors, either individuals or formal venture capital funds, seem to be much more comfortable with a team than an individual entrepreneur. This may be a good enough reason to form a team even when it might not otherwise be needed. If your business has to do any bank borrowing, you will probably find that bankers are also more likely to lend to companies formed by a team of entrepreneurs.

Improved likelihood of success

In his excellent book entitled *Entrepreneurs in High Technology*, published by Oxford University Press, Prof. Edward Roberts of MIT suggests that the failure rate of technology companies formed by teams of entrepreneurs is much lower than companies formed by individuals, especially if the team includes a marketing person. A recent study of fast growth companies showed that only six percent were founded by one individual, 54 percent had two founders and 40 percent had three or more.

Hewlett-Packard and Teledyne are classic success stories of companies started by teams. More recently Apple Computer, Microsoft, Ben & Jerry's Ice Cream and Genentech are a few of the more notable ventures started by teams of entrepreneurs.

Factors against teaming

Dilution of ownership

Many entrepreneurs are unnecessarily generous in sharing ownership in their new venture. Contributing to this is the common belief that the stock in their venture has no value. Gordon Baty in his book *Entrepreneurship for the Nineties*, published by Prentice Hall, suggests that stock in their venture, such as a share of the ownership, may be the most valuable thing a new company has. Clearly, it is unwise to give away ownership unless the recipient can contribute in a meaningful way.

He also suggests that sharing ownership, either as an outright distribution or as an option, should only be done with key people as a way of providing incentive for future contributions, not as a reward for past contributions. There are other, less expensive ways to give rewards.

Possible serious conflict

I have never seen a start-up business that did not, sooner or later, suffer from conflict among the team members. In my mind the question is not whether there will be conflict but how bad it will be.

Conflict can be caused by the emotional strain of running the new business, a feeling that one partner is not carrying his or her weight, simple personal incompatibility, a spouse who feels their marital relationship has been hurt by the demands of the business, and on and on. I have seen such conflict range from a disagreement that can be resolved by a candid discussion to one so serious that the only solution was selling the company. Recently I read about two partners in a business who actually resorted to fist fights with each other to resolve their disagreements.

Inequalities in responsibility

In most companies formed by a team of entrepreneurs, one is usually selected as president. The others may hold lesser key positions such as vice president of research or vice president of marketing, but all are almost always directors of the firm as well. On the board of directors everyone is equal. The problem results from the president being boss part of the time and an equal at other times. This can be a difficult relationship to deal with.

Bad decisions are hard to undo

When you bring in a team member as an officer and director and give that person stock in the firm, it represents a commitment both for the individual and for the company. You may hope the commitment is greater for the individual but, in fact, it may be greater for the company. If team members do not meet performance expectations or if their degree of commitment changes, it is difficult to remove them from the job, even harder to remove them as directors, and it may be impossible to get the stock back. So be careful.

Let me describe two rather bizarre teaming arrangements as extreme examples of the situations in which otherwise rational people find themselves. In one company that I had business dealings with there were four founders with essentially equal ownership. They agreed that the presidency would rotate among the group annually, with each taking a turn. As you might imagine this worked great for one year until it was time for the first president to step down. In another situation, a spin off from an aircraft company, there were 17 almost equal founding partners. It would take another book to describe the problems this caused, but it took years to unravel.

In summary, teaming arrangements in most start-up companies can be a powerful strength that greatly reduces the risk and increases the probability of success. But they almost always generate problems of some sort that may be hard to resolve. To be aware of this is, to some extent, to be prepared.

Chapter 10

Stolze's Law: The Peter Principle in Reverse

In my reading of books, periodicals, and articles relating to entrepreneurship and the management of new ventures, I have never seen any mention of the Peter Principle and its effect on the competitive behavior of a start-up business. The discussion in the following paragraphs is of immense importance and represents one of the most valuable competitive strengths of a new company.

First let's talk about the Peter Principle. This comes from a book entitled *The Peter Principle*, by Dr. Lawrence J. Peter and Raymond Hull, published by Bantam Books. I recommend this book highly to any student of management. It is a very easy read and quite humorous, but its conclusions are indeed serious.

Dr. Peter suggests that in a large organization, managers tend to be promoted to positions that they are no longer qualified to hold, and then they are not promoted again. He says that in a mature organization most positions are held by individuals who have reached their "level of incompetence."

You can reasonably ask whether this principle is real or nonsense. You better believe that it is real and the larger and more bureaucratic the organization, the more real it is likely to be.

The second question you might ask is whether the Peter Principle applies to start-up ventures. It absolutely does not and, in fact, the opposite is likely to be true. In most start ups that I know of, the key managers have stepped back from much more responsible positions in larger companies, and this gives the new company an immense competitive advantage. I call this Stolze's Law.

At RF Communications, three of the four founders came from the Electronics Division of General Dynamics, in Rochester, N.Y. There, I held the second senior marketing position as General Product Manager in a business unit with about 6,000 employees. Two of the other founders were Chief Engineer and Assistant Chief Engineer of the Communications Laboratory.

What were our jobs at RF Communications? In my case I had the title of President but my job was salesman—plain and simple. My main responsibility was to get orders. How did I do this? I wrote the sales literature, compiled mailing lists, dug out prospects, visited potential customers, made sales calls, wrote proposals, prepared quotations and, most important, closed orders. At General Dynamics, I supervised a product management department of about 40 people. At RF I was a salesman and spent most of my time trying to get orders.

How about the two engineers? At General Dynamics, they supervised a group of about 150 people. At RF Communications, they worked at the bench designing our products.

Why is all this so important to the start-up company? It means that most of the people in the small firm, at least for a while, have stepped back in position. They are working below their highest skill, not above their highest skill. As a result, they are much better at their jobs. As a practical matter, managers of smaller firms almost always know their markets better, know their customers better, know their products better, make decisions faster, and work much more effectively than their counterparts in their larger competitors.

Notice that I say "counterparts," not the same positions. RCA was one of our competitors but my counterpart at RCA was not its president, it was the salesman calling on the same customers in the U.S. government that I called on. And, I was better at that job than he was.

A big company has many competitive advantages over the small firm, but this is one instance in which the smaller firm clearly has the edge, and it is a very important edge.

Chapter 11

The Theory of Distinctive Competence

It is always valuable to look at companies that you consider to be exceptionally good and analyze the reasons for their success. Ask the questions, "What is this company really good at that distinguishes it from its competitors?" and "What represents its most important competitive strength?" Try to identify its distinctive competence. If you do this in a totally objective manner you will be surprised at some of the conclusions you draw.

An example that I especially like to use is the Coca-Cola company. When I ask students to name the distinctive competence of Coca-Cola, they usually suggest:

- Secret formula.
- Youthful image.
- Unique advertising program.
- Taste.
- Distribution system.
- Licensed franchised bottlers.

Which do you think is the best answer? In my mind the distinctive competence of Coca-Cola, by far, is its distribution system. There are over two million outlets for Coca-Cola soft drinks, more than for any other product in the world. Wherever you may be on the face of this earth, if you decide to have a Coke you can usually find one within a hundred feet or so.

How important is this immensely powerful distribution system? My guess is that Coca-Cola could put anything into a bottle or can and within months it would be among the top 10 soft drinks.

Now stop and think for a moment of the problem you would face if you decided to start a company with some kind of new soft drink as your product. You would surely have to think of some way to overcome the power of the Coca-Cola distribution system. It would be hopeless to try to compete with them head on. One approach might be to develop a unique soft drink product that served a market niche that did not depend upon such intensive distribution. Gatorade accomplished this successfully.

A few years ago a new company entered the soft-drink market with a product called Jolt. Its distinctive quality was high caffeine content. Their motto is "Twice the caffeine." They did this at a time when most soft drink companies were emphasizing low caffeine and low sugar. Jolt was an immediate success, attracting national media attention. Their strategy is described in more detail in a later chapter.

Several years ago, Judy Columbus, the founder of one of the most successful real estate firms in Rochester, spoke to my entrepreneurship class. I define her company's success in terms of sales per employee not in terms of total sales volume or number of employees. Her people usually average $3 and $4 million of sales a year, just about the highest of any realtor in the Rochester area. If her employees don't measure up to this they do not last very long.

Before starting her own company, Ms. Columbus was one of the top real estate salespeople in the entire United States; however, now she no longer handles clients herself. If she no longer sells, what does she do that makes her company so successful? She hires, she trains, and she supports her staff of very competent, highly motivated producers. At one time her distinctive competence was selling, now it is hiring and training. To her firm, this is a much more important skill than selling.

Try listing the distinctive competence of a few other companies. You will find that the larger the company, the more likely its distinctive competence will be some aspect of marketing. This is important from a small company viewpoint, because marketing is one of the most difficult and time-consuming competences to develop. Marketing, by and large, depends upon relationships—relationships between a company and its customers, between a company and its distributors, etc. Establishing relationships takes time. They must be earned, they cannot be bought. Time is the one thing a new company has least of.

As an entrepreneur, you can consider the issue of distinctive competence from two directions. First, you can examine your personal skills and the skills of others in your organization to determine how they can be used as the basis for a strategy. Or you can examine the market you wish to address and the competitors you will face, and try to identify the skills and competencies that are needed to succeed in that market.

Another quality found among the great companies of the world is that they tend to concentrate their activities in relatively narrow areas—narrow niches. In recent years, there have been as many examples of large companies selling off lines of business to un-diversify as there have been of companies diversifying.

Recently I read an article telling how Honeywell made a major comeback after years of poor performance. You may recall that Honeywell tried very hard to diversify into and become a major player in the computer business. They devoted vast resources and spent huge sums of money on computers only to abandon the program not many years later. The article mentioned that now Honeywell's key products are process, heating, and air-conditioning control equipment. Honeywell is a smaller but very profitable company today. They went back to their basics and it apparently worked.

Not too long ago Kodak made a major effort to enter the pharmaceutical business by purchasing a number of large drug companies. When it became obvious that this strategy was not working, the board of directors removed the head of the company and hired George Fisher, then president of Motorola. One of his early moves was to sell most of the pharmaceutical companies it purchased just a few years earlier. Kodak is again concentrating on photography, both chemical and digital, and succeeding—another example of a company returning to its niche.

It is also important to recognize that not only is it possible that the distinctive competence of a firm will change over time, but it is likely. I have often thought about the distinctive competence of Xerox. At the beginning, it was clearly superior technology—the electrostatic imaging process they acquired from the inventor, Chester Carlson. Several years later, when they introduced the fabulously successful Model 914 Copier, they expected considerable sales resistance because of its high cost. Their ingenious solution was to not try to sell copiers but to sell copies instead. Their sales pitch was, "Let us put a machine in at no cost—just pay us 10 cents a copy." Customers did not have to make a front-end investment to have the use of a Xerox copier.

Today Xerox is still a great company but everyone has access to its basic technology, and selling copies rather than machines is no longer fashionable. So what is Xerox's present distinctive competence? I think it is two things. One is an outstanding line of advanced, high-end copiers with a multitude of very sophisticated features, and the other is its marketing force which is still about the finest in the industry.

So, when developing a business strategy for a new company, it is very important to identify or develop some special, unique competence that distinguishes you from those with whom you compete. This can be in the area of product, marketing, pricing, manufacturing, service, etc. In most new companies, the main thrust is a unique product or service, but the other areas may be just as significant.

Of crucial importance here is that it is not necessary for you to be good at everything. But, it is extremely important that you be very good at something.

Chapter 12

Why Small Companies Are Better

When developing a fundamental strategy for a start-up business, give a great deal of serious thought identifying the intrinsic strengths of small companies compared to the intrinsic strengths of large companies. Where are small companies stronger? Where are big companies stronger?

Then, when you develop a strategy and select products and markets for your new firm, you should try very hard to maximize the advantage you get from your intrinsic strengths and do whatever you can to minimize the effect of the intrinsic strengths of the larger firm. You cannot hope to completely overcome the strengths of the larger company, but you may be able to reduce the advantage it gives them. This process will also make you more aware of obstacles you may have to face.

Let's talk first about the large firm, and try to identify those areas where large companies have an intrinsic advantage over smaller companies.

Intrinsic strengths of large companies

Financial resources

This, without question, represents the most important competitive advantage of larger companies. The lack of financial resources influences every decision in a small business. Some advantages that large companies get from their greater financial resources are:

- Economies of scale. Large firms can build large plants and manufacture their products in large quantity, thereby benefiting from economies of scale. High production rates usually mean lower cost and, probably, lower prices.

- Full product line. The large firm can have an extensive product line rather than isolated products. In a start up you must first develop, build, sell, and generate cash flow from one product before you have the resources to consider a second. To develop a meaningful line may take years.

- Investment in product development and marketing. Large companies can undertake product developments that require millions of dollars and years of time. They can establish large sales organizations and undertake huge introductory marketing promotions. These are completely out of the question for a small firm.

Momentum/marketing

Big companies have momentum. In business this is the ability to go through down periods or survive bad decisions with a minimum of disruption. It's the ability to weather a recession, a bad product, changes in management, etc. In my view, momentum is achieved by strong marketing, which is one of the most difficult, time consuming, and costly skills for a small company to develop.

Credibility

If you want to know the importance of this, try selling an expensive product to someone who has never heard of your company. You will soon learn how difficult it is to persuade a tough purchasing agent that your company, operating on a shoestring, will stand behind its product when it is far from certain that you will even be around next year.

Structure

Large firms have support organizations carrying out functions that are almost invisible when you work there, but require big investments of time and money to duplicate in a start-up company. Included are quality control, purchasing, incoming inspection, publications, and many others.

Early in the history of RF Communications I received a call from a customer asking about the status of a recent order. I said I would find out and call back. To my amazement and embarrassment, I learned the order had somehow been lost between marketing and manufacturing and that work had not even started. Obviously, we did not have, and desperately needed, an order entry system.

Together these represent a powerful set of advantages that large companies have over small companies. As a practical matter, the small company can do nothing other than become large.

Intrinsic strengths of small companies

At this point you might wonder how the small firm can hope to compete when all these chips are stacked on the other side of the table. Well, all is not lost because there are some areas in which small companies are stronger than big companies. They are just as important, though harder to identify.

Senior people working below their highest skill

This was discussed in an earlier chapter. It may be the most important strength of a small company. You have to replace the Peter Principle with Stolze's Law.

Greater flexibility

Small companies are more flexible and have the ability to react much faster on almost any issue than can a large firm. You can respond rapidly to changes in your competitor's product line or marketing strategy, you can customize your product to better meet your customer's unique needs, and you can make decisions in almost every aspect of the business in days rather than weeks, months, or years.

After years as president of Abbott Laboratories, Kirk Raab became president of Genentech, the incredibly successful biotechnology company. According to Raab, it took about 100 meetings to change Abbott's course a noticeable amount. At Genentech, he said, being president was like being at the helm of a PT Boat.

Determination to succeed

I was once asked what I considered to be the most important factor in the early success of RF Communications. After a few moments I answered, "Our compulsive desire to succeed." I cannot be certain that this was the most important factor, but it was significant. My guess is that employees of large companies never hear the words "compulsive desire to succeed" used by a senior manager. Like Avis, small companies try harder.

More fun

Finally there is the intangible factor that working in a small start up can be more fun. People who truly enjoy what they are doing are likely to do it better. An atmosphere of fun and excitement can be a powerful strength. This is one reason so many large companies are desperately trying to introduce "entrepreneurial spirit" into their operations.

These factors should influence the basic strategy of a start-up company. Clearly, you should avoid those areas where the large company has an intrinsic advantage and emphasize those areas where the small company has an advantage. The small firm holds more chips than most people realize. As a practical matter, there is nothing a large company can do about these except become small, which is their least likely response.

Chapter 13

Start Up Strategies That Work: Picking Your Product and Market

All new companies must make two very important initial decisions: The selection of the product or service that the new company will offer and the selection of the particular market to which it will be offered. These are by far the most important decisions in a new venture.

In deciding on your product or service and selecting the market you intend to address, you should strive to develop a strategy that is different from the strategy of your potential competitors, concentrate in fairly narrow niches, and be innovative in significant ways. Remember these words. Write them on your sleeve. Engrave them on your consciousness.

- Differentiate.
- Concentrate.
- Innovate.

If you can figure out how to include these three ingredients in your new venture, the probability of succeeding will be greatly enhanced.

Differentiate your offering, be it product or service. Rarely is it possible to achieve conspicuous success by following others. Offer your customers benefits that are significantly different than other solutions to their problems. This is very important.

Concentrate your efforts on a fairly narrow offering in a fairly narrow market niche. It is not possible to be good at everything. By concentrating in a narrow or specialized market niche, you may be able to avoid head on competition with larger, well-established firms. Attack your competitor in his toe, not in his heart. This is very important.

Innovate your offering in meaningful ways. Innovation of product or service is obvious. However, it is possible to innovate in anything—pricing, promotion, customer service, distribution, etc. This is very important.

All exceptionally successful companies do these things well—the more you can do, the better. You might ask, "How can a small start-up company with almost no resources achieve these qualities in actual practice? What specifically can it do? How should it approach the problem?"

We have already discussed the issue of distinctive competence. Identify what you and your associates are really good at, and select a market in which these competences will be valued. Next, I suggest you think again about the intrinsic strengths of a small company compared to the intrinsic strengths of a large company. This will help you develop a business strategy that avoids those areas in which large firms have a natural advantage and concentrate on those areas where small firms have a natural advantage.

From here on, this chapter will try to identify a number of specific issues related to product/service selection and market selection that are of paramount importance to the small firm. It includes a lot of do's and don'ts and a number of examples that should help you address the very important questions of what product or service should be offered and what market should be served.

You may have noticed by now that I am a product person. My experience is largely with companies that sell physical products rather than services. However, the things that I say apply to service businesses equally as well as to product businesses. The ideas that I am trying to develop and the principles I describe are the same for both.

Product/service selection

First we will list several things that a new company should avoid when selecting its initial product.

Advanced technology

It is my belief that new companies should not try to pioneer advanced, new technologies. Pioneering a dramatically new technology usually takes a long time, requires substantial capital and involves great risk. This seems to be the natural turf of large firms even though there are some notable exceptions—Polaroid, which pioneered both polarized optics and instant photography, is one, and Xerox, which pioneered electrostatic imaging, is another. Many people will probably disagree with this position, but I still think the risk and cost are usually not right for a startup.

New concepts

Pioneering a new concept is different from pioneering a new technology even though the impact is similar. For example, the new cellular telephone system was a dramatically new concept that utilized existing technology. Only a very large company like AT&T could have successfully introduced such a concept.

Volume production

A very large investment in plant, equipment, and working capital is needed to build almost anything in large volume. Where scale is important, only large companies can succeed.

What then should a new company do if it cannot offer new technology, promote new concepts, or manufacture in large quantity? There are a few things.

Operational innovation

This is not obvious. What I mean by this is to offer products that, even though functionally similar to competitors, have unique operational features. Make your product smaller, lighter in weight, easier to use, easier to install, easier to service, and so forth. Emphasizing operational innovation can provide powerful benefits to your customers, and is perhaps the most effective product/service strategy for a startup.

The following are a number of examples of companies that used the concept of operational innovation as the main thrust in starting a business. If you were to ask the managers of any of these companies whether operational innovation was their main start-up strategy they would probably not know what you were talking about even though they seem to be doing exactly as I suggest. I've have never seen this approach to an initial strategy mentioned in other books about entrepreneurship, yet it represents one of the best ways for an entrepreneur, with limited financial resources, to get a business off the ground.

In the product area the early Apple II personal computer is a classic example of operational innovation. It was built with parts readily available from an electronics parts distributor and employed computer architecture and programming techniques well known for years. I read recently that the Apple II was discontinued in late 1993, after 16 years and production of over five million units.

Digital Equipment Corp. (DEC) is a company that built up sales to the $8 billion range. It was started in the 1950s by Ken Olsen, an MIT engineer, and two partners. Olsen's idea was to build minicomputers—small dedicated machines intended for specialized applications such as monitoring engineering experiments and controlling factory processes. These computers were fairly inexpensive and located right in the work place. Before DEC pioneered this idea, most computers were large mainframes, installed in environmentally controlled computer rooms, and run by trained computer staff. DEC revolutionized an industry. It was years before IBM responded to Olsen's operationally innovative strategy.

Today the personal computer, and all of its variations, has largely replaced minicomputers but for many years DEC almost dominated the computer business.

Compaq Computer is a company that came into existence in 1982, with a personal computer product competing with three well established companies—Apple, IBM, and Radio Shack. Compaq had sales of more than $100 million in its first full year in business and became one of the fastest growing companies in U.S. industrial history. Compaq's first product was a portable computer. All the pieces were packaged into a single unit with a handle so the computer could be lugged around without too much difficulty. Even though it weighed about 30 pounds, the product was an immediate success. By today's standards a 30 pound PC is the equivalent of an elephant, but then the concept was unique.

Until recently, Compaq was able to stay ahead of the competition with a series of new products that were a little more operationally innovative. They were faster, smaller, more versatile—no big technical breakthrough—just more ingenious and imaginative. A few years ago Compaq went through some hard times, but after a number of major management changes they are again one of the leaders in their industry.

A small company, Terry Precision Bicycles For Women, came into existence in 1985. Georgina Terry, the founder, is an avid bicyclist and a mechanical engineer with an M.B.A. degree. When she started her company she routinely cycled 5,000 miles and more a year.

At that time, all bicycles were designed for men, and gave little or no consideration to the different physical characteristics of women. Generally, a woman has longer legs and a shorter torso, narrower shoulders, shorter arms and wider hips than a man. This means that to fit properly, a bicycle intended for a serious woman cyclist should be longer from the saddle to the pedals, shorter from the saddle to the handle bar, and have a narrower handle bar and wider saddle. Even though a bicycle such as this is straightforward to produce, none were available on the market. Georgina Terry formed her company to custom manufacture bicycles, priced in the $1,200 to $1,500 range, for serious women cyclists.

After several years she decided that to increase sales, her company must have a lower priced line than was possible with a small, custom manufacturing operation. She entered into an agreement with a Japanese manufacturer of quality bicycles to supply her with a line of products, built to her specifications, that could be sold for about half of her previous price. Over time she shifted entirely from manufacturing to distributing and her business has grown to about $1 million in annual sales. Interestingly, the Japanese partner was so impressed with Terry's conceptual knowledge of cycle design and ability to distribute such a product that it arranged a loan for her through a Japanese bank to finance inventory.

Several U.S. manufacturers offered similar products for a few years but have since dropped out. For all practical purposes, Terry now has this specialized niche market to herself.

More recently Terry has developed another new and unique product that is very successful. It is a bicycle saddle designed specifically for women. I won't try to describe its features but it seems incredible to me that a product so obviously desirable should have taken so long to reach the market. Georgina Terry clearly understands the needs of serious women cyclists and it took someone with her skills and knowledge to design and introduce this new saddle.

In the service area, H&R Block provides an excellent example of operational innovation. Its business is the preparation of income tax returns for tax payers with uncomplicated returns. H&R Block has more than 9,000 offices, about 40,000 seasonal employees, and is the most successful firm in this business on a national basis. It offers the same generic service as tens of thousands of public accountants, but it better meets the needs of its target market. Service is fast, inexpensive, and provided by trained specialists. As a result H&R Block has an incredibly high percentage of loyal customers who come back year after year. My daughter, who has her own accounting firm specializing in taxes, has nothing but good to say about H&R Block.

Domino's Pizza, headquartered in Ann Arbor, Mich., rocked the pizza industry when it introduced fast home delivery as a key part of its operating strategy. Today almost every neighborhood pizza shop provides the same service. The popularity of home-delivered pizza was at least partly a result of the popularity of microwave ovens. Some people think the most important reason to buy a microwave oven is to reheat home delivered and leftover pizza.

A friend of mine, the former owner of a video rental store, introduced a new twist to this business. He made a deal with a local pizza shop in which they would deliver both a pizza and a video rental at the same time. People staying home on Saturday night to watch a rented movie with the family may very well be interested in both. Why this idea did not succeed, I do not know, but it strikes me as being very innovative and sensitive to the needs of a focused market segment.

Perhaps the best example I know of a service business that used operational innovation as their initial business strategy is Paychex, Inc. It provides payroll preparation services to companies with between one and 200 employees. Tom Golisano, the founder of Paychex, previously worked as sales manager for a large, well-established firm that provided similar services but mostly to large clients.

For a small business with only a handful of employees, the weekly or semi-monthly paychecks can certainly be done by the boss's secretary in just a few hours. There are several simple PC software programs now available that help with the task. But the problem that Paychex identified was the preparation of the many complex reports required by federal and state governments. Companies have to report income tax withholdings, Social Security, disability, unemployment, etc. In New York State, for example, every corporation must file about 42 reports a year. Some states require a larger number. Now this is something a secretary cannot do in a few hours.

You could make the point that while these reports are admittedly difficult for the small business, why don't they just have their accountant do them? But even for the accountant it is both time consuming and expensive. In fact, a high percentage of Paychex's new clients are referrals from accountants who realize this is an area of specialization best done by a specialist. Paychex now has offices all over the country and prints more than two million paychecks a week for its 320,000-plus clients.

Did Paychex have a revolutionary idea or great invention? Absolutely not. What Tom Golisano did was identify a need in a very focused market that was not being served by companies already in the business. Through his very astute planning and brilliant management, he built one of the most successful start-up companies this country has seen in many years. A later chapter of this book includes a more detailed description of Paychex and the problems Golisano faced getting his company off the ground. It provides a superb example for any entrepreneur who wants to learn the right way to start and build a company.

The ability of small companies to conceive and develop operationally innovative offerings is largely a result of the entrepreneur's better understanding of users and their problems.

Customer accommodation

When a large company sets up an elaborate manufacturing facility and produces a product in large quantity, it completely surrenders the ability to modify or adapt that product to meet the specialized needs of a small market segment or individual user. You cannot have economies of scale and production flexibility in the same package. Because the small company cannot have economies of scale, it should adopt a strategy that emphasizes flexibility.

Early in the life of RF Communications I traveled to Washington to demonstrate one of our products to the chief engineer of a large U.S. government agency. When the demo was over I asked him how he liked our radio. He said, "It looks great but it does not meet our requirements." When asked what he meant, the answer was that they wanted the cabinets of all the communications equipment in their radio room to be the same color—green. Our radio was gray. What do you think I said? Obviously, my answer was, "We'll make it green."

There were a few other more technical changes he also wanted which we agreed to for a small additional charge. The sales people of our larger competitors would not even know who in their organization to ask for such modifications.

Through the years RF secured many very large orders because of its willingness and ability to adapt its very complex products to the unique requirements of individual or small groups of customers. Many new ventures have been built on a willingness and ability to accommodate small market segments and even individual customers. This can indeed be a powerful strength of the small company to which the large firm simply cannot respond.

Market selection

Here are a number of factors in the area of market selection that can be of value to a new firm.

Identifying market opportunities

Many new entrepreneurs spend a great deal of time and effort designing the product or service they intend to offer and almost no time confirming that a market exists or can be created for that product or service. This is frequently true of engineers. The best way to identify market opportunities, in my opinion, is preliminary research. The entrepreneur should spend whatever time necessary visiting potential customers, talking to people already in the business, and generally becoming as knowledgeable as possible in the market in which they have an interest. This is true even if it is a business in which they are already working.

Several small companies that I counseled recently used formal market research studies to try to ascertain the existence of a market by having the work done by an outside consultant after the company was under way. This was clearly wrong. First, it is a waste of financial resources to be investigating market opportunities after the company is under way. This should have been done during the early planning stage of the business. Second, formal market research usually provides a lot of data but little knowledge. Unless the entrepreneur already knows a lot about the industry and market, he or she will be unable to interpret the data intelligently.

In the software area, a company whose strategy I find very impressive is Intuit, a Menlo Park, California, firm, whose product is a simple check writing program called Quicken. In its original form Quicken did one simple job and did it extremely well and that was to manage a personal checking account. It set up a file of the names and addresses of the payees to whom checks are regularly sent, printed the check, maintained a check register, assigned each transaction to a category, and included a simple procedure for printing reports. It did not attempt to be a double entry accounting system, an inventory management system, or an investment advisory system. All it did was manage a checkbook. Intuit successfully avoided head-to-head competition with much larger software firms by identifying a very focused market opportunity.

Intuit's marketing strategy was also quite ingenious in that it sold the program at a very low price, somewhere in the $30 to $40 range. In general I do not like the idea of emphasizing low price as a key selling strategy, but Intuit had something else going for it. Many of its customers wanted pre-printed checks to use with the program and these Intuit sold at industry competitive prices. In effect it became the Gillette of the software industry. Give away the razor but sell plenty of blades.

Over the years Intuit added many other features that made the product easier to use and more versatile; that helped sell a lot of upgrades. I use Quicken to manage both my personal and business checking accounts, and I recommend it to all of my family and friends. Even my tax accountant uses Quicken. It drastically reduces the time I need to do my income tax summaries and it's fun to use.

My guess is that there are thousands of computer programmers with the skills to write a program like Quicken. But there are very, very few computer programmers with the skills to identify the need for, and so successfully sell, a program like Quicken.

An interesting problem recently faced by Intuit is that with more and more computers being used by small businesses and in the home, check book management software has become a very attractive market opportunity for some of the giants in the industry. For example, Microsoft, the world's largest software company, recently introduced a product that directly competes with Quicken, and they put a large effort into promoting the product. To date, Intuit seems to be one of the few companies in the software industry able to successfully survive a direct assault by Microsoft. A year or so ago Microsoft tried to acquire Intuit to strengthen its position in this market. But, the deal was never consummated because of regulatory concerns.

Nothing can replace the intuitive knowledge and experience of the entrepreneur when it comes to recognizing a market opportunity, but it is necessary to spend the time and effort to be sure the information is properly used.

Niche markets

By concentrating in a small, highly specialized niche market, a start-up company can eliminate the need for an extensive distribution or sales organization. Niche markets can be efficiently served by a new company with limited resources.

Several years ago I spent time with two very creative scientists who were considering starting a company. They described four products they thought could serve as the basis of their new business. The products were a camera that could photograph the inside of an eyeball, a fiber optics skylight for department stores to bring natural daylight into a clothing department, an infrared system for locating tanks on a smoke-covered battlefield, and an aerial mapping system. All of these seemed like very unique and innovative ideas.

When they asked my opinion I suggested that trying to introduce all of these products into four totally different, completely unrelated markets at the same time was a sure way to guarantee failure. Any one of the ideas alone could serve as the basis of a successful venture. Attempting all four would probably be their downfall.

As an alternative, I suggested that a possible way to capitalize on their obvious creative streak was to start an "inventing business." Their products would be ideas, carried to prototype stage, and then sold or licensed to others who had the marketing skills and resources to develop them into a business. As it turned out, they did not take any of my advice. Early in the Star Wars program, they obtained several major government research studies, which was perhaps the best niche of all for their inventive skills.

In addition to simplifying the marketing process, by concentrating on niche markets it is possible for a new company to minimize the advantages that large firms get through volume manufacturing.

A great example of a company that identified and found success in a niche market is Southwest Airlines, which began operations in 1971. It was founded by an attorney named Herb Kelleher. He had an extremely difficult time getting Southwest "off the ground" because of legal challenges from other airlines that were finally resolved in the Supreme Court.

Most airlines use the hub-and-spoke concept and try to serve their large markets with flights going into and out of a few hub cities. To travel on American Airlines from any northeastern city to the southern states you will almost surely go through Raleigh-Durham. To travel across the country on United Airlines you will almost surely go through Chicago.

Southwest's strategy is different—it serves many midsized and smaller, regional markets and operates city to city directly. It started out by using only a single type of aircraft (the fuel thrifty Boeing 737s), and had found ways to reduce time on the ground way below competitors. Other cost saving strategies? It offered no connections, no luggage transfers, no meals, and most of its planes made 11 trips a day. Because of these and many other efficiencies, its fare structure is below competitors. Yet in some years, it is one of the few profitable airlines in the country today. I read recently that Southwest could set prices 25 percent below its larger competitors...and still operate at a profit. Dallas-based Southwest Airlines made money for over 20 straight years. Wow!

Agency Rent-A-Car Company addresses a niche market generally ignored by the giants such as Hertz and Avis. If your car is damaged in an accident and your insurance coverage provides for a rental car, chances are your agent will refer you to one of several rental cars companies you never heard of. One of these is Agency. They are the nation's largest renter of insurance replacement rental cars. They have no rental booths at airports, they are usually not near hotels or in downtown locations but, because of the unique insurance situation they operate under, their rates are likely to be very low.

In general, offering a narrow line of products or services that by their nature are directed at fairly narrow niche markets is a better strategy for the new firm than trying to get too big too fast. Start by being very good at what you do and growth will come.

A friend of mine, who is both a very successful entrepreneur as well as a venture investor, says that every business, not only start-up businesses, must adopt a niche strategy to have any hope of achieving exceptional success. Trying to be "everything" to "everybody" just does not work.

Several years back Eastman Kodak learned this lesson when they attempted to become a major factor in pharmaceuticals and Xerox learned it when they acquired a major insurance company. Both of these "diversification" strategies failed.

One word of caution: The ultimate niche market is one that has only a single user. Designing a product or offering a service where there is only one potential customer clearly has a lot of risk and in most cases should not be done. What I suggest is that you should seek niche markets that are the "right size" for your specific situation. They must be large enough to be meaningful to your company yet small enough so as not to attract too many larger competitors.

Use of external selling channels

Since a small company cannot reasonably expect to have a large direct sales force, it should not try. It must either select markets and/or products that do not need extensive selling organizations or use channels external to the firm. In almost every industry, there exist representatives, distributors, agents, wholesalers, dealers, etc. that are geographically diverse and well-established with their target customer base. These individuals or organizations are often willing to represent small firms. I strongly encourage new companies to try to locate and use external selling channels as a way to rapidly increase its marketing strength at a minimum of cost. This subject is discussed in more detail in another chapter.

The following story is an indication of what an innovative mind can do to overcome the powerful distribution system of a huge competitor. Some years ago I read that Dr Pepper and Coca-Cola were battling in court over whether Dr Pepper, the soft drink, was legally defined as a cola. I remember thinking that while the world may have many overwhelming problems, the question of whether Dr Pepper was a cola did not seem to be one of them. As I recall, Dr Pepper, which was a small company at the time, won the case and their soft drink was officially not a cola.

Shortly after that, I attended a management seminar and sat next to the president of Dr Pepper at dinner one evening. I asked him what the big deal was in the dispute with Coca-Cola. He said it was extremely important to his company, because he had managed to persuade a number of franchised Coca-Cola bottlers to distribute Dr Pepper. The problem was that these bottlers would not be permitted to handle the product if it was a cola. Gaining access to Coca-Cola's distribution system was clearly a major achievement for Dr Pepper.

The Internet

The Internet is a relatively new information service in which people with access to personal computers can get information about products and services of almost every kind imaginable. This information is available through what is known as Web sites. Almost every organization, company and government agency on the face of the earth now is on the Internet. There are literally thousands and thousands of Web sites. It is hard to think of anything you might want information about that cannot be found somewhere on the Internet. A later chapter is devoted to a more detailed description of Internet and its possible importance to your new business.

Here I only want to mention its importance as a way for a new company to market its products. One of the more successful companies using the Internet as its only method of selling is Amazon.com. Amazon.com is a seller of books on every imaginable subject. I have heard that over 1.5 million titles are available from Amazon.com in a matter of days at discounts of up to 25 percent off the cover price.

The users of Amazon.com are frequently people who want to purchase books but who do not want to or have the time to go to book stores. Entrepreneurs starting new businesses should be sure to become familiar with the Internet to determine whether it is a form of marketing they should use.

A final word

In closing this chapter let's review the principles that a new company might follow in selecting its products/services and markets.

- Start with a well defined distinctive competence that can be used as the basis of the business. You should identify what you and your associates are really good at that distinguishes you from your competitors.

- Think about the special strengths of small, new companies compared to big companies. Try to take maximum advantage of those that represent intrinsic strengths of small companies and avoid those where large companies have an advantage.

- Differentiate your offering in meaningful ways and concentrate in a fairly narrow product area and market niche so that your limited resources can be used as efficiently as possible. In this way, you will avoid head-to-head confrontation with much larger and well-entrenched competitors.

- Be innovative. Most people think of innovation as applying only to products or services. But, as you will see, it is possible to be innovative in almost every aspect of a business including pricing, personnel policy, distribution, sales promotion, and so forth.

- Emphasize the benefits your product or service provide your customers and avoid a strategy that emphasizes low price as your most important competitive thrust. This particular issue is discussed in more detail in another chapter.

Although large companies have competitive advantages that seem impossible to combat, small companies have many strengths that the larger firm cannot duplicate. The challenge faced by the start up is to select an offering and identify a market that takes advantage of these strengths.

Chapter 14

Product/Market Matrix

A helpful tool in selecting the product offering and target market for a new company is a "Product/Market Matrix." An example is shown below.

Along the horizontal axis I show product categories: Existing Products, Modified Products, and New Products. Along the vertical axis, I define market conditions: Existing Markets, Identifiable Markets, and Unknown Markets. Written in each cell of this matrix is a specific product offering. I tried to pick examples based upon the conditions that existed when the product was first introduced, not the situation that exists today. Think for a few moments about the specific products as we go through the discussion of the comparative attractiveness of each cell for a new company.

Existing product/existing market

Start-up companies should avoid this cell at the top left on the chart at all costs. Why should you knock yourself out trying to do better what is already being done well enough? Entry costs into such a market are likely to be very high and profit potential questionable.

Product/Market Matrix

	Existing Products	Modified Products	New Products
Existing Markets	Women's shampoo	Alternative greeting cards	Solid-state still camera
Identifiable Markets	Clothes for professional women	Overnight package delivery	Specialty sports car
Unknown Markets	Mobile pet grooming service	Personal computers	Laser discs

53

An example I use here is women's shampoo. I was staggered when I learned that a number of years ago Gillette, a major consumer products firm, sent out 20 million free samples to introduce a new shampoo product named "Silkience."

When entering an existing market with an existing product about the only competitive moves available to build sales is to lower price. This is almost never an acceptable strategy. For a start up to compete in this cell is almost hopeless.

New product/unknown market

Shown at the bottom right of the chart, this is very dangerous territory for a new firm because of the large uncertainly in both the product area and the market area. The example I use, the old video disc, has been a disaster business for a number of companies. Both RCA and N.V. Philips invested huge amounts of money trying to introduce competitive technologies. Both failed. The market at the time did not want a cumbersome and expensive product that could play video but not record. On the other hand, the video cassette recorder (VCR), with which you can both record or playback, was a huge success.

Modified product/existing market or existing product/identifiable market

For a new business these two cells (top middle and left middle), probably represent the lowest risk. The examples I use are alternative greeting cards and clothes for professional women.

The greeting card industry is dominated by three giants, Hallmark Cards, American Greetings, and Gibson Greetings. Over the past 15 years, dozens of small entrepreneurial card companies have come into existence featuring niche themes not addressed by the big three. These include such things as love themes, humor, inspirational messages, and sex. Many of these startups survive and thrive up to sales levels in the $1 million to $10 million range. At that point, they encounter a common problem: Gaining sufficient distribution in the face of the large marketing organizations of the entrenched giants.

Liz Claiborne launched her clothing business in 1976, selling fashions for professional women. The business has been extremely successful. Claiborne identified this probable market opportunity long ahead of others and tried unsuccessfully to persuade her current employer to switch from junior dresses to clothes directed to fashion conscious, highly-paid working women. They refused, and Liz Claiborne, Inc., was born shortly thereafter.

Existing product/unknown market, modified product/identifiable market, new product/existing market: In these cells, from bottom left to top right, we take a step up in risk—and a step up in opportunity. All things considered, these may be good cells for a start up. They give ample room to differentiate, concentrate, and innovate. The opportunity for reward is high and the risk reasonable.

The three examples used here are a mobile pet grooming service, overnight package delivery, and solid-state still cameras. The first is an easy entry service business. The others would require large amounts of capital, but all might be good opportunities under the right circumstances.

Modified product/unknown market or new product/identifiable market—Many dramatically successful new ventures are in either of these two cells, bottom middle and right middle, as are some notable failures. High-potential rewards are combined with high risk. Generally speaking, these two cells take considerably more vision and guts than you are apt to find in a large firm, yet the risk level may be acceptable for the more venturesome entrepreneur.

One of the examples I use here is the personal computer, which was a huge success for Apple Computer and many companies since, including the Compaq, Dell, and Gateway computer companies. Who would have guessed at the time Apple introduced the Apple II that it would revolutionize the way business is done throughout the world?

The other example is the DeLorean Sports Car. This was a car of unique design introduced by John DeLorean and manufactured in a factory in Ireland. It was introduced with a huge amount of publicity but never sold well and the company soon ceased to exist. Apparently, the car buying public had no interest in such a radical new design. This car program was a disastrous failure for John DeLorean.

This type of analysis is far from failsafe. It is often difficult to decide in which cell a product fits best, the cells can be moving targets, and the process might be criticized for being too simplistic. Yet I still believe that thinking through your fundamental strategy in this way can only be beneficial.

Notice that I have not included price as part of the product/market matrix decision process. Nor should you.

Chapter 15

Supply-Side Strategy

When developing a strategy for a business, most entrepreneurs look at the market they intend to serve and try to identify characteristics and needs of existing or potential customers to which competitors have not responded. This is, of course, a good way to develop a strategy, but it is not the only way.

Another approach is to put yourself in the position of the customer and to look back at the suppliers from the user's perspective. Try to identify ways that suppliers can serve their customers better. This can help you identify opportunities your competitors may not be aware of. I call this "supply-side" strategy.

The following are some situations that might indicate an opportunity for a new business:

- No recent entries in the market.
- A reasonably large market being served by a small number of suppliers.
- The only suppliers are large firms.
- Little or no recent change or innovation in the products or services being offered.
- An existing network of distributors or dealers who do not have access to a product.
- Complacency among suppliers, possibly a result of some kind of government regulation.
- Suppliers that treat customers poorly.

Here are several examples of what I mean:

During the late 1970s, three U.S. companies dominated the market for office copiers—Xerox, IBM, and Kodak. All three sold their products using large, direct-sales organizations. At the same time there existed in the United States, an extensive network of independent office equipment distributors. These organizations sold to the same people in the same companies as the Xerox, IBM, and Kodak salespeople. Yet these office equipment distributors did not have access to a line of copiers with which to compete with the big three.

When Japanese copier companies came into the U.S. market, they discovered that they could get access to an existing network of quality distributors who were anxious to add a line of copiers to their offering. This gave the Japanese firms an instant sales capability that in many ways may have been better than those of the big three, especially for smaller, inexpensive copiers. Today, 20 years later, some of these Japanese copier companies have switched to direct selling, but others stayed with the distributors.

Another example is Federal Express, which provides overnight parcel delivery anywhere in the United States, as well as several other countries. It accomplishes this by having its own fleet of cargo planes pick up parcels at the end of the day at airports all over the country. These planes then fly to Memphis, Tennessee, where the parcels are sorted. Within a few hours, the planes take off again, heading for outlying cities. The parcels are delivered by local truck early the next business day.

This concept was revolutionary at the time. During its early history, Federal Express had a lot of difficulty raising sufficient capital. It took a series of large outside financings, mostly from venture capital firms, and two or three close escapes from the edge of doom before its unusual service produced a satisfactory revenue stream. Today, Federal Express is an important part of the business communications system. It is hard to imagine the business world functioning without Federal Express.

What had Federal Express done? Well, it certainly identified a market opportunity that it addressed in an aggressive and extremely innovative manner. But it also entered an industry with at least three of the supply-side characteristics listed earlier:

* No recent entries in the market.
* Little innovation in the services being offered.
* Customers being treated poorly.

A couple of years ago I sent an Express Mail Letter from Rochester, New York, to a destination in Indiana. Express Mail is the U.S. Postal Service's competitive response to Federal Express. Delivery is guaranteed the following day, or you get your money back. The fee was something like $11. The letter was not delivered the next day as promised. As a matter of curiosity, I decided to see how hard it would be to get a refund. It was harder than I expected. This is what happened:

1. I telephoned the person to whom the letter was sent to get a copy of the receipt showing the time of mailing and the time of delivery.
2. I mailed this to the post office branch from which the letter was sent requesting a refund.
3. The response I got was a special form that had to be filled out and mailed to a central refund processing location. I did this.
4. Next, I received a call from a person, who did not identify himself, telling me to come in for my money. Unfortunately, I was not in the office and took the call from my telephone answering machine.
5. I confused the name of the branch where I was to pick up the refund. When I got there I was directed to the correct branch.
6. I went to the correct branch and asked the clerk for my refund. I was told in no uncertain terms that I could not get a refund until I filled out a special form and sent it to the central processing point along with evidence of late delivery.
7. I tried to no avail to explain that I had already done that.
8. By coincidence the postmaster of the branch walked by and heard an argument developing. He interceded and said he remembered the call and that I could have my money. That's service?

Several weeks later, I decided late in the afternoon to send a package that day to Florida by Federal Express. The package had to be there the following morning. This is what happened:

1. I called the local Federal Express office and was told to call an 800 number.
2. When I did this a woman on the other end asked if I could get the package to one of their deposit boxes before 6 p.m.
3. I said I could not and she said they would handle it. An hour or so later a Federal Express truck arrived at my office and picked up the package.
4. When I tried to pay in advance the driver said they would bill me. I said I had no account with them. He said that was all right, they knew my name and address.
5. The package was delivered the next morning, on time. That's service!

I do not recall what Federal Express charged for this pick-up and delivery. I do not care. I do not know how hard it is to get a refund from Federal Express. I never had to try.

I could give many other examples of companies who discovered an unexpected opportunity by putting themselves in their customers' position and looking back at the suppliers who serve these customers. This can be a somewhat offbeat but very effective way to develop a strategy for a new business.

Chapter 16

Fads vs. Trends

A fad, by definition, is a short-lived but widespread phenomenon. A trend, on the other hand, reflects a relatively long-term direction.

It is extremely important for entrepreneurs to decide whether the business they are considering is a fad or a trend. In either case it may be a good opportunity, but your operating strategy must be entirely different if you hope to succeed. The basic distinction between the two are short term versus long term. If you guess wrong, you could be in for big trouble.

Relatively early in the life of RF Communications, we had to decide whether to enter the citizens band (CB) radio business.

The cost of a CB radio was only a few hundred dollars and many private citizens used CB for emergency communications while on the road. To a large extent, CB has been replaced by the now popular cellular telephone.

At the time, our products were single sideband, long-range, radio communications equipment for military, commercial, and industrial customers. When we faced this decision, the CB market was experiencing explosive growth and U.S. companies serving the market were expanding by leaps and bounds. They were all very profitable.

I personally felt nervous about entering the CB business. We had the technical skills and financial resources, but I was unsure that the market would last. Was citizens band radio a fad or a trend? If it was a fad, we had no interest, if it was a trend, we had no alternative.

Since we did not have good market research skills in our company, we sought counsel from a large management consulting firm that had just completed a major, multi-client, international communications market study. Their conclusion was that CB was here to stay and that within a few years most new cars would include a CB radio as original equipment. They predicted that the market would continue to grow for the foreseeable future. In effect, they suggested that CB was a trend and that we had better move fast.

I still felt uncertain. Because we had several other opportunities at the time that were more attractive than the CB radio business we decided not to enter that market. Within a year or so the CB market collapsed and many companies in the business went down the tubes. I do not know whether we were lucky or smart but in hindsight, I guess it doesn't matter.

More than 20 years ago, Apple Computer pioneered the personal computer—a dramatically new and innovative product sold into a market that did not exist a short time earlier. Predictions were rampant that within several years we would find a PC on every office desk, in every classroom, in every home. Was the personal computer a fad or a trend?

Even though I was not in the business at the time, I concluded that it was probably a trend. Shortly after that, IBM apparently made the same decision...and the rest is history. It is hard to think of a new product that so quickly became a necessity in almost every aspect of our lives than the personal computer.

Another interesting product that looked like a fad when it was first put on the market was the Walkman Personal Cassette Player, introduced a number of years ago by Sony. I remember reading that all of the market research that Sony did indicated that the world did not want this product. However, the Chairman of Sony felt the world *did* want this product. Obviously he was dead right. Years later, the Walkman and countless variations are still extremely popular.

I learned a few years back about a company named Safety First Inc. that sold over four million of the yellow and black diamond-shaped signs that say, "Baby on Board!" These were usually put in car windows. This sign was definately a fad! When sales of the sign tapered off, however, Safety First began selling other safety products for babies that they marketed through several large national retail chains, supermarkets, and drug stores. Safety First apparently thrived with a fad type product that gave it the resources and impetus to expand into a more attractive, long-term type of business.

On the other side of the coin, we might think about Pizza Time Theater, a California based company founded by Nolan Bushnell, who previously started the Atari video game company. Chuck E. Cheese/Pizza Time Theater was a chain of company owned and franchised pizza restaurants featuring animated cartoon characters, including Chuck E. Cheese, and a large room full of video games, as well as the food. The quality of the pizza was excellent, the cartoon characters unique, and the video games interesting.

Business boomed for several years and then the parent company failed as did many of the franchised, privately owned Pizza Time restaurants. I am not certain of all the reasons but two things seem clear. One was that the concept was too dependent on the popularity of video games, which itself was a fad and the other was that the world can only support so many specialty restaurants of this type. What Bushnell and his investors apparently thought was a trend seems to have been a fad.

A few years back another company took over Pizza Time Theater, modified the concept somewhat, and cut back drastically on the number of restaurants. I spoke with the owner of five franchises and was told that business is good and the organization is growing again.

It is easy to suggest, with 20/20 hindsight, that the answers in these situations should have been obvious. But believe me, when RF Communications decided not to enter the citizens band radio market, it didn't feel obvious.

Take another example. Approximately six years or so ago, the Internet appeared on the scene big. At the time, it was difficult to decide whether the Internet was a fad or a trend. Many companies were unsure whether or not they should try to use some of the features of the Internet in the conduct of their business. As I write this fifth edition of *Start Up* in early 1999, it is hard to imagine anything in the history of the world that has had a bigger effect on the way business is conducted. I don't know of any company that does not utilize some of the features of the Internet in carrying out its business. For many it is the heart of its strategy.

Several issues are important here. One is whether a fad type of business is ever right for a start-up company. You can make a very strong point that a start-up firm has a number of qualities that make fad businesses attractive. For instance, they are willing to take risks, they are responsive, they can move fast, and so forth. Surely, to succeed in a fad business these qualities are essential. Yet my personal belief is that it is usually best for a new company to avoid fad type businesses. To succeed, management has to have the foresight to get out at the right time and the skill to get out fast and decisively. These are rare qualities.

In thinking about the fad vs. trend question I tried to list a number of notable fad type products. They are hula hoops, Nehru jackets, quadraphonic sound, and electric carving knives. You can surely think of others. All were bringing forth business at one time...but try to buy any of them today. For some companies these may have been profitable businesses for a short time but my guess is that they had to be pretty fast on their feet to come out whole. A year or so ago I spoke to a meeting of a local business group. At the end of the meeting, they gave me an electric carving knife as a gift. I could hardly believe my eyes.

Trend-based businesses are clearly attractive. They permit sensible planning, have desirable long-term benefits, greatly reward the creative and responsive entrepreneur, and do not require skills unlikely to be found in a start-up company. The big problem in deciding between a fad business and a trend business is telling them apart early enough. In chapter 4, I tell how being street smart or having instinctively good moves is an important personality trait of successful entrepreneurs. This is a business area where being street smart can really save the day.

Chapter 17

Product/Market Zig-Zag

Entering a new market with a new product or service is a very difficult challenge for any business. The risks of doing this are always high and it is an excellent example of "leading from weakness." When you introduce a new product or service, you can never be sure that it will perform satisfactorily or have the right features. When you enter a new market, you can never be certain that your product or service will meet the customer's needs.

Every company starting in business is faced with the challenge of entering a new market with a new product or service. Usually, the company is trying to sell something that it has never sold and it is trying to sell to users who have never before bought anything from that new company. This is one of the many reasons why starting a business is so difficult.

As you overcome this difficulty and your business grows, before long you will seek new opportunities for expansion. You'll try to develop new products and services and identify new market opportunities. My very strong advice is that it is almost always wrong to try to do them both at the same time. A better strategy is what I call "Product/Market Zig-Zag."

Let us assume that after a year in business, your firm has successfully introduced its initial product. Call it "Product A." It has been accepted by your customers, it can be produced efficiently, and all the bugs are out. This product is being sold into what we will call "Market A." You have a small sales force that calls on the customers in this market, you have established a series of strong distributors and you are competing effectively. Everything is great. Product A is selling well in Market A. However, you have some extra financial resources that you want to invest in growth.

My advice is to either take your existing product and try to sell it to a new group of customers or develop a new product and sell it to your existing group of customers.

- New product to an old market.
- Or, old product to a new market.
- But **never, ever**, a new product to a new market.

This is shown in the chart on the following page.

After you have established the new product or have penetrated the new market, you can consider doing the same thing again. This time, you will be doing it from a stronger base. Zig-zag between product and market.

Paychex, Inc. is a company that provides payroll preparation services to many small businesses. The market that it targets are

```
Product A  ──▶  Present Strategy  ──▶  Market A
         ╲         ╱        ╲         ╱
          Acceptable Strategies
         ╱         ╲        ╱         ╲
Product B  ──▶   Bad Strategy   ──▶  Market B
```

Product/Market Zig-Zag

companies with between two and 200 employees. Paychex is a fast growing, very profitable and very successful company by any standard.

A number of years ago, Paychex decided to diversify by introducing a service called "Jobline." Jobline tried to match individuals interested in changing jobs with companies interested in hiring. This was done on an experimental basis in the Boston area.

Paychex collected and published long lists of condensed resumes. When a firm had a need, it could contact Jobline and, for a fee, get a list of candidates who might be qualified for the position. This business did not succeed and after a few years, the project was abandoned. This is a good example of the difficulty of trying to penetrate a brand new market with a brand new offering.

More recently, Paychex began packaging fringe benefit programs, such as health, disability, and workman's compensation insurance, that could be offered to the client base that buys its payroll service—small companies that do not have benefit specialists on their staffs. It also began selling employee handbooks customized for individual users. Here Paychex has put together several innovative offerings that are sold to its existing customers. These programs are a success.

Another example is Xerox. At one point, Xerox made a major effort to enter the computer business. As I recall, it paid something like $1 billion to purchase Scientific Data Systems, a fast growing, West Coast computer company. Over the years, Xerox made other major moves to enter into this market. For example, its Palo Alto research center is credited with pioneering the use of graphical user interfaces in personal computers, a technique that was so successful in Apple's Macintosh and in Microsoft's Windows. Xerox was one of the early companies on the market with a personal computer product.

Perhaps now you should ask, "How important is the computer business to Xerox today?" As best I know the answer is, "Not very." Xerox is still the world leader in photocopiers, introducing new and totally revolutionary products on a regular basis...but its computer-related business is very small. I believe that the reason for Xerox's failure with computers was that it was trying to enter a market it did truly did not understand with products it truly did not understand. Computers are completely different both in technology and in marketing than copiers.

Introducing a new product or entering a new market is always a formidable challenge for a business. If you try to do only one at a time, you have the benefit of at least some strength and experience helping the process.

Chapter 18

Buying a Franchise: Another Way to Own a Business

Buying a franchise in an established business is another way to become an entrepreneur. However, buying a franchise is a very specialized undertaking. There are numerous books and magazines devoted to franchising and you should read some of these. There are also lawyers, accountants, and franchise consultants who are expert in the field who you should consider using before you sign on the dotted line.

In the middle 1990s there were about 540,000 franchised outlets in operation in the United States accounting for about one-third of all retail sales. The franchise industry employed more than seven million full-time or part-time people. There are over 4,000 companies from which franchises can be bought representing about 60 different industries. From this data you can see that franchising is big, big business.

The larger franchise companies, such as McDonalds, Holiday Inn, and Wendy's frequently require investments in excess of $1 million and, as a practical matter, simply are not an option for the average person interested in owning a business. On the other hand, there are other franchises available, where the investment is modest.

Lists of franchise opportunities are included in franchise guides and handbooks that can be obtained from most libraries and many bookstores. If you are seriously thinking of buying a franchise, be sure to read some of these at the very beginning of your search to get a feel for the scope and diversity of franchise businesses.

There are two different types of franchises: One is a *product* franchise where the franchisee obtains the rights to purchase and sell the product of the franchiser, perhaps operating the business under his or her own name rather than the franchiser's name. The most common of this type is an automobile dealership.

If you want to buy a new Chevrolet you don't go to a Chrysler dealer. However, in recent years it has become more common for a single dealer to offer more than one brand of automobile, such as a U.S. brand as well as a Japanese brand. In these cases, they must obtain separate franchises for each brand, each with its own restrictions.

The other type of franchise is a *business format* franchise. Here it is usual to operate the business under the franchiser's name. Typical of these is a McDonalds or Holiday Inn franchise. In these cases, it is often difficult for customers to know whether they are in a franchised or a company-owned unit.

The main advantage of buying a franchise rather than starting a business from scratch is that the failure rate among franchised businesses is lower than among independently created businesses. You are buying a proven business idea and you get a lot of help running it.

In a franchise, you begin with a known product or service, you usually receive training and expert guidance in the operation of the business, you benefit from the advertising and promotional efforts of the parent company, you may receive volume buying economies, you follow standardized procedures and operating methods that have proven successful for others, and you may get the benefit of new products or services developed by the franchiser. All of these can give you a valuable head start. In effect, you are in business *for* yourself—not in business *by* yourself.

Some of the disadvantages are that the up-front costs may be considerable, there are probably continuing carrying costs in the form of royalties and advertising sharing fees, and you will probably have to accept many restraints and limitations on your freedom to zig and zag in directions you evolve on your own. These restraints may reduce the upside potential and long term financial rewards. And if the franchiser goes bust or gets into financial difficulties, your life can become very complicated.

All sellers of franchises are required by the Federal Trade Commission to give the potential buyer a document called a Franchise Offering Circular. This provides detailed information about the franchiser's business and is intended to protect the buyer. Be sure to read it carefully. Many states also have laws that regulate the operation of franchises. Learn about these.

If you are serious about buying a franchise you should consider attending one of seven or eight expositions or trade shows held each year which will have as many as 400 franchise companies exhibiting.

Other organizations that support the franchise industry include these:

- American Association of Franchisees and Dealers, 800-733-9858
- International Franchise Association, 202-628-8000
- Annual Franchise Directory, 716-754-4669

Buying a franchise is far from a fail-safe way to have a business. You should go about the selection of a franchise in a thorough and rigorous way. Evaluate the product or service, analyze the market, study your competitors, and learn all you can about the business from others. Write a business plan of your own. The contents of the plan may be different than for other types of businesses, but the importance is equally as great.

When buying a franchise, you are free to talk to other franchisees who have gone down the same path you are considering, and the likelihood is that they will be willing to share their experiences. One important thing to know is how many units of that franchise were abandoned or sold by the owners within a short period of time. Also, you should be sure that you have reasonable geographic protection and that the franchiser cannot open other units so close as to negatively affect your sales. I read an article recently where a disenchanted franchisee of a major fast food chain was quoted as saying, "It's just buying a hard, low-paying job with long hours."

In summary, I view buying a franchise as one of a number of acceptable ways of being an entrepreneur. But you should be just as careful and just as diligent as you would in starting a business of any kind.

Chapter 19

Why People Buy: Value, Benefits, and Price

This section is about pricing. But before we get to the details, I suggest you make a list of what you consider to be the five or six best companies in the United States. Define "best" in any way that you like. List any type of companies from any industries. Write down your choices before reading further. My list includes the following companies:

- Microsoft.
- Bristol-Myers.
- Hewlett-Packard.
- Bloomingdale's department store.
- Coca-Cola.

Your list is probably entirely different. One quality common to all of the companies on my list is that rarely do their customers make their purchase decision because of price. In no case are these companies the low price player in their industry and in many cases they are the high price player. Yet, they are almost always the most profitable. How do you explain this?

I explain it by using the following very simple formula:

$$\text{Value} = \frac{\text{Benefits}}{\text{Price}}$$

This formula suggests that buyers, when making a purchase decision, select what they consider to be the best value—all things considered. And it suggests that value is equal to the benefits they perceive divided by the price. Price is only one part of the purchase decision process.

If you want to increase your customers' perceived value of your product, you can do so by either increasing the benefits or decreasing the price. It is usually preferable to work on the benefits, which should make it possible to sell at a higher price. Unless you do this, the likelihood of your company being reasonably profitable is small.

Surely, at this point, some readers will suggest that these companies are either lucky or that they can only demand high prices because they dominate their markets. First, I reject the idea that luck has anything to do with it. Consistent winners are always lucky. As Malcolm Forbes, Sr., once said, "The harder you work the luckier you get."

Second, I reject market dominance as the key issue. Instead, I suggest that all the companies on my list, and probably your list as well, follow the pricing approach described above as a deliberate strategy. They surround their offering with so many benefits of such great value to their customers that they invariably can command a higher price.

It is because of this that they are able to dominate their market. Anyone who suggests that good companies can justify higher prices because of market dominance has the cart before the horse. It may be possible in the short-term but in the long-term, it just is not true. A large, dominant company that is going bad may be able to demand higher prices for a while based upon its reputation; however, unless it keeps its offering sharp, this dominance will not last.

For a new company, the only way to get high prices is to have an offering that provides benefits for which users are willing to pay a premium. Doing this is the best way to gain market share and be profitable at the same time.

Another way of looking at this is to consider what happens if your offering (product or service) is identical to your competitor's. In this case, the only thing you can do to increase sales is to cut your price. Your competitor's reaction is predictable (dropping prices further than yours). And you have only one move. In the long term, selling price seldom works.

If you permit your company to develop the mindset that emphasizing price is an acceptable strategy, sooner or later your business will be in trouble. The alternative to price cutting is to increase the benefits of your offering.

How can you do this? You can include innovative features in your product that your competitor does not have (as does Microsoft). You can offer a continuous stream of new products (as does Bristol-Myers). You can build an extremely effective marketing organization with a great product offering and concentrate on being a safe, dependable buy (as does Hewlett-Packard). You can offer a combination of unique products and an exciting buying environment (as does Bloomingdale's). Or you can concentrate on extensive distribution and availability (as does Coca-Cola).

You can reasonably stop me here to point out that the benefits I list are things that are often not available to a small start-up firm. Extensive distribution systems and the perception of dependability take years to develop. True. But earlier, we identified a number of strengths of small companies. The ability to customize products for small market segments or individual customers, fast response to changes in the market, and better understanding of customers' needs are just a few of the ways that small companies are better than big companies. Convert these strengths into benefits.

In summary, I suggest that the only pricing strategy that makes sense is to work very hard to surround your product or service with benefits, both tangible and intangible, both rational and emotional, both large and small, that will cause your customers to perceive a value that is greater than their alternative. Then, you will have justified a higher price. Companies, large or small, that continually emphasize low price as a competitive strategy are almost always lousy companies that sooner or later either reverse the strategy or find themselves in very serious trouble.

In discussing this approach to pricing to business groups or classes in entrepreneurship, I am always challenged by someone who names companies that seem to be exceptions. Usually they are retail chains that, through volume buying and a willingness to operate at lower margins, are able to sell at lower prices. My response is to accept the fact that there may be exceptions, but I also name a long list of similar companies who also emphasized low price as their main strategy that are no longer in existence.

My point is that by emphasizing benefits rather than price you are more likely to have a profitable, successful business.

Chapter 20

Marketing Means Selling

It is an absolute truth that unless a start-up company can sell its offering (and sell it fast) it will not survive. Getting orders, selling your product or service to paying customers, is of crucial importance to a new firm. I cannot emphasize this enough.

You would be amazed at the number of entrepreneurs who simply do not understand both the importance and urgency of getting orders. For a company to survive it must have positive cash flow. Sooner rather than later, its cash receipts from orders must be greater than its cash expenditures. Early on, cash is generated by the personal investment of the entrepreneur, by borrowing and/or by raising outside equity capital. But these sources only last for a short time. It is imperative that the new firm generate positive cash flow through the sale of its offering to paying customers, before its sources of capital are depleted.

The only way to do this is to get orders. Getting orders is the main game in a new business.

Many people in both the business world and in academia go to a great deal of trouble to differentiate between *marketing* and *selling*. They consider marketing to be more dignified than selling and in fact, many marketing programs do not even include selling as part of the agenda. My solution to this is that you can call the process anything you want, but the basic problem remains the same, especially for a small or new company, and that is getting orders. Exactly what you do, which element of the marketing process your choose to follow will vary depending on the exact nature of your business. But whatever you call the process the goal remains the same: That is to get orders.

How does a new start-up company go about getting orders? Well, you do not do market research or quantitative competitive analysis or consumer surveys. These should have been done before you started the company. You do not develop long-term marketing strategies, and you do not do computer modeling.

However, you *do* communicate information about your products and services to as many potential users as possible and, most importantly, you sell. Finally, you do all this in the most efficient and effective way possible within the financial constraints of the small firm.

The reality is that selling, influencing the decisions of others, is something we spend more time doing, in both our business and personal lives, than almost any other activity. Let me give a few examples:

- You get up in the morning and ask your two year old what she wants for breakfast. She says, "ice cream" and you say, "cereal." You have to sell!
- You ask your boss for a raise. The response is, "Why do you think you deserve a raise?" You have to sell!
- Before you leave the office in the evening you call your spouse and say, "I have had a hard day, let's go out to dinner." He or she answers, "Great, where will we go?" You say, "How about McDonald's?" Your spouse says, "I sort of had Chez Paree in mind." You both have to sell!
- Hopefully, as an entrepreneur, you are also spending a lot of time selling your customers.

If you think about it you can only conclude that our entire lives are devoted to "sell, sell, sell!!!" Having emphasized how important selling is, I will now tell you what a difficult job it is for the small firm and suggest some things that might be done.

Selling direct

Many large companies sell with a direct sales force of company-employed sales people. This is very expensive and takes years to implement. The only way a small firm can hope to sell direct is to focus on a very narrow niche market that can be addressed by a small number of people. I have already stressed this point.

High-level selling

In a startup, the head of the company is almost always an effective salesperson. He or she knows the customer better, knows the product better, works harder, and can make decisions on the spot. Every buyer likes to deal with the head of the firm. When making a call or setting up an appointment, few people will refuse to see "the president." Clearly, this is one of the most effective uses of the time for the head of a start-up company. Getting orders is crucial and the best person for getting orders is the boss.

Ross Perot was a star IBM field salesman before he started Electronic Data Systems. Later he continued as a star salesman for EDS while being an effective chief executive as well.

Another good example is Bill Gates, the founder and head of Microsoft, the world's largest software company. Yes, Bill Gates has a great knowledge of computers and computer software but what he really does well is to promote Microsoft products using every form of marketing and selling ever invented. In my opinion, the main factor in the amazing success of Microsoft is Bill Gates's selling skills and understanding of the market for its products. In many big companies, the president rarely sees a customer.

Using external channels

The next alternative, and most small companies follow this course, is to use some type of marketing channel external to the firm. Use marketing intermediaries, such as agents, representatives, distributors, jobbers, wholesalers, retailers, dealers, and so forth, whichever are appropriate in your business. The number of marketing intermediaries available in the United States is great, and they are available to sell almost every imaginable product or service. Shown below are some of the pros and cons of a small firm selling through independent marketing intermediaries.

Pros

- No fixed cost, they are only paid when they get orders.
- They can be put into place fast.

- If they have complementary lines, the strength of their offering may be greater than yours alone.
- They will often handle training, installation, warranty, and service.
- As a new and unknown firm, you can benefit from their reputation with their customers.
- They know the territory.

Cons

- It is difficult to train and monitor external marketing organizations.
- They tend to emphasize the things that are easy to sell, which may not be yours.
- If they are very successful they become hard to control.
- Your customers may have more loyalty to your representative than to you.
- They require a lot of support.

In most situations the pros far outweigh the cons. However, managing an external marketing force is complex. Here are a few key issues:

- A large part of your selling effort must be devoted to finding, managing, and keeping top-quality members of your distribution channel.
- Philosophically you should operate as if the selling intermediary is part of your organization, not an outsider.
- You must compete constantly for their attention and effort.
- You must treat them fairly by such actions as paying generous commissions, paying commissions promptly, backing up your product, being responsive to their inquiries, and keeping your promises.

Managing external channel members is a specialized skill that requires maximum attention.

Licensing and private-label resale

Other alternatives that I used successfully on a number of occasions are private-label resale and license arrangements. If you have a very strong product offering and limited marketing and selling skills, you may be able to find an established company that will purchase or license your product to resell it under either its name or yours.

In recent years a number of small software companies with products such as spelling checkers, data compression techniques, virus detectors, and so forth, have licensed the use of their very specialized products to larger, better known software companies with better marketing skills either for incorporation as a feature in their products or to sell as part of their product line.

The advantages and disadvantages of these arrangements are:

Pros

- Access to skills that might take years to build in your own company.
- Single large order, with delivery scheduled over an extended period.
- No credit risk or collection problem.
- Possible ability to negotiate advance payment.
- Quick access to the market.
- The larger firm's reputation carries over to your product.

Cons

- You don't develop marketing strength in your company.

- You may be subject to price pressure.
- You build no reputation for your firm with the end user.

The Internet

Hardly a day goes by that when you open any magazine or newspaper that you do not see at least one article about the Internet. In some industries the ability to sell products and/or services over the Internet has virtually resulted in a revolution. I am not referring to Internet companies as an investment but as a way to reach customers and get orders for whatever product or service you are trying to sell. This has become such an important channel in so many industries that I will cover the subject in more detail in the following chapter rather than here.

Franchising and multilevel marketing

These are two somewhat different ways of selling, which have become very popular in recent years. Chapter 18 gives a description of each along with its pros and cons.

Advertising/sales promotion

Promoting your offering and communicating information about it to potential customers is another complex problem. The traditional way of doing this is through media advertising—trade journals, magazines, newspapers, television, and radio. This is expensive. As an alternative, small companies should make extensive use of new product releases—which trade magazines usually publish at no cost, papers in professional journals, and presentation of papers at seminars and meetings.

If you decide to use paid advertising, choose your media with care and imagination.

I had a very interesting experience that really opened my eyes on how innovative you can be in the area of product promotion at very low cost.

RF Communications' products, as I mentioned earlier, were two-way radios sold to military and government customers throughout the world—a very hard market to target indeed. Even though we made no products used by amateur radio operators, our most effective advertising medium turned out to be a magazine called QST, the official monthly publication of the amateur radio fraternity. Why would we advertise in this magazine when we made no products bought by amateurs? Because most communications engineers in countries all over the world are amateur radio operators! You could see QST lying around radio rooms everywhere. Only a tiny fraction of the readers of QST were potential customers, but almost all of our potential customers were readers of QST. And, because it was the publication of a private society, space costs were fairly low. Through the years, RF Communications received a number of very large orders that could be directly traced to these ads.

Direct mail selling

For a small company, direct mail is another selling alternative that should be considered. It can be efficient and cost effective in focused markets. I read recently that in 1990 over 50 percent of American adults purchased products through mail order—more than twice as many as in 1983. In any one year there are over 8,000 different catalogs mailed out in the United States. Consumers and businesses spend over $175 billion on mail order products. My guess is that many of these buyers are now using the Internet, but direct mail surely still represents a huge market.

Incidentally, if you have trouble finding a mailing list contact your advertising agency. There are lists available for every specialized market segment imaginable. Here are some examples of lists that you can purchase at very modest cost:

Mailing Lists

Category	Number
Sperm banks	20
Rubber band manufacturers	30
Windmill wholesalers	80
Air ambulances services	80
Dude ranches	240
Spiritualists	430
Tattoo shops	500
Banks with assets between $5 and $9.9 million	950
College bookstore managers	3,545
Baptist churches	55,520
Medical specialists	614,146
Small businesses	2,300,000

And, of course, another source of lists is other users of lists. Almost every magazine and every company in the mail order business is willing to sell you its list of customers. I have heard that for some companies in the mail order business, selling its list of customers is a more profitable business than selling its products.

Mail order selling requires you to have a good catalog or brochure describing your offering and probably an 800 number over which you can take orders. In addition, you must be able to accept payment with credit cards and have the facilities to store, pack, and ship your products. During the starting phase, these services can all be purchased from specialized outside organizations at fairly reasonable prices. These are called "Fulfillment Companies." As your business grows you will undoubtedly decide to do some of them yourself.

Incidentally, when you do this kind of mailing be sure that the letters are signed in blue ink, and that they always include a postscript. Experience has shown that people usually read postscripts, often before they read the body of the letter. Also, some mailing experts recommend that stamps be used for postage rather than bulk rate pre-printed mailing envelopes. Envelopes with stamps are more likely to be opened rather than thrown in the trash barrel—even when bulk rate stamps—are used. My personal preference is to send all your mailings first class, however, mine are usually fairly small.

Selling by mail (or mail order marketing as it is now called) has been the strategy of many very successful companies in recent years. One that I find especially intriguing is Lands' End. It was founded in 1962 by Gary Comer, a copywriter at Young & Rubicam and an avid sailor. Initially, Lands' End sold specialty yacht hardware, but soon found that men's and women's clothing and high quality canvas luggage were more profitable. Today, it mails out millions of its monthly catalog, employs over 6,000 people, and is one of the premier firms in this highly-competitive industry. It emphasizes quality products, outstanding service, competitive prices, and a return policy with no questions asked. I have never purchased anything from Lands' End without being completely satisfied with the experience.

Another interesting example is Calyx & Corolla based in San Francisco. This company, founded by Ruth Owades in 1988, sells fresh flowers and plants with a mail order catalog. She sends out six seasonal catalogs a year. Sales in 1995 were about $20 million. Calyx & Corolla has 50 full-time employees and many part time people during the heavy selling seasons—Easter, Valentine's Day, Mothers Day, and other holidays. When an order is received, it is forwarded to one of 25 growers in both

Florida and California with whom Calyx & Corolla has a strategic relationship. The flowers are shipped in insulated boxes by Federal Express. Owades has been quoted as saying that flowers are the ideal gift. They are "non-fattening, low-cholesterol, moderately-priced, and even politically correct."

Lillian Vernon is another big-time mail order player. It mails out over 179 million catalogs annually to over 12 million people and has annual sales of over $200 million.

The Direct Marketing Association is a source of information and material about this form of marketing. Its publication entitled *The DMA Catalog Start Up Resource Guide* is a collection of tips and guidelines for starting a mail order business. It is available from the association at 212-768-7277.

Infomercials

Over the past few years, another selling method has emerged that made it possible for several new companies to achieve amazing success over a very short period of time. An "infomercial" is a 15 minute or longer television program produced by the selling company and put on the air or on cable as a paid advertisement. These are often aired during the late night hours when rates are lower. Those that are most successful seem to use well known personalities as part of the program. Even though the viewers may never have heard of the company or its product, they will have heard of the individual promoting the product.

Two good examples are Victoria Jackson Cosmetics, which sells a line of facial foundations and other makeup products, and Anthony Robbins, who sells a program for increasing ones self-confidence and self-esteem. Victoria Jackson uses movie personalities, such as Ali McGraw, and Anthony Robbins uses football star Fran Tarkenton.

I read recently Victoria Jackson had a great deal of difficulty raising initial capital for her venture. She was quoted as saying, "Anyone who takes no for an answer isn't an entrepreneur."

Recently, I have noticed many more infomercials on TV and cable for some type of exercise or body building equipment. They all seem to include a muscle bound man and a very shapely young woman explaining how you can improve your physique and general health by purchasing one of their odd-looking machines.

Whether infomercials are appropriate for your business depends on the nature of the business. But many companies now using this innovative approach have achieved outstanding results.

Publicity

Although most entrepreneurs begin marketing their companies through advertising, direct mail, telemarketing, or trade shows, one of the best and least expensive ways to generate interest in a company's product or service is through publicity. You need to get your name in a newspaper article, get interviewed for a TV newscast, or perhaps participate in a radio program. Anything you do that gets a mention of your company, your product, your service, or your employees in the media is considered publicity.

It may surprise you that a large percentage of stories appearing in your local newspaper come directly from press releases and information provided by publicity-seeking organizations. Be sure to take advantage of every opportunity to communicate with the media alerting them to interesting happenings at your company. Publicity is often called "free advertising" because you are featured in a published article or broadcast, but you don't pay for it. The advantages of publicity are:

- It's free. Your only costs are for sending out information to the media in the form of press releases, announcements, or letters.
- Articles and editorials are considered much more credible than advertising. You receive implied endorsement from the publication or station just by being mentioned.
- You often have more space in an article (versus an ad) to explain exactly what your company does or what your specialty is.
- The more publicity you get, the more successful you are perceived to be.

Some of the disadvantages are:

- You have no control over the content of a news story or article. Editors will use the information if they have space, and it may or may not say what you want it to.
- There is no guarantee that if you are interviewed for a story that you will actually be mentioned. Sometimes editors will cut out part of an article because of space constraints or may even discard it altogether.

Like other marketing methods, publicity can help generate sales leads, educate potential customers regarding what you are selling, and project a company image of professionalism and success.

My most convincing example of the power of getting your name out happened when I was trying to sell the first edition of this book which I self-published. I was a guest on a Saturday morning program called "Sound Money" on National Public Radio which was carried by about 95 stations throughout the country. When I got back to my office from New York City on Saturday afternoon, I had about 40 calls on my answering machine from people wanting to purchase copies. I sat taking calls the rest of Saturday and all day Sunday and Monday and sold several hundred books all at the cover price. And this was without an 800 number. So you can see the power of publicity.

Make It Easier For Your Customers To Buy

Finally, an approach to selling that I never read about in the marketing literature is, simply, to make it easier for your customer to buy. Analyze the buying practices and habits in the markets that you selected. Try to identify the things that make life difficult for the person making the buying decision and then do everything possible to remove those obstacles. Make his or her job easier.

Selling to communications customers in places such as Nigeria, Tanzania, Saudi Arabia, and Indonesia was difficult for RF Communications. We analyzed the problem and discovered that the buying process was unbelievably complex. Consider the problem of the director of communications for the army in any one of these countries. First of all, he is not sure what he needs to buy. Then, when he figures that out, he has difficulty finding out where such equipment might be available. After that, he must design the system—select operating frequencies, antenna locations, and so forth. Then comes the preparation of a purchase specification and competitive bidding. He must get the purchase approved at a very high government level, perhaps even by the president of the country. Funds must be put into the national budget, and foreign exchange established (extremely hard for some countries). After a supplier is selected, the order must be placed and confirmed. Then, letters of credit set up (the normal payment process) through at least two international banks. The equipment must be inspected before shipment and cleared through the buying country's customs.

Finally, all that remains to be done is unpacking, installing, and putting into operation in some remote area of the world an elaborate configuration of high-tech electronics, some of which might have been damaged or lost in shipment.

How do you like that for a buying process? What an opportunity for a creative, innovative seller! Some of the things we did were to prepare instructional material that helped the customers' engineers design the system. We also wrote a detailed specification in our brochure that was good enough for procurement purposes. We included in our standard catalog and price list every accessory and piece of installation material that they could possibly need, we offered a variety of spare parts kits so that the entire package could be bought from one source, and we offered training in either our plant or the user's facility. In short, we tried very hard to simplify the buying process for the user and make RF Communications a more attractive supplier.

Why companies fail

In closing this chapter, I want to say a few words about why companies fail. Early in my career I worked for a man who told about a company he and his brother started. He said that the business was a great success, but it failed because they ran out of money. I had little management experience at the time but what he said bothered me. Something about it seemed wrong.

Years later, after I started my own business I think I figured out why his statement bothered me. First of all, being a success includes not running out of money. That seems pretty obvious.

Second, I do not believe that companies fail because they run out of money. They fail because they run out of orders. Sure, his company ran out of money, but that was not the cause of the problem—it was the result of the problem. I do not know what their business was but it seems to me if they were halfway decent managers and had been more successful selling whatever it was they were making, they would not have run out of money and the business might not have failed.

A few years ago a company started in Rochester with the intention of bringing a new, very high tech product to market for use by the semi-conductor industry. I was told that they raised a total of approximately $72 million from individual investors, venture capital firms, private placements, New York State guaranteed loans and other sources before they ceased operations. Unfortunately, I was one of their individual investors. Was this company's problem a lack of capital? I seriously doubt it.

In summary, the problem of getting orders, selling, is crucial, yes crucial, to any new business. It must be done well, and done fast, if the firm is to have a hope for survival.

Chapter 21

Using the Internet for an Entrepreneur

I want to thank Mr. Peter Davidson, president of APEX Information Management Consultants, Inc. (716-342-9420) for his assistance in writing this chapter.

This chapter of the book is devoted to the Internet (the Net) and how it can be used by an entrepreneur in starting a business.

The Internet has become very popular in the past few years. Literally millions of people both in the United States and throughout the world use the Net for many different purposes. I am far from being a computer expert and will not try to tell you how the Internet came into existence or how it works. This chapter will be limited to describing some of its important features and how they can help an entrepreneur. The particular items I will discuss are these:

1. **E-mail.** This is a feature that makes it possible to send messages, files, photographs, and other information to other users of the Internet. E-mail makes it possible to send messages at very low cost and usually in a matter of seconds, minutes, or hours—much faster then the U.S. Mail or overnight delivery services such as Federal Express or UPS.
2. **Sources of information.** By using the World Wide Web (WWW) you can have access to information on almost any subject known to man. Many government agencies, universities, private organizations, magazines, newspapers, companies, etc. all have Web sites which are usually available in seconds and minutes and usually at no cost.
3. **How you can promote your business.** If you have your own Web site, you can provide other Web users (read: potential customers) with information about your company and your products and/or services so that they can make purchases either at retail outlets, through distributors, or directly from your company.
4. **Selling your products and services over the Net.** Whether this is applicable to you depends on the nature of your business and what you are selling. Some industries (such as books, travel, the stock market, and many others) have almost been revolutionized by their ability to sell their products and services over the Internet.

Access to the Internet

To use the Internet for any purpose, you must first gain access through an Internet Service Provider (ISP). There are many of these all around the country. I personally use America Online (AOL), the country's leading information service which has about 15 million subscribers. At a modest cost, currently about $22 per month, you can get an e-mail address and unlimited use of that service, and unlimited access to the Internet, in addition to AOL's other services. There are other organizations that provide access to the Internet with some benefits not available from AOL. One of the reasons I use AOL is that I travel frequently to various parts of the country and almost everywhere I go I can usually find a local telephone number to reach them without incurring a long distance charge.

E-mail

To use e-mail you must know the e-mail address of the person with whom you want to communicate. Most business people include their e-mail address on their letterhead along with their business address. Also, almost every advertisement in almost every publication includes an e-mail address as well as a telephone number. Another benefit is that to send copies of your message to others with e-mail addresses all you need to do is list their addresses and copies automatically go to them. Finally, if you receive e-mail messages and want to send a reply you simply click your computer mouse on the reply symbol. You do not have to enter the other person's address.

One of the disadvantages of e-mail occurs if you get on any number of junk mailing lists. This will result in your having a bunch of e-mail messages every time you turn on your commuter. This is a practice frequently referred to as "spamming."

From this simple description you can see how e-mail is in the process of revolutionizing business communications.

Sources of information

I have used the Internet often as a source of information in the writing of my two books. Because I include many examples of companies and how they got started it is important that I be as certain, as I can that the things I say are correct. The Securities Exchange Commission has a Web site (www.sec.gov) which includes every report filed by every publicly traded company for as long as that company has been filing reports electronically—which in most cases is many years.

It is usually easy to obtain copies of recent annual reports and other information about the company by writing or telephoning. However, it is not so easy to obtain copies of annual reports from eight or ten years ago, or information they filed at the time they had their Initial Public Offering. This is all public information but under ordinary circumstances is not easily obtainable. By using the Internet, it is a cinch.

Another Web site I use fairly often as a source of information is the U.S. Small Business Administration (SBA) Web site (www.sba.gov). This site includes a list of all published SBA documents. Again, this is all pubic information but without the help of Internet would be difficult to identify and difficult and time consuming to obtain.

Throughout this book, I refer frequently to Internet Web sites where entrepreneurs can obtain many other types of information. Nowadays, it is hard to think of an organization that does *not* use the Internet to disseminate information about its various activities. Almost every magazine, book, or newspaper you read these days includes many names of Web sites that many people will find of interest.

Promoting Your Business

Regardless of what business you are in it is probably desirable to have your own Web site as a means for disseminating information about your company and its products and services. This is more commonly known as e-commerce. How important this will be as a marketing tool depends on the nature of the business, but it is hard to imagine how it can be bad. To generate a Web site you can purchase software and do it yourself, or you can hire the service of a company whose business is designing Web sites. There are hundreds of these Web designing companies throughout the country. From what I understand the cost of this service is not excessive and, unless you are a computer expert, the quality is likely to be much better than you could do on your own.

For you to have a Web site, you first need to register a site name. This can be done for you by your Web designer. Finding an available name is becoming more and more difficult as more and more people are using the Net which is why you are beginning to see some very odd Web site names. Obviously, you would like a name that describes the name of your company or the product and/or the service you are trying promote. This suggests that you should register your site name even if you do not intend to develop a Web site for some time in the future.

When you select a Web designer they will want to know what your goals are in having a Web site, how many people you forecast will use it, how many things you want to include in the site, how often it will be changed, and so on, and so forth.

In selecting a firm to design your site, it is usually best to select one that can provide you with an entire package. This does not mean they will sell you everything themselves, but they know other service providers and the software you will need and can follow through with all of the tasks required to complete the project. The biggest advantage of selecting one firm to implement the entire package is that it allows you to hold them accountable to deliver the final Web site.

They will work with the service provider and software to develop the site to your specifications and can assist in getting your new site publicized over the Net. They can develop a site that can be easily maintained because they will be using all standard software. They will submit your Web site to various search engines such as Yahoo, Altavista, Lycos, HotBot, and InfoSeek, etc. Being on these search engines will make it much easier for interested people to find your site.

It is important that you develop a trust that the consulting firm and the Internet service provider will be there when you need them.

Selling over the Internet

Finally and perhaps of greatest importance is that many companies are using the Internet to sell their products and/or services and to obtain orders directly from people using the Net. Whether this applies in your situation may depend on your company's ability to obtain orders over the Internet. Perhaps the best known at this time is Amazon.com. This is a Web company that sells books, CDs, and other products in direct competition with companies such as Barnes & Noble (www.bn.com) and Borders (www.borders.com). Through Amazon.com a buyer has access to over 1.5 million titles, can browse excerpts and reviews of books, and delivery is usually made by mail, in just a few days. For people who do not like to go to bookstores, this is a good way to buy books. Another benefit is that Amazon.com discounts most titles by about 25 percent.

Selling over the Internet has an additional requirement and that is that you will want a safe way of being paid by the buyer. One approach is to take the order over the Net and bill the buyer before or after you ship the merchandise.

Possibly a better approach is to permit the buyer to pay by credit card. You can have the Web site automatically submit the card number to a card service for validation and send back an authorization number. Make sure your service provider can guarantee the security of this transaction for both you and your customer. And make sure you have an agreement with your credit card bank to handle these transactions. This is similar to a purchase in a store where the clerk slides your card through a card reader and gets a telephone response to validate the card. Using a credit card for an Internet purchase can usually be completed in 15 to 20 seconds.

One of the biggest benefits of selling through the Internet is that the buyer will probably make the purchase decision while on-line and not spend the rest of the evening thinking about it.

This sounds complicated, but it is not as bad as it sounds. The firm you pick to design your Web site will be able to give you a lot of advice and help in putting this system into operation.

Even though I think there will be a shake-out of companies selling through the Internet you should consider very carefully whether this could be an effective way for your new business to market your product or service.

Chapter 22

Other Ways to Market: Franchising and Multilevel Marketing

Two other ways for a small company to sell its products or services are franchising and multilevel or network marketing (sometimes called direct selling). Both of these are fairly complex. They are often under attack by regulatory agencies and require considerable care in setting up in order to avoid problems at a later date. I strongly advise anyone considering either approach to consult an attorney, expert in these areas, at an early stage. An amateur proceeding on his or her own is almost certain to encounter some difficulty that could have been avoided by seeking advice and counsel from a specialist. Caution is strongly suggested.

The subject of franchising in general terms and from the viewpoint of the franchisee are discussed in an earlier chapter. We are now talking about the other side of franchising, but the fundamentals are similar. They will not be repeated here.

Multilevel marketing is a selling approach where the company sells its product to others, who are frequently called independent distributors or independent consultants. Typically, they buy products from the company and resell to the ultimate user. This is often done through house parties, group sessions, door-to-door selling, selling to friends, relatives, neighbors, and acquaintances. The product, when purchased by independent distributors, is discounted from the retail price so they can realize a profit on the transaction. Normally the distributors operate as independent contractors rather than employees of the company. They take title to and pay for the product in advance of making a sale.

There's even more appeal to this selling approach. The independent distributors are then encouraged by the company to recruit other distributors and, in return, receive a percentage commission on the sales of their recruits. They cannot be paid a fee for finding a recruit. Their payment must be in the form of a commission on the sales of the recruit.

This arrangement may extend through several levels. If you're good at recruiting others to sell the product, you don't have to sell as much yourself to have a good income.

Amway, Mary Kay Cosmetics, and Tupperware are several of the better known companies using multilevel marketing as their main distribution method. I have heard that there are about 2,000 companies that use this approach, most of their independent distributors work part-time and about 80 percent are women. Information and very good publications about multilevel selling can be obtained from the Direct Selling Association at 202-293-5760.

From the company's viewpoint, there are several key benefits from both franchising and multilevel marketing:

* The company can recruit a large sales force without the expense of adding full-time employees.

* You can view either of these approaches as an inexpensive way of securing capital for your business. Both the franchisee and the multilevel marketing distributors are independent contractors, owners of their own businesses. Little investment is required from the company. In fact, the franchisee usually pays a fee in advance and then raises the capital to build the facility to carry out the franchisor's business. In the case of a Holiday Inn, for example, the cost of building a hotel may be in excess of $50,000 per room. Holiday Inn has about 1,400 franchises. I have no idea how many rooms there are in the average Holiday Inn, but you can see the immense capital investment that would have been required to accomplish this through normal financing channels.

* Franchisees and distributors tend to be entrepreneurs or individuals working part-time to augment their income. They are likely to work very hard. They will often have more drive, enthusiasm, and spirit than will regular, full-time employees

Both of these methods of selling have come under criticism recently for different reasons. In the case of franchising, this happens when the franchiser establishes a company-owned operation in the same area after the buyer of the franchise invested a lot of money and years of effort establishing the market, or when the franchisor holds back on the training and management assistance that was promised. Also, if the franchisor goes out of business this could leave the franchisee without the support it already paid for and expected to receive.

This means that if you are selling franchises to others you must take it as serious business, not a windfall source of capital. The franchiser has an obligation to fulfill its commitment and to do everything possible to help the franchisees succeed. One thing not too many people selling franchises do is to qualify the buyers. This means you should be sure the franchisee has the necessary knowledge, experience, and capital and is committed to being successful. One seller of franchises that I read about receives over 5,000 requests a year for information. After initial discussions it invites about 200 to informational meetings and ends up selling franchises to only about 50.

In the case of multilevel marketing, the company must have a valid product or service. However, a frequent criticism here is that some of these situations may resemble a pyramid scheme where the people who get in early can get rich but the latecomers are taken for suckers.

Another criticism of multilevel marketing is the great emphasis on recruiting new distributors. This implies that, because of the override commissions across several levels, the distribution costs become excessive. In most cases, I do not believe this is a valid criticism. For example, it is not unusual in the normal distribution of consumer products to have a company sales person selling to a commission representative selling to a distributor selling to a retailer selling to a consumer. Add all the markups in this conventional distribution process and you may find the costs are similar to or even higher than those in the multilevel process. And, the multilevel marketer will usually deliver the product to the user's home at no cost, which in some cases may be an important benefit.

In both cases, these objections can be overcome by the franchiser and multilevel marketer by their doing business in an open and ethical manner and making sure that the buyer knows and understands the risks involved. Not every kind of business is suitable for franchising or multilevel marketing. For those where it is suitable, it may provide an opportunity to greatly leverage your marketing and selling capability in a way that would not be possible to do on the company's own resources.

Chapter 23

Forms of Business

I want to thank Mr. William R. Alexander, an attorney specializing in corporate law, for his assistance in writing the chapter.

"What form should my business take? Should it be a sole proprietorship? A partnership? A corporation?"

These are the first questions the start-up entrepreneur should ask. These questions have many legal and tax implications and vary greatly from state to state. From time to time, each has been the subject of numerous books, pamphlets, and articles. My intention here is to review briefly these various forms in general terms and then suggest that probably the best answer is to incorporate.

Sole proprietorship

In a sole proprietorship, the individual entrepreneur owns the business. For example, in the State of New York, all that seems to be necessary is to go to a county clerk's office, pay a small fee, and register the business as a "DBA," which stands for "Doing business as..." This permits you to operate a business under a name different than your own.

This is simple, fast, and inexpensive. The main drawback is that all assets owned by the entrepreneur may be at risk if the business runs into trouble. This could include house, car, savings account, etc.

In a service-based business, you may be able to secure business liability insurance to protect you from this risk. In a product-related business, insurance of this sort can be prohibitively expensive—if available at all. In a sole proprietorship, the profit and loss of the business flows through to the owner each year for tax purposes.

Partnership

This is similar to a sole proprietorship but has more than one owner. Typically, a partnership agreement is desirable to define the relationship. Normally, a partnership ends at the death of any partner, but this problem and other situations can usually be provided for in the partnership agreement.

All partners are liable for the acts of all other partners, which can be a serious drawback considering the insurance situation. This is known as "joint and several liability." Should you decide on this business form, one piece of advice I can give that may save you a lot of grief later is to discuss and put in writing at the beginning exactly how the partnership will be dissolved, considering as many different circumstances as you can think of. You will find that it is much easier to reach an agreement when the business is worth nothing than later on when real money may be involved.

Some legal experts suggest that the spouse of each partner also be asked to participate in and sign any agreement because they may suddenly become involved in the event of a divorce or estate situation.

This form is not quite as simple as a sole proprietorship because tax returns must be filed for the partnership even though the partnership pays no taxes. Profit and loss from the business flow through to the partners, in proportion to their ownership.

Limited partnership

This is a special form of partnership in which the general partner has liability, but the limited partners do not as long as they refrain from managing the business. Profits flow through each year to all partners in proportion to their ownership. Again, the partnership must file a tax return even though it pays no taxes. Not too long ago, this was a popular business form. However, recent tax law changes have reduced its attractiveness, except in special situations.

C-corporation

This is a business form that has a life of its own. It is usually chartered by and subject to the laws of the state in which you incorporate. Many publicly traded companies incorporate in Delaware because its business law is considered more "friendly." Incorporating in Delaware has no distinct advantage to privately held companies located in other states. A corporation is owned by shareholders whose liability (with several exceptions) is limited to the assets of the corporation. The C-corporation is required to pay income tax on its earnings.

Some of the advantages of a corporation, in addition to limited liability, are that its shares can be sold to others as a way of raising capital and the company survives the death of individual shareholders. Its shares can be traded, with various restrictions, providing some degree of liquidity to investors. Profits and losses stay inside the corporation unless they are paid out in dividends and/or capital distributions.

The downside of incorporating for a small business is that there are significant overhead costs. Everything that you do seems to become more complex. I once had a small software business that I formed as a hobby and made the mistake of incorporating it too soon. It cost me $500 to form the corporation, about $1,000 a year in franchise tax and legal and accounting fees, and finally, it cost about $1,000 to terminate the corporation.

Subchapter S corporation

This is similar to a conventional corporation except that profit and loss flow through to the shareholders each year for tax purposes in proportion to their ownership. The corporation files a tax return, but it pays no taxes. Sometimes companies start as Subchapter S corporations when they expect to lose money and then convert to a standard C-corporation when they get into the black. This transition can only be done once. Like the limited partnership, the popularity of Subchapter S corporations is influenced by prevailing tax laws.

Limited liability company

All 50 states permit businesses to use a new business form known as a limited liability company (L.L.C.). It has some of the advantages of a corporation, is less complex than a Subchapter S corporation, and may afford the tax advantages of a partnership without the liability. It provides greater flexibility while avoiding some of the complications of corporate reporting. It is a little more costly to form than a corporation.

Because an L.L.C. is neither a partnership or a corporation how it is taxed depends upon how the L.L.C. operates and how it is organized.

Some legal experts believe the L.L.C. will be the predominant business form in the not-too-distant future. Because the details of what a business must do to qualify as an L.L.C. are somewhat complex and vary from state to state, it is recommended that the entrepreneur consult a lawyer familiar with L.L.C.s before making a decision.

Joint venture

This is a special business form where two or more individuals or corporations associate with each other for the purpose of performing a specific task or business activity. The joint venture usually ends when the task is completed. A joint venture agreement defines the tasks each party will perform, their responsibilities to each other, how profits will be divided, and under what circumstances the venture will be terminated.

There may be other alternatives of which I am not aware. My advice to an entrepreneur is to consult both an attorney and tax adviser to be sure that all the implications of this decision are fully understood. The legal and tax aspects are complex, and vary considerably from state to state and from time to time.

Chapter 24

Setting Goals

There are two approaches to setting goals for a business. The first is to set goals that are difficult to achieve, representing a very tough challenge for your entire organization. The second approach is to set goals that are realistic, or even on the conservative side, that you have a good chance of both meeting and exceeding. I like the second approach.

Most entrepreneurs lose all sense of reality when making sales and profit projections and setting goals for their company. They seem determined to set goals, they have almost no possibility of achieving. This is bad for a number of reasons. If you consistently fail to meet your goals you will quickly lose credibility with your employees, with your investors, with your bank, and everyone else for that matter. It is demoralizing for an organization to work hard and always fail to meet its goals. Nobody likes to be a loser.

On the more practical side, consistently missing goals has a devastating effect on profits. High-expense budgets tend to go hand-in-hand with high sales projections. You can be assured that most people are very good at meeting expense budgets. However, if your sales fall short of projections and expenses are not cut back quickly and decisively, you are certain to have large losses. Cutting back is a very disagreeable task because it usually means laying people off. Therefore, the temptation is to hold off on expense reduction until it is so late that such cuts no longer produce the results you need.

As an alternative, suppose you set conservative sales goals—goals that you are almost certain to meet or exceed. You should budget expenses consistent with these conservative goals so that if this is your actual level of operations, you will have a modest profit.

Now let's assume you exceed your sales goals by a significant amount. Expenses are not likely to expand as fast as sales and the result will be an exceptionally profitable company. This is called "planning for the worst and hoping for the best."

There is always the possibility of having more orders than you can handle and thus facing cancellations or loss of business to a competitor. This doesn't happen very often. Most organizations have a way of rising to the challenge of coping with excessive orders. Somehow or other they fumble their way through.

When I talk to entrepreneurs planning to start a business, I always ask what they consider the most serious problem they are likely to face. You would not believe how often they answer, "Expanding production fast enough to handle a sudden inflow of orders!" Of all the problems that I enjoy having, it is trying to keep up with unexpectedly high orders. What fun!

If you routinely set conservative sales goals and set expenses accordingly, you will have discovered one of the best ways to have a very profitable company. Another way of saying this is that expenses almost always lag revenues. If expenses lag revenues when revenues are increasing, you will have a very profitable company. If expenses lag revenues when revenues are declining, you may lose your shirt.

This approach is frequently criticized as being too short-term oriented. I am often asked how I balance short-term performance against long-term performance. Many managers pressured by their company for short-term profits become confused when trying to plan for the long-term. I have no problem with this, it all depends on how you define good long-term performance. I define good long-term performance as good short-term performance five years in a row.

I once fired a division manager for unsatisfactory performance. His explanation was that he would never sacrifice long-term goals for short-term profits. I did not debate the question...but that was exactly the reason I fired him.

Long ago, I concluded that there are three kinds of people in the world. They are winners, losers, and nonwinners. Winners and losers are easy to identify: They are obvious. It is the nonwinners, the people who always fall just short of success, who are the real menaces in the business world. If you are successful in weeding out the nonwinners from your organization, you will have a far better company.

Run your company so that it achieves profitability early and stays profitable. The way to have a profitable big company is to grow it from a profitable small company.

At RF Communications, we decided early that operating the company at a profit was a very high-priority goal. I would like to take credit for this approach, but it was really the contribution of one of the other founders, who was a very profit-conscious manager. As a result, we reached profitability in our second quarter of existence and stayed there for the eight years we were an independent company. We ran RF Communications to make a profit. Before long, every employee understood that no other way was acceptable.

The philosophy of goal-setting that I describe here will help you put your business in the black and keep it there.

Chapter 25

What! Me Write a Business Plan?

More has been written on the subject of planning and the preparation of business plans than almost any other business discipline. An immense amount of material is available telling you how to write a business plan. I urge you to read as much as you can. Some of it will be great, much contradictory, and some wrong. None of this matters. The more you read, the better understanding you will have of the process. After reading, follow the suggestions contained here. It is good advice that will put you well on the road to having a good business plan.

How important is the business plan? It is crucial! I urge everyone even thinking about starting a business to write a business plan before you go very far down the road. Modify and change it when necessary, but do not try to run your business without one. It has been said, "If you don't know where you're going any road will get you there."

There are samples of two good business plans in the appendices. These will give you an idea of what several entrepreneurs used to guide them in planning and/or starting and/or managing their businesses.

Recently, I have thought a lot about this subject and came to the conclusion that I should differentiate between a "plan for the business" and a "business plan." Many would say that these are the same but I would suggest that they are different. A plan for the business implies a strategy, which may or may not be in writing. A business plan implies a written document. You can reasonably ask which is most important. Is not the process of thinking it through and making the fundamental strategic decisions more important than putting it in writing? The thinking process is much more important than the document. But the discipline of putting the plan on paper will make the thinking process more effective and you will end up with a better plan for the business. In addition, a written plan can be shared with others.

Before you prepare a business plan for your company, you must decide on the main purpose of the plan. In general, you prepare a business plan for one of two reasons: as a road map for managing your business, or as a sales document for raising capital or securing a loan. The information in either of these plans should be substantially the same, but the emphasis will be different. For example, a plan intended to be used as a road map does not need to include detailed biographies of the key management. In a plan intended as a sales document for raising capital or obtaining a loan, the background and experience of management may be the most important part. I suggest that you first prepare a business plan to be used as a road map, an operating plan for running the business. This can then be modified for use as a sales document.

How long should a business plan be? How many pages should it have? Many entrepreneurs rebel at the prospect of writing a business plan, but when they finally decide to do so they write one about 200 pages long. Most business plans are far too long and far too detailed. As a result, they are less effective than they might be. It is my belief that 40 or 50 pages is long enough—perhaps even too long. Longer plans are much less likely to be read.

Consider the problem of presenting a 200-page plan to the venture capital firm from which you are seeking an investment. Even a medium-sized venture fund is likely to receive several dozen business plans each week. With this number to review, and investment decisions to be made, the following is apt to be the sequence of events:

1. Four out of five plans will be reviewed and discarded in 10 to 15 minutes or less after a cursory scan.
2. Of the remainder, four out of five will be read thoroughly (an hour or more) and then discarded.
3. The rest may be of sufficient interest for the venture investor to either visit the company or invite the management to their office for further discussion. Many of these plans then will be turned down.
4. The remainder of the business plans originally submitted, may survive to the point of serious discussion and perhaps negotiation of detailed terms. Most of these will fall short.
5. In most cases, only one or two out of several hundred plans submitted will result in an investment.

The general partner of a medium-sized venture fund told me recently that he sees about 1,200 investment opportunities a year and invests in four or six. This means that your business plan better be a pretty darned good selling document to have a prayer of surviving to the end.

There is also the question of who should write the business plan. Many entrepreneurs are uncomfortable writing such a formal document. Engineers and scientists in particular are often intimidated by the process. They frequently assign the task of writing the business plan to others such as a business plan consultant, their lawyer, or their accountant. I advise against using a lawyer or accountant to write your plan. However, hiring a professional business plan writer may be the right thing to do. But please remember that the planning decisions for an enterprise must be the effort of the key person or small key group if it is to make any sense at all. Get help with editing, get someone to correct your spelling and grammar—even get someone to write the plan for you. But be sure that the key strategic decisions about the business are yours. Any knowledgeable reader will know in an instant when a business plan was prepared entirely by a surrogate.

At the end of this chapter, there is a brief section prepared by a specialist in business plan writing about some of the benefits of using her services.

As far as the format of the plan is concerned, I again suggest caution. Today we are in the age of desktop publishing and multimedia. Computer magazines are full of articles about how to include graphics, color, different typefaces, many types of charts, and other elements in your written documents. Physical appearance is fast becoming more important than content. I suggest you forget all of this and keep your plan simple. Use only one or two different typefaces. In the text, use a typeface with serifs, such as Times, with proportional spacing to make it easier to read. Use graphics only where they add meaning to the plan—not for the purpose of adding flash.

Another thing to consider in writing a business plan is whether or not to use a PC software program which guides you through the process. There are quite a few available at prices near $100. I have some experience with one of these and it did a pretty decent job. In essence, what these programs usually consist of is a simple word processor, an outline for a plan, and one or more sample plans.

Shown below is an outline of a business plan that I like. This is an outline of a plan intended to be a selling document. There is nothing magical or unique about it—it just covers all of the bases and puts the contents in logical sequence.

Outline of a business plan

- Title page.
- Table of contents.
- Executive summary.
- General description of business.
- Goals and strategy.
- Brief background.
- Product/service description.
- Market description.
- Competition.
- Marketing and selling.
- Manufacturing/quality.
- Organization and management.
- Board of directors.
- Financial plan.
- Present stock ownership.
- Capitalization plan.
- Return to investors.
- Assumptions and risks.
- Supporting material.

The rest of this section will include brief comments on each part of the plan and a description of its purpose.

1. Title page

Obviously, the title page should include the name of the company and the words "business plan." What isn't obvious is that it should also include an address, telephone number, fax number, and e-mail address. On a number of occasions, I have had to call the information operator in order to learn the telephone number of the company whose plan I was reading.

2. Table of contents

This should be only a page or so long, and is more important than you might think. Many readers have hot buttons. They like to read about cash flow, marketing strategy, or some other narrow interest, before reading the entire plan. The table of contents directs them to the right place. Obviously, the pages must be numbered.

3. Executive summary

Here you must capture the entire essence of your business in one, two, or three pages—at the most. Some people write this first—others write it last. I think last is better. It is a critical part of the plan and the only part some audiences may read. Many will read no further if the executive summary does not whet their curiosity. You cannot spend too much time working on this section.

4. General description of business

Here is where you present the "Big Idea." What is your offering (product and/or service) and what market will you address? Why did you choose this offering and market, and why are they attractive? Be sure to comment on your distinctive competence and how it supports your selections.

5. Goals and strategy

State briefly the goals you have for your business and the general strategy you intend to follow to achieve these goals.

6. Brief background (optional)

This is to set the stage for the remainder of your business plan, if it is appropriate. This could include a description of other ventures in which individuals on your team have been involved in and anything else you may want to highlight by way of introduction.

7. Product/service description

This and the next section are the heart of your business—and the heart of the business plan. Identify the important attributes of your product/service and the benefits that it provides to your customers. Be certain your proposal differentiates, concentrates, and innovates in meaningful ways.

8. Market description

Include comments about the resources you need and what you consider to be the major success factors. Forecast how you expect your market will grow or change over the next few years. Brief descriptions of market research studies and projections by industry experts might be included to substantiate your projections.

9. Competition

List your competitors and identify their strengths and weaknesses. Include estimates of their market shares and profit levels, if possible. This section will give the reader an idea of how tough it will be to get your business going. One venture investor I know says that when he sees the words, "We have no competition," in a business plan, it is a sure predictor of failure.

10. Marketing and selling strategy

This should be an action plan on how you expect to get customers to buy your product or service. The selling strategy is a serious weakness in many plans. Make it a strength. Describe available distribution channels and how you intend to use them.

11. Manufacturing and quality control

Include some comments on how you will produce your product or deliver your service and how you will assure continued good quality. While this will become an important operating problem in the future (you hope), it is not often a key part of the business plan.

12. Organization and management

This is considered an extremely important section by many investors. Include a description of your organization and how you expect it to develop over the next few years.

Your management team is of critical importance. Be sure you have identified the key skills that are needed and that you have first rate players covering these key skills. I am a strong believer in including references in a resume or biography...especially if you can use people who are known to the intended reader. Include addresses and phone numbers because you want it to be easy for the reader to contact your references if they choose to do so. Do not make individual resumes too long. Academics are the worst offenders. They often equate quality with length.

13. Board of directors/advisors

List the people you have or expect to have on your board of directors or board of advisors. Do not load your board with either relatives or employees. Investors like to see a fairly small board, which includes successful business people with strong skills in functional areas key to your business. Tell how often the board meets and whether the directors/advisors have a financial commitment to the company.

14. Financial plan

Financial projections are a key part of a business plan. They provide the reader with an idea of where you think the business is going. Perhaps more importantly, they tell a lot about your intrinsic good sense and understanding of the difficulties the company faces.

Financial projections are often optimistic to an outlandish extent. They are always prefaced with the words, "Our conservative forecast is..." Do not use the word "conservative" when describing your forecast. Be careful not to use the "hockey stick" approach to forecasting (that is, little growth in sales and earnings for the first few years followed by a sudden rapid upward surge in sales and totally unrealistic profit margins). Many are the business plans I've read where after tax margins of 40 percent and higher are projected in an industry where 10 or 15 percent is considered good performance. Excessively optimistic projections ruin your credibility as a responsible business person.

Include monthly cash flow projections (remember, this is different than profit), and quarterly or annual order projections, profit and loss projections, and capital expenditure projections. In making financial projections it may be a good idea to include "best guess," "high-side," and/or "low-side" numbers.

15. Present stock ownership and investment

Include a list of all present shareholders with a comment about what they contributed to get their stock—money or otherwise. If the list of shareholders is too long, use a summary, but be sure to include the large shareholders. Investors like to see the founders of a company have a cash investment in the business in addition to "sweat equity." The level of this investment should have a reasonable relationship to their personal resources. But remember, your chances of raising capital from others will be much easier if you have invested some of your own money.

16. Capitalization plan

This is the financial deal you are trying to sell. Tell the potential investor how much money you're trying to raise, which should be consistent with your cash flow projections, and what percentage of the company they will own in return for their investment. This can be done in terms of number of shares, percentages, or both. Be specific in describing the type of security you're trying to sell (common stock, preferred stock, warrants, and so forth) and other alternatives you will consider.

17. Use of funds

Include a description of how you expect to use the money and of any major capital items you need to get the business going. On large items it may be appropriate to show actual quotations from credible sources.

18. Return to investors

Sensible investors want to know what returns they can expect and especially how they will achieve liquidity. Tell them, again perhaps with alternatives.

19. Assumptions and risks

This is another very important part of the plan, even though I suggest it be placed toward the end. It could be a good idea to suggest other strategies you might consider to reduce risk in the event your original assumptions do not materialize.

20. Supporting material

Brochures, short magazine articles, technical papers, summaries of market research studies, references from people acquainted with the company or the founders can be included. Be careful not to go into too much detail.

You may ask how you can possibly pack all of the above in 30 to 50 pages. The answer is, "With great difficulty." But remember, people who read business plans appreciate brevity and view it as an indication of your ability to identify and describe in an organized manner the important factors that will determine the success of your business. If the plan is so long that it intimidates the reader, you are the one who suffers.

Using professional business plan writers

This section was written by Marcia Layton Turner, president of Layton & Co. (716-256-6224), a Rochester-based business and marketing consulting firm. Layton & Co. provides small and midsized companies with guidance in growing their businesses through improved marketing, increased sales, and/or additional capital. Marcia is a graduate of Wellesley College and the University of Michigan M.B.A. Program. She is the author of "Successful Fine Art Marketing" and co-author of The Complete Idiot's Guide To Starting Your Own Business.

While I agree with Bill Stolze that you should never have a "surrogate" develop your company's business plan, I do not believe that all business plan writers are surrogate planners. The majority of business plan writers that I am aware of would never attempt to prepare a business plan without significant input from the entrepreneur or business owner. And when I say 'significant input," I mean participation in the form of face-to-face or phone interviews, providing important business documentation, and going through several iterations of editing and revising a plan.

Extensive interviewing is necessary because you, the business owner or entrepreneur, need to have your words in the plan. Your business plan should reflect your goals and personality.

Business plan writers do **not** make business decisions for you, nor should they. It is foolish and even potentially dangerous to hire a firm or consultant to write a business plan and turn over all the goal-setting and decision-making activities to that person. Only **you** know what you want to achieve with your business and how you want to go about it.

A plan writer can tell you what your plan is missing, asking questions that can help you make decisions about your business. Through these questions, the plan writer can lead you to a more complete plan that addresses all the important issues you will have to deal with.

For those of you who are unfamiliar or uncomfortable with financial statements, a business plan writer can help you prepare reasonable projections for your business. With your input and guidance, the business plan writer can create the financial statements your banker, venture capital group, or investors will want to see.

Working with someone who can speed the process of organizing and writing a plan can be beneficial.

Benefits

Some of the major benefits of working with a professional business plan writer may include:

1. **Saving time.** If you are a slow writer, you can have someone who writes business plans for a living work with you and speed up the process. If you have never written a plan before, you can potentially spend hundreds of hours researching and studying the process, or you can choose to hire a professional who does this on a daily basis to help you. Even if you have written a plan before, you may simply not have the time to devote to running your business and writing a plan. By working with a business plan writer, you can make progress in getting it done without investing countless hours yourself.

2. **Better quality.** While a business plan that you write on your own may be successful in helping you secure financing and manage your business, it can also hurt your chances for funding if you haven't done a thorough job.

   I've heard from many bankers and financiers that the quality of a business plan can play a major role in their decision to provide financing. If the plan is well-written, easy-to-understand, and demonstrates that the entrepreneur has carefully thought through the potential opportunities and problems the business will face, the banker or investor comes away with the sense that the entrepreneur is capable. But often, business plans that bankers and financiers review are not thorough or easy-to-read, and so they may end up sitting on someone's desk for days or weeks.

   By working with a knowledgeable consultant who specializes in preparing business plans, you can feel confident that the information that your banker or investors need to see is going to be in the plan. In many cases, this significantly improves the readability of the plan and success in financing.

3. **Direct access to financiers.** Most business plan writers I know maintain close contact with financing consultants, brokers, venture capitalists, investors, and bankers as a normal part of doing business. Business plan writers need to be aware of what the financing community wants to see in a business plan so that they can prepare a plan that meets the standards and needs of the bankers and investors who will ultimately be reviewing the plan.

Selecting a business plan writer

By working with a business plan writer, you get advice and direction to financing sources you would otherwise not have met. For many entrepreneurs, this network can save time and money. If you are considering working with a business plan writer to complete your plan, make sure that they are qualified to assist you. Just because someone can write or create financial statements does **not** qualify them to advertise themselves as a business plan writer.

Ask to see samples of their work, which should demonstrate an understanding of the format and presentation of a business plan, as well as their educational background and training. Do they have financial knowledge, marketing training, writing experience, and so forth, that is necessary to understand and create a comprehensive plan? Or, do they have work experience directly related to business planning? The answers to at least some of these questions should be yes.

As business plan writers, they should be qualified to provide suggestions regarding issues you have not yet encountered or considered, so make sure you would feel comfortable taking advice from them. Working with a business plan writer who takes your vision and communicates it clearly on paper for you can save you time and money and improve your chances of securing financing.

Chapter 26

Homemaker's Theory of Cash Flow: Forecasting Capital Needs

About 17 years ago, I began teaching a course entitled "Entrepreneurship and New Venture Management" to second-year M.B.A. students at a prominent business graduate school. To my amazement, I discovered that the students had virtually no understanding of cash flow—particularly as it applies to a start-up venture. Since then, I have read informational booklets written for entrepreneurs by several national public accounting firms. To my further amazement, I found that the discussion of cash flow in some of these booklets was almost useless to an entrepreneur.

Cash flow is by far the most important element of financial control in a start-up venture and just about every small business. Every entrepreneur must fully understand its significance.

The accounting definition of cash flow is net profit plus depreciation, both being noncash items in the operating statement. A better way to define cash flow, at least for a start up, is that it is the difference between cash receipts and cash expenditures—the difference between the money you take in and the money you spend.

It is imperative in planning a new business (or in managing a growing business), to do a cash flow projection on a regular basis. A cash flow projection must be a key part of your business plan. It is the only way for you to have any assurance you will be able to meet the financial obligations of your business. It is the only way to be sure that you will not come to the office some day and suddenly discover that the business is insolvent. Some people describe managing a start-up venture as "a race against insolvency," and they are right.

The most useful way to forecast cash flow in a meaningful way is to first project cash receipts from all sources. Subtract from these the projected cash expenditures. This is a very simple concept. Keep track of the cash input to the firm and subtract the money that you spend. I call this the "Homemaker's Theory of Cash Flow."

The average homemaker is a master at managing money. This includes the housewife, professional woman or man—whoever is managing the finances. This person doesn't worry about profit and may not even know what depreciation means. What he or she does know is that if more money is spent than is taken in, there will be troubles ahead. It is the same with a new company. Almost every new company begins its life with limited capital and it is necessary to project and manage cash flow carefully to manage the business intelligently.

Cash receipts are deposits of cash in the bank. Orders are not cash receipts and invoices that you send out are not cash receipts. A deposited check is close to a cash receipt. Cash receipts are cleared checks—and even here, you run some risk that you will have returns.

On the other side, a purchase order placed with a supplier, a bill, or even a mailed check is not a cash expenditure. A check that clears your bank account is a cash expenditure. By keeping all of the above in mind, you can forecast cash flow in a reasonably intelligent manner.

As an example, the illustration below shows a cash flow projection for a typical start-up company.

When projecting cash flow, you must consider when orders will be received, shipping schedules, and collection delays. In this

Sample Cash Flow Projection

	Jan	Feb	Mar	Apr	May	June	July	Aug	Sept	Oct	Nov	Dec
Receipts												
Product A												
Units Ordered	5	5	7	7	9	9	9	9	9	9	9	9
Units Shipped	0	3	6	7	8	10	10	9	9	9	9	9
Cash Receipts	0	0	0	24	48	56	64	80	80	72	72	72
Product B												
Units Ordered	0	0	2	5	5	5	3	3	4	4	4	4
Units Shipped	0	0	2	3	4	4	4	4	4	4	4	4
Cash Receipts	0	0	0	0	10	15	20	20	20	20	20	20
Product C												
Units Ordered	1	1	3	3	3	3	3	3	5	5	10	10
Units Shipped	0	0	0	1	2	2	2	4	6	8	8	8
Cash Receipts	0	0	0	0	0	10	20	20	20	40	60	80
Total Cash Receipts	0	0	0	24	58	81	104	120	120	132	152	172
Expenditures (All cash)												
Rent	5	5	5	5	5	5	5	5	5	5	5	5
Salaries	10	15	20	30	40	40	40	40	45	45	45	45
Benefits	2	3	4	6	8	8	8	8	8	8	8	8
Telephone	2	2	3	3	3	3	3	3	3	3	3	3
Materials	2	2	8	10	12	20	50	50	50	50	50	50
Capital Equip		15				8					10	
Misc.	1	2	2	4	1	1	2	2	2	2	2	2
Total Cash Expenditures	22	44	42	58	69	85	108	108	113	113	123	113
Net Cash Flow	-22	-44	-42	-34	-11	-4	-4	12	7	19	29	59
Cumulative Cash Flow	-22	-66	-108	-142	-153	-157	-161	-149	-142	-123	-94	-35

example, I assume the company has three products that go into production within a few months of each other. I also assume a collection cycle of two months. Expenses, of course, start almost immediately. A personal computer and a spreadsheet program will be an immense help in projecting cash flow. This example is somewhat oversimplified and may be unrealistic in a real life situation.

These projections are very difficult to make with any degree of confidence. The only thing you can be sure of in a forecast of cash receipts is that it will be wrong. Should that stop you from making the forecast? Absolutely not! What it does tell you is that projections of cash receipts must be constantly reviewed and updated.

On the other hand, projecting cash expenditures is easy. Most expenditures are both known and controllable and can be projected with a fair degree of accuracy. Here again, they should be constantly reviewed—not so much for accuracy but to be certain that your spending rate is consistent with the most current projection of cash receipts.

Any dunderhead can forecast expenses, but it takes someone with real business sense to project orders, shipments, and cash receipts. Students doing a business plan for the first time invariably get bogged down when they try to project cash receipts. They simply cannot deal with the uncertainty.

I suggest doing these projections on a monthly basis—and they might even be done weekly. For a new company, a quarterly or annual cash flow projection is of no use. The bottom line in the projection is cash flow on a cumulative basis.

I find cash flow most understandable when plotted as a graph shown on the next page.

A critical point for all small businesses is when cumulative cash flow reverses direction and starts to head north from negative to positive. This is a milestone that every company must reach sooner or later and the sooner the better!

The cash flow projection is also important for forecasting the capital needs of the company. The lowest negative point in the graph indicates in simplest form how much capital the company will need.

In planning the financing of your firm, you should obviously include a safety factor when using this system to allow for contingencies. I already suggested that the only thing you can be sure of is that these projections will be wrong. This means that when you begin raising capital, you should aim at raising 25 percent or 50 percent more than your projections indicate will be needed. For example, where the projection shows that about $160,000 will be needed, you should probably try to raise between $200,000 and $250,000.

This approach to forecasting is a simple yet effective way to project the capital needs of a business that will be of great value to the entrepreneur.

Finally, you might ask who in the new company should make these projections. The only one qualified is the head of the company. Do not let your accountant do the job. He or she may be able to handle the expense projections but is sure to panic when trying to project orders, shipping schedules, revenues, and cash receipts.

That is all there is to cash flow. Do not let anyone tell you that it is complex. It is not. It is extremely simple in concept, yet crucial to the new firm.

Sample Cumulative Cash Flow

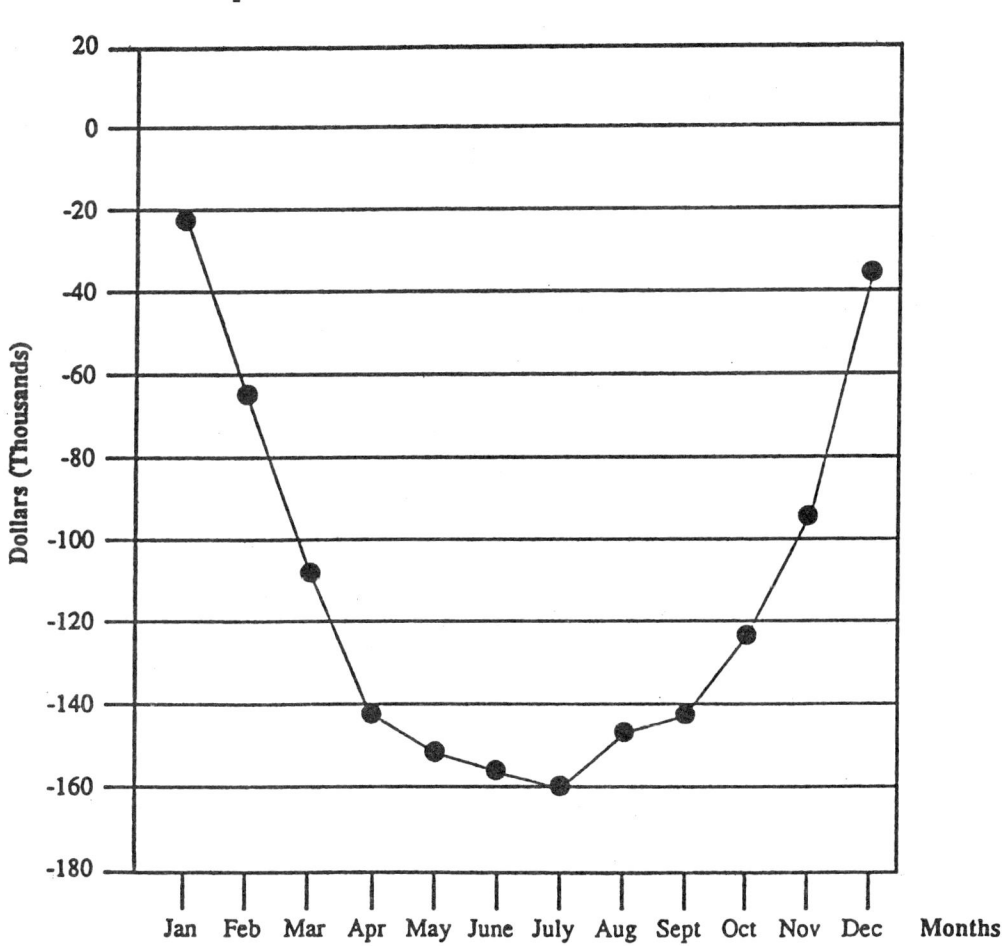

Chapter 27

How Much Money Is Enough?

The previous section suggested a way of estimating the capital requirements of a new business by using detailed cash flow projections. This gives you an idea of the capital you can expect to need based upon the scale of operations suggested in your business plan. It is the amount of capital that you would like to have to get the business underway. Ideally, you would like to approach a venture investor and say, "Please let me have $...," and walk away with a check. It's not that simple. The capital projection is only a first step.

The next step you need to take is to try to determine how much capital you can raise and what you should do if you cannot raise the amount you think you need. Further questions include: Should you try to raise all of the capital you need at one time or should you do it in stages? And, is it desirable to raise more capital than you require?

For the sake of example, you think you need $200,000 to get your business going as planned and find you can only raise $100,000. What next? Well, you have two choices. One is to take the $100,000, get the business going as best you can in accordance with your plan, and then attempt to raise additional capital at a later date.

Another alternative is to go back to the drawing board. Go over your business plan and try to devise a different strategy that requires only $100,000. You should carefully examine both the projected cash receipts and projected cash expenditures and try to figure out what you can do to speed up the receipts and delay the expenditures.

An important strategic decision a new business must make that greatly affects cash flow is whether to be a product company, a service company, or an advice company starts to head north. Many start-up businesses follow two or even all three of these options.

We faced this decision at RF Communications in developing our initial strategy. If we were to be a product company—that is, to try to have a line of proprietary radio communication equipment—we had to design the product, build prototypes, set up a manufacturing facility, get orders, and make shipments before we could expect our first cash receipts. This process takes at least 12 to 18 months and requires a lot of capital. As an alternative, we could have become a service company. We could have gone to the Army, Navy, and Air Force to try and get development contracts and studies. Government contract business is the high-tech equivalent of a service business. We would be selling man-hours of staff time to design military products to government specifications. The advantage of this strategy is that you perform the work, send an invoice once a month, and in a few weeks pick up a check. Not much cash is needed up front.

To us, the major difference between a product business and a service business was the timing of cash flow. The product business is capital-intensive. It needs a lot of initial investment before cash receipts can be expected. With a service or advice business, positive cash flow can be expected fairly early, frequently within weeks or just a few months.

Our goal at RF Communications was to have a line of proprietary products. We believed this would result in a more profitable and stable business. We thought we could raise enough capital to do this, but were not certain. As a hedge, we also aggressively pursued contract work at the same time, and within a few months had several large contracts. In effect, our game plan emphasized the product business and used contract work to provide cash flow to keep the company running until our products came upstream. From time to time we also did consulting for other firms as a way to generate both cash and sales leads for our products.

Even if you have a product business, there are strategies that can reduce the capital needed. A new company should buy as many components and sub-assemblies as possible, rather than setting up its own manufacturing facility.

Take one of the most successful games ever invented: Trivial Pursuit. The inventors, Scott Abbott and Chris Haney, were two Montreal journalists. They started their business with only a small amount of capital. Rather than manufacturing and distributing the game themselves, they contracted the assembly and distribution to companies in Canada, United States, and Europe. This was a good way to get a business going by taking advantage of the capital resources of suppliers.

I suggest you do a careful job of estimating the amount of capital you need for the kind of business you want to have. If you don't like the answer, shift the strategy as much as you must to match the capital you can raise. Forecasting the capital needs of a start up is an empirical process. You may have to do it many times before you are satisfied with the result.

Now, let's suppose you encounter the opposite situation where you are able to raise more capital than you need. Suppose for example, that you can raise $500,000 when you think you need only $200,000. What then? Surprisingly, this too can be a drawback! First, if you raise more capital than you need during you start-up time, you may be selling your stock too cheap. It may be better to take $200,000, the amount you forecast. One or two years later, if you are meeting your plan, you should be able to sell stock for a higher price. This means that fewer shares and less dilution will be required to raise the additional $300,000.

Secondly, having more money than needed takes the pressure off the management of a new business. Offices will be larger, facilities will be more elaborate, salaries will be higher, more support services will suddenly appear, and so forth. All of these consume cash and none contribute in meaningful ways to the success of the business.

A third (and more subtle) reason why a start up should not raise more capital than it needs relates to the skills of the entrepreneurs. One of the major risks in a new venture is the uncertainty as to whether the team of entrepreneurs has what it takes to run a business. If they do, more money should not be difficult to obtain. The sooner they learn and stop trying, the better. I believe there is such a thing as a right amount of start-up capital for a new venture: Not too much and not too little.

Paul Hawken, in his book *Growing a Business*, said that they started the very successful Smith & Hawken garden equipment mail order business with $100,000 even though they had access to much more at the time. This was the amount they were comfortable with and the amount they thought necessary to do the job they had in mind.

Few financial experts are likely to agree with these comments. Almost no business failures occur because of lack of money. The real reason businesses fail is because of poor product selection, poor market selection, poor marketing, or just plain poor management.

In discussing the financial needs of new companies in his book, *Winners*, Carter Henderson quotes Mary Kay Ash, the founder of Mary Kay Cosmetics, as saying, "It takes more than money, you must also know what you are doing."

Of all the advice entrepreneurs may seek from various specialists, the advice they get from financial experts will probably be the least consistent. On many occasions throughout my career, I have sought financial counsel, particularly on methods and specific problems relating to raising capital. I consulted commercial bankers, investment bankers, venture capitalists, vice presidents of finance of major corporations, and other entrepreneurs. Rarely have any two been even close to giving the same advice.

Chapter 28

Where and How to Look for Financing

Many (if not most) entrepreneurs need outside financial support of some sort to start a business. This support is usually either a loan of some sort or an equity investment resulting from the sale of stock in the new business. The level of difficulty in getting financial support depends upon many factors, but I think it is safe to say that raising money is seldom, if ever, easy.

Some experts suggest that raising money has a seasonal quality. For example, it is probably a waste of time to approach wealthy individuals for equity investments either in the middle of the summer or the middle of the winter. People with large amounts of capital to invest are likely to be away on vacation during the summer months and in a warmer location during the winter months. The right time to approach them is likely to be in the spring or fall.

Other experts say that raising money is more cyclical than seasonal, and they too are also right. A number of years ago I did some research and found that in the upstate New York area during the 1960s, almost 100 new companies raised their initial outside capital by going public. Some used an underwriter, most did it themselves.

A more recent study I conducted showed that during the 1980s, in the same region, a larger number of companies raised more initial capital from private investors than from any other source. In the early and mid-1990s there has been a sudden surge of Initial Public Offerings (IPOs) done mostly through underwriters both large and small.

And, during the last few years, a number of new Venture Capital Funds have come into existence with many millions of dollars to invest. I have been told by a friend of mine who manages a midsized fund that there is beginning to be competition among funds for deals. This means that they have to pay a higher price for stock in the companies in which they invest or they find themselves investing in more risky situations. Obviously this makes Venture Capital Funds a more attractive source of capital for new businesses seeking early investment

First, a course on selling

Before listing and commenting on various sources of financing, I would like to describe a recent experience I had that substantially altered my view of this important issue.

In late 1991, I spoke at an outplacement seminar at a state university in New York. Schools in the state system faced substantial reductions in financial aid and were in the process of making staff cuts to balance their budgets. This seminar, which lasted two days, was organized to help those facing termination with finding a job. My role was to describe starting a business as an alternative.

One of the other speakers was discussing making contacts, writing a resume, and being interviewed. A man in the audience, very upset by his situation, raised his hand and said, "I know nothing about finding a job. I have not done it in many years. Every time I apply anywhere there are 30 or 40 other applicants for the same job. What am I to do?"

Even though this was not my assigned subject I could not restrain myself. I interrupted him and said that whether he liked it or not he had just changed professions. Last week he may have been an assistant registrar or a data processing specialist but this week he had suddenly become a salesman. And, he had only one product to sell—himself. He may not like being a salesman but if he wanted to find a job during difficult times, he had better get used to the fact that he was now a salesman.

His next question was, "What is the state going to do to help me?" I answered, "Probably nothing." Then he asked, "What would you do if you were me?" I suggested he do the same things I did early in my career when I made the transition from design engineer to salesman.

I would immediately find a course in selling that I could take. Go to the library where they undoubtedly have several shelves full of books about selling. Read them all. Soon you will understand that selling is a process that has well-established techniques and procedures that are followed by almost every successful salesperson, and these techniques work. Learn them and apply them. This will be an immense help in finding a job because your competitors, the other 30 or 40 applicants, almost surely have done nothing to improve their selling skills.

Why am I telling you this complex story as part of a chapter on where to look for financing for your new business? The reason should be obvious. When you, as an entrepreneur, decide to try to raise outside financial support for your business you, also, have just changed professions. You are no longer an entrepreneur, or design engineer, or the distinguished founder of a hot new start-up company. You are now a salesperson whether you like it or not.

The product you have to sell is a little different than in the previous example. Here you are selling your concept of a business. You are selling your management team, your idea for a product or service, and your assessment of a market opportunity. In short, you are selling your plan for a business. To raise money today you had better learn how to sell. If you don't, your chances of success are virtually nil.

What do I mean by selling? First you develop leads, then you separate the prospects from the leads. A prospect is someone who needs what you are selling and who can afford what you are selling. This is a little tricky to comprehend when your goal is raising capital, but it must be done.

Next, you analyze your competition and plan your approach and your salespitch. Then you figure out how to answer the objections and negotiate and close the deal. All of these things are standard selling techniques. They are skills you seldom learn in business schools, but you had better learn them now if you expect to raise capital, whatever its source.

Where do you look?

At last we get to the main subject of this chapter. This discussion assumes that the entrepreneur has determined how much capital is needed to launch the new business. The question to be resolved is how to find that much money. This is a complex question for which there is no right or wrong answer. Possible sources of early capital for the entrepreneur include:

1. **Personal savings and borrowing**

Most entrepreneurs finance the early start-up stage of their business with personal savings. If the company is formed by a team, it is their combined personal contributions. This amount of money, though often quite small, can sometimes pay the cost of building prototypes of products, limited market research, filing a patent application, getting a service business off the ground, incorporation, and the preliminary steps of more formal financing.

Personal borrowing is also a possible source of start-up capital. However, any loans you are able to get will probably have to be secured with a personal guarantee. Many entrepreneurs become upset when they are unable to borrow from a bank to get their business underway. Another chapter of this book describes some of the things an entrepreneur can do to increase the odds of getting a loan.

Several years ago, I met an entrepreneur who had started a very successful market research firm. Unable to obtain a bank loan, she used credit cards. As I recall, she had about a dozen cards from different banks, each with a $5,000 line of credit. Five times 12 equals $60,000, a significant amount. The downside of this is that credit card interest rates tend to be very high—at that time they were about 18 percent. When I met her she had 15 employees and was operating at a profit. I encouraged her to try again for bank financing and suggested that if she had trouble with her own bank to shop around. She acquired a bank loan with no trouble and was out of the credit card loop.

2. **Friends and associates**

If more capital is needed than is available privately, the first sources many entrepreneurs turn to are family, friends, or close business associates. At this point, you will have to begin to think about some agreement with your investors. Chances are you will need an attorney to formalize the arrangement in acceptable legal form. As you bring in more and more outside individual lenders or investors, you will probably decide to incorporate. As we discussed, this form of business permits you to share ownership by selling stock.

3. **Venture investors**

There are three separate and distinct kinds of venture investors: individual venture investors, formal (institutional) venture capital funds, and corporate venture investors. The amounts of capital that can be raised from these sources varies from as little as $5,000 or $10,000 up to $5 million and more. Venture investors tend to be quite sophisticated, and a later chapter is devoted to a discussion of various venture capital sources.

4. **Going public**

Selling stock to the public is usually not considered as a reasonable approach to raise capital for most start-up businesses. Almost every financial expert you ask will advise you against even thinking about this alternative. However, I suggest you do think about it as many companies have gone public very early in their corporate lives, either using an underwriter or on their own.

5. **Federal, state, and local governments**

The federal government, most state governments, and many local governments have financial programs intended to encourage people to start businesses. They also provide financial support to help existing businesses grow. The purpose of most of these programs is to create jobs. Creating jobs may not be your highest priority as an entrepreneur. But that in no way conflicts with the government's goal, because if you succeed in your business, the probability is you are also creating jobs. Both sides win.

There is no right answer

Which of these approaches is best? Well, it's hard to say. There is seldom a right or wrong answer, and the best you can hope for is an answer that works.

In 1988 I conducted a study of venture capital sources in the Rochester, New York, area and surrounding counties. A list was compiled of all firms that I could identify that raised their first outside capital between Jan. 1, 1980 and March 31, 1988. A second list was compiled of the companies among this original group that raised capital a second or third time during the same period. I included five sources of venture capital: individual investors, going public, formal venture capital funds, corporate investors, and minority small business investment companies.

Table I, following, summarizes how 65 companies raised their first outside capital. Table II lists how 29 among these 65 companies raised capital a second or third time during the same period. A fairly high percentage of the companies on this list continue to operate. I don't know if the situation in other sections of the country is similar to Rochester, but I see no reason for much difference.

Table I: Sources of First Outside Capital

	Number	Percentage	Dollars
Individual Investors	42	65%	$22.5 Mil
Going Public	16	25%	30.3 Mil
Venture Capital Funds	5	8%	6.8 Mil
Corp. Venture Funds	0	0%	
Minority SBICs	2	3%	0.2 Mil
Total	65		$59.8 Mil

Table II: Sources of Later Capital

	Number	Percentage	Dollars
Individual Investors	8	28%	$11.3 Mil
Going Public	8	28%	37.3 Mil
Venture Capital Funds	8	28%	14.4 Mil
Corp. Venture Funds	5	17%	31.0 Mil
Minority SBICS	0	0%	
Total	29		$94.0 Mil

Although this survey is not entirely up-to-date, it does gives an entrepreneur some guidance as to how a large number of new businesses raised early capital.

Scams

In recent years with so many new companies trying to raise equity capital, some of these firms have become the target of unscrupulous scam artists. These vary from people who agree to raise the capital you need but require large advanced payments, to others who in fact do sell the companies stock but then proceed to manipulate the stock price in ways that can seriously endanger the company for which the money was raised.

Some states have begun holding seminars to advise entrepreneurs on the process of raising money. In at least one case, the manager of the seminar estimated that about 20 percent of the attendees were unscrupulous promoters looking for their next sucker.

The February 12, 1996 issue of *BusinessWeek* included an article that suggested a number of things a small business can do to avoid being ripped off. They are:

- Beware promoters promising easy venture capital or business loans, particularly if they ask for fees up-front.
- Check references by getting written evaluations of the firm's service from former clients. Phone references may be accomplices.
- Check credentials with state securities or banking regulators. Be especially careful if promoters are in another state.
- Beware if someone wants to sell shares or reincorporate your company out of state, or do a large stock split. These hallmarks of the penny stock scam are now being applied to small cap stocks.
- Have a lawyer read the fine print of any agreement. Some contain fees that must be paid in cash whether or not your company receives capital. Others require turning over up to 10 percent of equity.

This same issue of *BusinessWeek* describes a number of specific examples where small companies have been badly hurt, and even driven out of business.

Chapter 29

How to Obtain a Loan: Improving the Odds

This chapter was written by Victoria Posner, a Trainer and Consultant based in Rochester New York. Victoria has 10 years experience in commercial lending and teaches banking and finance to bankers, investment managers, and other financial professionals. She also teaches a number of workshops on financial planning for small business. Victoria sits on two nonprofit microloan committees: the New York State Rural Venture Fund, sponsored by Rural Opportunities, Inc., and the Minority and Women's Revolving Loan Fund, sponsored by the Urban League of Rochester. She writes a monthly column for the newsletter Small Business Success. *She holds a B.A. from Connecticut College and an M.B.A. from Wharton.*

Getting a loan is a hard road

Borrowing to start a business is not easy. The problem is often not that there is no money available but rather that many people do not want to put in the time and effort necessary to submit a good package to potential lenders. Lenders ask for an awful lot of information. It takes a great deal of work to put it all together. You may wonder why so much information is requested. Well, lenders need to know as much as possible to make a good decision.

No lender should take inordinate risks. There is a great deal of "downside risk" and virtually no "upside" potential for a lender. If the business fails, the loan goes down the tubes. If it succeeds, the lenders gets the money back with a little interest, but it is important that the lender be prudent. There are no windfall profits to offset losses.

At the same time, it does not benefit you to take on debt that cannot be repaid. The likely result is a failed business and often personal bankruptcy. Of course, everyone thinks that his or her idea is a sure winner. But the failure rate of start-up businesses tells us otherwise. As unpleasant and as disappointing as it may be, getting turned down for a loan may be the best thing that can happen to you. It should make you stop and rethink your whole idea again. That doesn't mean that you should give up, just that you need to do more work.

The need for personal information and guarantees

Because your business is a start up, lenders rely on your ability and integrity. Therefore, they need to know as much about you as possible. Most lenders will ask you for a lot of personal information in addition to information about your proposed business. Typically you will be asked for a complete resume, several years of income tax returns with all supporting schedules, a personal financial statement listing all your assets and liabilities, and a recent report from a credit bureau (unless the lender can access the credit bureau directly). Many people balk at these requests, however this is standard procedure.

You can also expect the lender to ask for personal guarantees from you and your spouse and a lien on any major assets such as a home. Don't be surprised, this is also fairly standard. If you want a loan you will have to supply the requested items.

There will usually be an application you must fill out. It may be one or two pages, or a long-detailed document. Many of the questions will already be answered in your business plan. You may be tempted to write "see business plan" over and over. **Don't do it!** As boring and as tedious as it is, answer each question fully and completely. Although you may not understand the need for this redundancy, there usually is a good reason. Banks must compile information on loan applications into statistical reports for regulators. Searching through your entire package would be very time consuming for them, so they ask for the needed information on the application document.

The business plan is critical

The heart of your package is your business plan. Having a good business idea but only some vague notion of how to accomplish it just won't work with lenders. Time and time again I see applicants come to the loan committees on which I sit with half-baked business plans. They follow the right format, but there is no meat to their plans. Just having the right chapter and section headings does not constitute a good business plan.

Sometimes people make such incredible mistakes when writing their plans that it seems insane that he or she cannot see them. However, they are glaring to the reader. When writing your plan, be sure to do the following:

1. **Make sure it is very clear to the reader just what the business is.** I have read many plans that never says exactly what the writer plans to do. Sometimes they use a lot of industry jargon thinking that they are being precise, but you can't expect everyone outside your industry to understand. Make it very clear what you are doing or making, and who the customer is. Lenders are not inclined to approve a loan if they can't tell what the business is. To help you write a simplified plan, pretend you're explaining your goals to a group of children.

2. **Do not make broad, unsubstantiated statements like, "It is a known fact that..."** If you can't support statements with solid data, don't make them. There is little room for opinions in a business plan. Lenders want real facts. *Document, document, document.* Spend time in the library doing research. Be able to support everything you say, including every number in your projections. Vague ideas and guesses just won't do. Don't rely on, "I've worked in this industry (working for someone else) for 20 years, so I know what I wrote is true." If you really know what you are talking about, you should be able to back up your assertions with facts from reliable sources.

3. **Keep your negativity in check.** "There is a dire need..." A dire need? Are people dying, is the world heading for eminent disaster because your product or service isn't available? Negative adjectives are particularly dangerous. For example, I had a client who made a number of negative statements about his largest competitor. However, that

competitor had been in business for many years so it must have been doing something right. Indeed, I had personal experience with the competitor and knew it to be a well-run operation. Knocking the competition does not build your case, so don't do it.

4. **Make sure your numbers make sense.** Many people who start businesses are product people (such as engineers) or marketing people. Almost everyone hates numbers. But the bottom line that determines whether the lender gets the money back is numerical. So you have to spend time with your numbers and make sure they make sense. Here are a few classic errors:

    a. *The numbers don't square with other sections of the business plan:* In another business plan I reviewed, the marketing section called for local television advertising. The financial plan showed $200 per month for advertising. This ought to buy about five seconds at 3 a.m. once or twice a month on the bowling channel.

    b. *Not anticipating price increases:* I reviewed a set of projections where utility bills remained at the same figure for three years. Even if you don't use more power over three years it is unlikely that the rates will stay constant.

    c. *Presenting only annual projections:* Preparing projections month by month for the first year is tedious. Some people shortchange the process by making an annualized projection, and then dividing the figures by twelve to fill in the blanks for each month. That defeats the purpose of monthly projections. Virtually every business has peaks and troughs—the lender wants to know if you can get through the slow months. If you can't, you're out of business and the loan is gone.

    d. *Not including a list of assumptions to explain how you got your numbers:* The lender wants to know how you arrived at your figures. This should be provided line by line, starting with a detailed discussion of your sales. You can't just pick a number—you must have good, solid reasons.

    e. *Numbers that don't make sense:* I saw a set of projections where the gross profit margin went from 35 percent in the first year to 60 percent in the third with no explanation provided. Gross profit margin in percent is defined as: (Sales − Cost of Goods Sold)/Sales multiplied by 100. It's possible, I suppose, but you'd better tell me how you plan to achieve that.

    f. *Not telling the lender how the money will be used:* It is important to let the lender know how you are going to use the money, dollar by dollar. You can't just say, "inventory, equipment, and working capital." You need an itemized list of exactly where the money will go supported by price quotations, price lists, and so forth.

5. **Failure to discuss risk.** It's great to have a positive attitude, but there is no business without risk. None. Risk is everywhere. If you don't discuss risk, then lenders are going to assume *you haven't thought* about risk. That scares them to death. They know you can't possibly plan for every single contingency, but they want to know that you've thought about the major risks and of some way to manage them.

    Of course, risk is not always negative. There is the risk of succeeding beyond your expectations. For example,

I reviewed a business plan once of someone who was going to manufacture sophisticated crafts. The product was beautiful and I could see where orders could well be way in excess of projections. Since it took some artistic skill to make the product, I wondered what the owner would do if that happened. Failure to meet orders on a timely basis usually means you don't get repeat orders. In the owner's plan he had identified several skilled people who could be hired if the need arose. I was very impressed and the loan was granted. The business has done well.

6. **Unprepared to answer questions about your plan.** The applicant whose profit margins went from 35 to 60 percent in two years said she was "not a numbers person," that the accountant had prepared the projections, and that she couldn't explain them. The loan was not approved. If you are going to own a business you have to have some understanding of numbers. How else will you know how you are doing and where the problems are? When you tell a lender that numbers aren't "your thing," what you are really saying is that you really don't want to own a business. You are better off working for someone else. You must be able to answer virtually any question about any aspect of your business plan.

7. **Excessive wordiness.** The reader of your business plan is a busy person. Don't waste his or her time with long florid passages when a few well-written sentences will do. I've read business plans that went on for 40, 50, 60 pages and more that could easily have been reduced to just 10 or 15 if only the writer had eliminated all excess language. Don't repeat yourself ad nauseam.

Stick to the facts, state them clearly, and don't repeat them unnecessarily. The point isn't to write a *long* business plan but a *good* business plan.

Reviewing the plan

Have your business plan read by as many people as you can. You want them to read for two purposes: mechanics and content. You would be amazed how many plans I see with gross spelling, grammar, and mathematical errors. I firmly believe that if you don't care enough about your business to do a great business plan, why should I care enough to put money on the line. Don't leave the important proofreading task to yourself alone. Get a couple of people to read your plan for the mechanics, even if they know nothing about business. Tell your kids you'll pay him or her 50 cents for each error found; it will be money well spent.

You also want at least one person to read your plan whose business judgment you trust and who you know will give you honest feedback. The best person for this job is a good outside consultant—someone who has seen a number of different business plans, who has experience lending money, and who won't worry about losing a friend by being truly honest. That will cost you more than a few dollars but will be well worth it in the long run. It is important to find out where your business plan falls short before you send it off to a lender.

And now the good news

Finally, here are a few words of encouragement. There are lenders out there who want to help small businesses. There are banks that will lend to you, although you may have to search around. Generally small, local banks are your best bet, although some larger banks might have funds available under their Community Reinvestment Act programs.

Also, the Small Business Administration has a program under which they will guarantee part of loans made by banks to small businesses. These guarantees are usually obtainable through a bank, not directly from the SBA.

Some of the SBA rules governing who can secure SBA guaranteed loans and under what circumstances are somewhat complex and change from time to time. You can learn about these rules and restrictions over the SBA Internet Web site (www.sba.gov). However, people at your bank are probably familiar with SBA and you can always contact any SBA office.

Recently the SBA has streamlined the application process and sometimes has been approving/denying applications within a few days—it used to take anywhere from a few weeks to a few months.

There are finance companies that specialize in small businesses. You must be sure to check these out carefully since there are bogus operators in the field. If a firm asks for a significant, up-front "application fee," run as fast as you can in the opposite direction. Before dealing with any of these companies, ask your bank or SBA office for references.

Interest rates charged by legitimate finance companies are usually higher than banks charge. But remember your problem is access to credit—a loan at zero percent interest isn't going to do you any good if you don't qualify for it.

Finally, there are a lot of nonprofit organizations with microloan funds. These are usually loans of less than $250,000 and can be as small as several hundred dollars. The SBA sponsors some of these; again call your nearest SBA office to see which ones are involved. Another way to find some local organizations is through the Association for Enterprise Opportunities in Chicago (312-357-0177).

The picture is far from bleak. If you do your homework carefully you should be able to find some money!

Chapter 30

Taking on Investors

To most entrepreneurs starting a company, the idea of raising capital from outside investors is very appealing. However, many do not fully understand the serious implications of such a move.

The benefits are fairly obvious. By using other people's money instead of your own, the financial risks are reduced considerably. And, by having more capital available than you can invest yourself or generate from earnings, you can adopt a more aggressive strategy and hopefully grow faster.

Two disadvantages of having outside investors are the questions of dilution of ownership and loss of control, which most entrepreneurs are far too concerned about. These questions are discussed in another chapter.

Another more important disadvantage, though, is that by having outside investors you, as the head of the company, assume a very substantial obligation to do all you can to provide these investors with a return on their investment consistent with the risk, and to provide them with liquidity—that is, a way to sell their stock.

Think of your relationship with an investor as being similar to the relationship between a borrower and a bank. An equity investment from a shareholder is a liability, and liabilities must be paid back. The main difference between outside investors and a bank is that investors have different expectations and are usually more patient. Venture investors typically expect a minimum of a five to 10 times return on their investment over a period of about five years. You should not even think about selling stock to outsiders unless your venture has reasonable potential for this kind of appreciation.

In addition, you have a strong obligation to find some way for your investors to achieve liquidity, to convert their stock into cash, within a reasonable length of time. As a practical matter, the two most common ways to accomplish this are for the company to either go public or merge with another firm.

Telling your investors that they will achieve liquidity from the dividends your company will pay or that you will buy the stock back according to a formula, is a good way to make it very difficult to raise capital. Venture investors do not make high-risk investments for the purpose of getting dividends. If that were their intention they would buy stock in a public utility. And they probably will not believe you or will find the formula unacceptable when you suggest the company is prepared to buy back its stock at some future date.

What I suggest is that when an entrepreneur accepts money from an outside investor, he or she assumes a very strong obligation to provide a return to that investor consistent with the risk and a very strong obligation to provide liquidity in a reasonable period of time. It probably requires that the company either go public or merge. If you cannot accept this, do not take on outside investors.

Chapter 31

The Importance of Control: Who Needs It?

Most entrepreneurs, when trying to raise capital from outside sources, seem to be obsessed with the subject of control. The 51 percent number is magic. Admittedly, it is desirable to own as much of the company as possible. However, this issue is not nearly as important as most people believe.

Digital Equipment Corp. (DEC) is a classic example. When Ken Olsen raised his first $70,000 of venture capital, he gave up about 77 percent of the company, keeping only 13 percent for himself and distributing the rest to other founders. Over the years, his modest share of the ownership of DEC achieved a value of millions of dollars.

My advice in negotiating with a venture investor or an underwriter selling stock to the public is to give up as little of your company as possible in return for the money you are trying to raise. But don't panic if your share of the ownership drops below 50 percent.

The bottom line here is that if you are doing a good job running the company, if your sales are increasing and you are realizing a good profit, and if you consistently meet the goals of your business plan, you have nothing to worry about regardless of whether or not you control a majority of the stock. On the other hand, if none of the above is happening and the company is floundering, you have plenty to worry about, even if you own all of the stock.

My point is that even the founder must earn the position of head of the firm. And you only earn it with good performance.

Assume, for example, you have to give up 70 percent of the stock to outside investors in order to raise the capital you require to start the firm. So what? When venture investors put money into your business they are investing in you and the team you put together. A major factor in the investment decision is their evaluation of your ability to build and manage a business. Many venture investors, when asked what the three most important factors were in their decision to invest in a start up, answer, "Management, management, and management." The last thing in the world they want is to run your business. If they thought that was likely to happen they would not invest.

Suppose the company isn't doing too well. You should be the first to suggest that someone else might be better than you at running the business. Perhaps you should play a different role (director of engineering or sales manager for example), rather than president. Let someone else run the show.

The management skills needed to run a successful business are different for a start up than for a $10 million company, and they are different for a $10 million company than for a $100 million company. Some entrepreneurs can make this transition—many cannot. More important in the long run for you, your employees, and your investors, is that the company survive and thrive rather than that you remain in control.

Do the best that you can when structuring a financial deal. Try to keep as much of the stock as possible. But don't forget: It's more important that you have the opportunity to start the company than owning 51 percent of the stock and remain the boss forever.

In addition, there is another more practical consideration that you should keep in mind. If you have any significant number of shareholders—say 10 or more—the likelihood of their joining forces against you is low unless you really screw up. If your company is publicly owned, the chances of a stockholder revolution is almost nil. We all know about publicly owned, multimillion dollar corporations in which the management holds only a tiny fraction of outstanding shares. Since they usually load their board of directors with friends and/or employees, they must be guilty of gross mismanagement for their job to be in jeopardy.

This has been challenged lately at IBM, Eastman Kodak, Apple Computer, and several other companies where the board of directors replaced the CEO with an outsider, but it is still generally true.

At RF Communications, the four founders first formed a legal partnership in which we were all equal. Then, we incorporated and divided the stock in proportion to our expected role in the company. My reward for being founder and president was to have a little more stock than the other three, or about 33 percent. Then we sold stock to the public to raise our initial capital and my percentage dropped to about 20 percent. Over the next eight years, we raised money on four other occasions each time further diluting my share of the ownership. When we finally merged I only owned a little more than 10 percent of the stock—but this was 10 percent of a very big pie! Had I insisted on maintaining a controlling interest in RF Communications, we could not have possibly achieved the results that we did. My personal rewards would surely have been much less. I can honestly say that I never worried about having control.

In the long run, if the company succeeds, there will be more than enough to go around and your rewards will be great. If the company fails, it does not matter how big a part of it you own. Set your ownership goals high, but don't be greedy.

Chapter 32

Watch Out for the Sharks: And Other Advice for Dealing With Venture Investors

There are at least three distinct kinds of venture investors. They are:

1. Individuals and informal venture groups.
2. Formal, institutional venture capital funds.
3. Corporate venture funds.

There are several other sources of venture capital that I have not mentioned, such as R&D Limited Partnerships and Small Business Investment Companies (SBIC). The R&D Limited Partnership seems to be out of favor because of changes in the tax laws. The SBIC is, for all practical purposes, a variation of the formal venture capital fund but it uses SBA guaranteed loans as its source of capital rather than venture investors and need not be discussed separately.

With this as background, let's look at the pros and cons of each:

Individuals and informal venture groups

This includes individuals or small groups that invest personal money in new ventures. They are often entrepreneurs who have started their own companies and have capital that they are willing to put at risk. Individual venture investors are either willing to or insist on being closely involved with the business as directors, informal advisors, or mentors. This type of investor is often referred to as an "angel." I read an article about venture investing and it said the angels invest about $10 billion a year in over 30,000 companies nationwide.

The major advantage of dealing with individuals or small groups of venture investors is this: If the entrepreneur can catch their interest, deals can be consummated rapidly and the deals are likely to be fairly straightforward. This type of investor may be more willing to finance an early start up than other sources of venture capital. In general, individual investors have goals similar to the entrepreneur. Having been entrepreneurs themselves, they understand the problems of starting a business, and their involvement can be valuable.

Finally, even though individual investors and informal groups are likely to be fairly sophisticated, they often make their investment decisions intuitively without too much due diligence investigation. The deals they cut will be less burdensome than the deals you are apt to get from a venture capital fund or corporate investor.

On the negative side, even though the total amount of money invested each year by individuals is very high, the amount they will invest in any particular deal may be limited. In addition, individuals or informal groups may have little interest in providing a second or third round of financing after making the initial investment. And, the contacts these investors have with the investment banking community may be somewhat limited.

Individual venture investors may be hard to find. There are few formal channels available to establish contact, and the entrepreneur may have difficulty in locating people with the kind of money required.

Until recently, this type of offering could only be made to a limited number of potential investors and the company had to establish investor criteria. This criteria included the minimum each investor must contribute and what income or net worth an individual must have to qualify. In effect, the Securities and Exchange Commission (SEC) permitted the sale of this type of high-risk security only to investors who were capable of fully understanding the risk and who had sufficient personal resources to afford a loss in the event the company goes under.

In 1992, the SEC amended its Rule 504, which controls this type of stock sale, substantially reducing or eliminating many of the restrictions previously in place. The purpose of the amendment was to make it easier for small companies to raise capital using this route. Among other things, it permits a company to promote the offering more broadly and to sell stock to greater number of buyers. It also makes it easier for the buyers to sell the stock they purchased, and eliminates the need for the Private Placement Memorandum in order to comply with all of the specific requirements of Regulation D, "Safe Harbor." It does not, however, reduce the company's obligations to make full disclosure under the antifraud rules of the federal securities laws.

My suggestion is that your first step in trying to raise capital from individual venture investors should be to prepare a document called a Private Placement Memorandum (even though it is no longer a legal requirement). These should be about 30 or 40 pages in length and present detailed information about the company. The information is similar to that contained in a conventional stock prospectus but with more emphasis on the risks associated with the venture. The information in a Private Placement Memorandum must be absolutely true, and should accurately describe both the positive and negative aspects of the business. Much of the information can be drawn from the business plan. An important part of this document is a description of the number of shares you want to sell, the price of the shares, and what you intend to do with the money.

Even with the changes in Rule 504, I strongly recommend that **under no circumstances** should you conduct a private placement without the advice of a knowledgeable lawyer completely familiar with security regulations.

You may conclude from what I have said that the private placement is just too complex to bother with. That is not the case. As mentioned in another chapter, in the Rochester area, between January 1980 and March 1988, 42 companies raised approximately $32 million from individual investors. I know many individuals who are interested in making this kind of investment—they understand and are comfortable with the risks. Their hope is that they may find a situation where their investment may appreciate 50 or 100 times.

Raising money through a private placement usually requires a large amount of time from the senior people in the firm. Many of the potential investors are likely to visit the company personally to meet the principals, see the facilities, and ask questions about the business. If you happen to include among your personal acquaintances a half dozen or so millionaires, this will be of immeasurable help. Failing this, I suggest you try to find one or two highly-visible, successful entrepreneurs who, if persuaded to come in on the deal, may attract others.

An example of a Rochester company that successfully used individual investors for its initial financing is Ormec Systems Corp., a manufacturer of high-tech precision motion control systems used in automated manufacturing. Its customers include Eastman Kodak, for its film manufacturing operation, Johnson & Johnson, for the manufacture of its pharmaceuticals, and the Harrison Division of General Motors, for the manufacture of automobile radiators.

I met two of the four founders of Ormec in an entrepreneurship class I spoke to. At the time, the two key people were engineers working for Eastman Kodak. After getting to know them and their business I decided to invest personally and brought together a group of four other successful entrepreneurs. Together we provided $300,000 of start-up money in return for a 40 percent interest in the company. The two key founders quit their jobs and the company was off and running. Three of the outside investors became board members.

Ormec has since raised about $1 million of additional capital in two private placements and now has about 130 shareholders. Over the past few years they made major investments in building a large national network of distributors and representatives and in developing new, advanced lines of products. Even though they have had some ups and downs through the years, sales are now in the $12 million range...and growing. They hope to soon reach the point where either a public offering or merger with a larger company should be considered.

Another example of a company started with funding from individual investors is Jolt Cola. Jolt was founded in 1985 by a man named C.J. Rapp at age 25. What differentiated Jolt from other soft drink beverages at the time is best described in the company's motto: "Twice the caffeine." This strategy was almost the exact opposite of other soft drink companies at the time which were emphasizing no caffeine and low sugar.

Rapp's initial financing was his personal savings, a six-figure loan from his father and about $100,000 of equity investment from 12 private investors. The loan from his father was paid back exactly two months after the first case of Jolt was sold. At the present time Rapp still owns an estimated 88 percent of the company and the remainder is still owned by the initial investors.

When he started Jolt, Rapp's target market was young people, 16 to 32 years of age, who live a very hectic lifestyle and want a product that provides the stimulation they need.

I recall vividly when Jolt first announced its high caffeine cola. The product was so unusual, that it received a huge amount of national publicity both in the press and on national radio and television talk shows. It was featured on *Late Night With David Letterman*. Over the years, Rapp has increased sales for his company to over $10 million. They have added a number of additional products to their line that sell in over 22 countries with a staff of 18 employees. The company is entirely debt-free.

How about the future? Rapp mentioned that he has been approached by several underwriters who suggest that he take the company public. To date, he has declined all offers.

Individual venture investors can be a good source of capital for a new business.

Formal (institutional) venture funds

The venture capital industry has been one of the major growth industries of the 1980s and 1990s. In the late 90s, about $40 billion of investment was managed by venture capital funds. Venture funds are usually limited partnerships where the bulk of the money is supplied by passive limited partners, such as insurance companies, college endowment funds, or corporate retirement funds. The investment portfolio is then managed by a general partner or group of general partners. They seek out and evaluate investment opportunities, negotiate deals, manage the follow-up activity, and participate on the board of directors of companies in their portfolio.

The formal venture capital industry has structure, and there are a number of directories available that list the various funds, amounts of capital available, industry focus, and addresses and telephone numbers of the managing partners.

One such source of information is Galante's *Complete Venture Capital & Private Equity Directory*, which is available from Asset Alternatives, 180 Linden St., Ste. 3, Wellesley, MA 02181 (617-431-7353) which contains an extensive list of venture funds along with their areas of interest. Its cost was $395 on either disk or hard copy or $495 for both. The disk version of this directory is compatible with many popular personal computer programs.

Another is *Pratt's Guide to Venture Capital Sources*, from Venture Economics, a Division of Securities Data Publishers, 40 W 57 Street, #1100, New York, NY 10102-0968, (800-455-5844 or 212-765-5311). The price of the 1997 edition was $325. It includes an introductory section about the venture capital industry and lists just about every venture capital fund in the United States and Canada and its area of specialization.

Even though these directories are fairly expensive, they both contain much cross referenced information that can save you hours and hours of effort trying to find a venture fund that may be interested in your type of situation.

A Directory of Small Business Investment Companies can be obtained from the Associate Administrator for Investment at the U.S. Small Business Administration, Washington, DC 20419, (202-205-6510, fax 202-205-6959).

Another way for a company to reach venture investors is by attending venture capital forums which are held on a regular basis in many sections of the country. They are intended to give entrepreneurs the opportunity to present their deal to groups of venture fund managers. Contact your chamber of commerce to learn whether there are any of these forums held in your area.

One of the more important advantages of dealing with an institutional venture capital fund is that they have access to large amounts of money. For example, in 1995 venture funds raised about $4.4 billion of new money, an all-time record. Since then, I understand they have raised even greater amounts. Except for the very small funds, their minimum investment is frequently in the $500,000 to $1 million range and they can often put together deals requiring $5 million or more. In addition, it is quite typical for this kind of venture investor to make second and third infusions of capital as the company grows.

Another important benefit that the venture funds offer is an excellent window on the investment banking industry. At such time that the company goes public, the managers of the fund can be a valuable source of help. In general, the goals of this type of venture investor are similar to the goals of the new enterprise. However, the venture fund may be more impatient to cash out on a deal, which could force the company into a merger or public offering sooner than it wants.

Finally, the general partners are usually diligent in their participation on the board of directors of the companies in their portfolio. Because they are frequently involved with other similar companies, they can be an important source of experience and expertise.

However, in spite of the above list of advantages, I urge new companies seeking capital from venture funds to proceed with caution. Entrepreneurs recognize the risks associated with starting the business. They may not be familiar with the risks of dealing with venture investors.

Among the disadvantages of trying to raise capital from a venture fund is that the process can be very slow. Venture funds are typically deluged by proposals and business plans from companies seeking money, and most funds operate with a limited staff of people who are all extremely busy. Their response time can be slow. Some people familiar with the venture industry suggest that a business plan submitted without a personal introduction has almost no chance of receiving attention.

Because they have a fiduciary responsibility to their limited partners, venture funds go through an extensive "due-diligence" process. Commonly, they retain consultants, expert in the specific industry, to investigate the products and markets of the new venture. This process can take weeks and months to complete and can be very demanding on the time of the entrepreneur.

Another disadvantage is that venture capital funds impose some very tough conditions that many entrepreneurs consider unacceptable. For instance, it is not unusual for them to demand some form of convertible preferred stock, the purpose of which is to give them preference over other shareholders in the event of liquidation. Also, they frequently require anti-dilution protection if stock is ever sold at a lower price, strong representation on the board of directors, control over salary levels of managers, and the latitude to take over the company if certain financial criteria are not met. These conditions are outlined in what is known as a "term sheet."

The advice I give to people beginning negotiations with a venture fund is to ask for a copy of their standard term sheet at the start rather than at the end, as this may avoid unexpected surprises and a lot of wasted time. You will likely be told they do not have such a thing because terms vary so much with the deal. Then, ask for a copy of the term sheet of several recent deals, or the term sheet of an investment they made in a company similar to yours.

Most burdensome, though, in dealing with venture funds is the valuation they set on the company, which determines the price they are willing to pay for the stock. My experience with venture funds is that they drive tough financial deals.

It is extremely desirable for entrepreneurs to negotiate with a venture fund at a time when they do not need the money too badly, and to have at least two sources of venture capital competing for the deal. It is not unknown for a venture fund to deliberately protract negotiations so long that the company is desperate for money, then nail them to the cross in setting a price. The expression "vulture capitalist" has some basis.

I already mentioned how diligent venture funds are in checking the credentials of potential investments. It is equally as important that companies seeking investment check out the credentials of the funds they are considering taking money from. One of the best ways to do this is to talk to the heads of other businesses that secured investments from the funds they are considering working with.

Entrepreneurs should be very careful in approaching venture funds to avoid the appearance that they have unsuccessfully approached a number of other potential investors. Communications between funds is fairly efficient and the fact that you have shopped the deal and have been turned down by two or three may make your situation untouchable to others.

From my contact with venture funds, I have concluded that when you get past the public relations hype, many of them are really not very venturesome. Part of this results from the fact that they must report regularly to the limited partner investors, who, in turn, are managed by financial types whose performance is continually under review. Either consciously or unconsciously they want investments that will make them look good in the short term. An entrepreneur trying to raise money from a venture fund to finance a raw start up faces a very hard road.

Entrepreneurs dealing with venture funds had better not be thin-skinned. A few years ago a friend of mine was invited by the manager of a large, well-known fund to come from Rochester to Boston to meet with the partners at 3 p.m. the following afternoon. After being kept waiting for two hours, he was told he had 15 minutes to present his story.

If you do approach a venture fund, remember that the managers control large amounts of money and the world seems to beat a path to their doors trying to relieve them of some. Financial power, like political power, can distort one's sense of values. Also, the general partners of venture funds are almost always incredibly busy. Typically they travel three, four and five days a week. They are overwhelmed with potential deals, some of their past deals may be in serious trouble, and they are deluged by telephone calls from impatient entrepreneurs. This frenetic existence can cause impatience and unintended slights.

In approaching an Institutional Venture Capital Fund the entrepreneur should remember that the main goal of the fund is to make a profit for themselves and their sources of money. This is probably your main goal, but if other goals are of equal or greater importance (such as providing a place for your children to work or providing some benefits to society in general) the chances of getting an investment from an institutional investor goes down dramatically.

Another thing to keep in mind is the various stages a company may go through during its corporate existence and that some of these stages are of much more interest to a venture fund then others. The stages businesses go through, in general, are these:

1. **Start-up.** This is the formative period of the existence of a new business. Some specialized venture funds will invest in the start-up stage of a company's existence but many will not.

2. **Development stage.** Here a company has probably raised some capital from private sources, completed the development of its main product, perhaps has secured a patent, has built some units, and possibly even sold some. This stage is of more interest to a venture fund, and if the heads of the company have a successful record starting other businesses, the chances of getting an investment may be pretty good.

3. **Growth stage.** In this stage the company is up and running and perhaps even operating in the black. They have gone through the initial period of getting some market acceptance and need additional funds to achieve growth. This

is the type of situation that many venture funds are looking for. It is not overly risky and the opportunity of participating in the fastest growth phase of the company can still be quite high.

4. **Running well.** Here the company is doing quite well and needs additional funds for such things as a new factory, an acquisition, and so forth. Venture funds may be interested in investing at this stage even though they may have missed the period of rapid growth and their chances of investing at a very low price is not too good.

5. **Other stages.** This would include helping an entrepreneur buy an existing unit of a company that it is trying to sell off, a turnaround situation where the company has been doing very poorly but a new management thinks it knows how to get the ball rolling again, and so forth. Here the likelihood of getting an investment from a venture fund varies depending on the exact situation.

So my advice to entrepreneurs seeking investment from venture capital funds is to be very cautious. Talk to other entrepreneurs who have been down the same road and, of utmost importance, try to do all of your money raising when you do not need the money too badly and while you still have options.

To give you the "other-side-of-the-story" about working with institutional venture capital funds, I asked a friend of mine who manages a large institutional fund to write a later chapter about how to improve the odds of attracting this type of investment.

Corporate venture funds

A third source of venture capital is the corporate venture investor. In recent years, a number of large corporations have established venture funds, sometimes formal and sometimes informal, for the purpose of investing in new ventures. In most of the cases that I know of, these investments are made in situations that are generally related to the main business of the investing organization. In some, the goal is to diversify the business, not expand it in areas in which they are already active.

Among the advantages of raising capital from a corporate investor is that they are a potential source of both technical and management expertise as well as money. They often have access to fairly large amounts of capital, they can be quite venturesome, and, because they have goals other than pure financial gain, they may not drive as hard a deal as a venture fund.

The major drawback of using a corporate investor as a source of venture capital is that they often want some way to eventually gain control of the company in which they invested. This will sometimes be in the form of a buy-out provision with price based on a predetermined formula. Obviously, this constraint can put a serious limit on upward potential for the entrepreneur.

In thinking about obtaining financing from a large company, the entrepreneur should keep in mind that large firms use at least two primary approaches to venturing. The first (and most common) is called "intrapreneurship." This is the process that many large firms use to encourage people already employed by the firm to identify and bring into existence new businesses or new products that will benefit the company. The companies assist and encourage people with entrepreneurial qualities to develop new ideas that can be financed and supported by the firm as a way to expand its business.

The second approach is to provide financing, similar to the way used by venture capital funds, to become involved in ventures outside of their present organization. These new ventures will usually not be 100-percent owned by the sponsoring company and may or may not be based upon ideas for products or services that originated within the company. Also, with this approach the entrepreneur may be able to own a reasonably large percentage of the equity in the new venture thereby greatly increasing the potential for financial reward if the venture succeeds.

Intrapreneurship

The purpose of this book is mainly to assist an entrepreneur in starting a business independent of a parent company, not as part of a company for which the entrepreneur is already employed. However, in some cases intrapreneurship may be a good way for an entrepreneur to proceed. Many large U.S. companies very heavily involved in intrapreneurial activities.

One of the most successful Intrapreneurial programs that I am familiar with is the Post-It program at 3M. It is an incredibly successful and profitable new product area that evolved entirely from within the company. It led 3M into a new business area that a few years ago did not exist.

In another case of intrapreneurship that I am familiar with that was not as successful as 3M's is a very large company that had an internal department whose function it was to locate potential entrepreneurs, mostly from within the company. They were seeking ideas unrelated to the company's current product offering. This was intended to give the company the opportunity of diversifying into other types of businesses.

They undertook about 16 of these new ventures in a period of about two years and provided them with considerable capital. Several years later the company decided that this system was not working well and they terminated the program. They either sold off the new businesses, reabsorbed them into some department of the parent company, or simply abandoned them. They spent millions of dollars trying to get into these new, unrelated businesses with this approach and it turned out to be almost completely unsuccessful.

External ventures

These are situations where the sponsoring company takes a substantial equity position, but not necessarily control, of a start-up business.

One interesting example of a new business whose initial financing was from a major corporate investor was Microlytics, which was founded by a former employee of Xerox. My familiarity with this situation is a result of knowing the entrepreneur who was seeking the investment and providing some counseling to him during negotiations.

This one seemed to have turned out badly for everyone involved since Microlytics recently filed for bankruptcy. However, from the entrepreneur's viewpoint, even though the company was not a success, it gave him a chance and the financing necessary to start a new business. If it had been a success he would have fared very well financially. It did not succeed and, I assume, he did not come out so well. I will tell you a little about the background of Microlytics because it is a very interesting situation.

The founder had a long background of running a number of his own businesses and seemed to have many important entrepreneurial qualities. When Microlytics came into existence its intention was to enter the computer software business. Its initial product was a program named "Wordfinder," a spelling checker and thesaurus. This was at a time before every word processing program included these as built in features. One of Microlytics' goals was to license its spelling checker and thesaurus software to companies offering word processing programs.

Initial financing was a $400,000 investment from the venture capital arm of Xerox. In making this investment, Xerox required that Microlytics raise a matching amount from private investors, which the company did without too much difficulty.

At the start everything seemed to go well. Several years later Microlytics merged with Minneapolis-based Selectronics, which had a line of hand-held spelling checker/thesaurus products. Because Selectronics was publicly owned at the time they kept that corporate identity. Over two million of these hand-held spelling checkers were sold. Unfortunately severe competition kept profit margins very low and the company ran into serious financial difficulties. The combined company name was then changed back to Microlytics and they abandoned the hardware business.

During several years of severe ups and downs, the company worked hard to expand its product offering and get the operation back into the black. Xerox helped them during these very hard times. A short time later the company filed for bankruptcy.

For the founder of Microlytics the corporate venture capital route was a good approach to its initial financing since it gave him the opportunity to see whether he had the skills and ideas needed to create a profitable business with a minimum of personal risk. He worked very hard for a number of years before leaving Microlytics. For Xerox and the other outside investors, it did not turn out so well.

My personal experience with these corporate investing programs is that they vary considerably from company to company.

In the situation I just described, the company had a formal venture fund that operated somewhat independently of the parent company.

Another approach I am familiar with is used by a company in the military electronics business. They became associated with an existing institutional venture capital fund which moved one employee to the city the company was headquartered. His job is to actively seek out possible venture opportunities within the company. The difference between this and the prior example is that the people in the venture capital fund were required to raise about half of the needed capital from other outside venture fund investors. From the sponsoring companies viewpoint this gave them at least some assurance that the specific deal had been reviewed by several independent and experienced venture investors, with each performing some due diligence. Hopefully, this will increase the possibility of the spin-off company succeeding.

This program has only been under way for a short period of time and I do not know what the results have been. My general feeling is that having the deals reviewed and approved by professional venture investors, unrelated to the sponsoring company greatly improves the chances of succeeding.

Of the two examples I described above where large companies provide financing to new businesses outside the company one is unsuccessful and one "too early to tell." But both summaries are both from the viewpoint of the investors not the entrepreneurs. In both cases the entrepreneurs successfully raised the capital needed to try to start businesses. One of them did not succeed, but at least he had the chance. My belief is that in most of these situations the founders would have had difficulty raising financing on their own. So even with all of the shortcomings they are a way for the potential entrepreneur to give it a try.

Another question that might be asked is, "What is the best way to locate a company that might be a source of early financing and what would be the best way to approach them?" This is a question to which I do not have a good answer. If I were trying to start a company using this route I would begin by regularly reading business publications such as *The Wall Street Journal*, *BusinessWeek*, *Fortune*, *Inc.*, *Forbes*, among others. Occasionally there are articles describing various companies financing new businesses. There are also several books devoted to large company venturing which describe the programs in a number of organizations. Then, I would contact someone within those companies, at a very high level with a personal introduction if possible, and send them a copy of my entire business plan or a brief summary. The business plan should be "customized" to match the interests of the company to which it is sent and carefully written to generate interest.

Determining the value of your business

In the early stages of a business, most entrepreneurs have a very difficult time trying to determine what their company is worth. A venture investor calls this the "valuation" of the deal. In effect, what you must decide is what percentage of your company you are willing to sell for how much money. Because start-up companies have no operating history, the valuation is set mostly by estimates. The following describes the process a venture investor is likely to go through.

The first thing a venture investor will do is to look at the sales and net (after tax) profit you project in your business plan five years or so in the future. Assume for this discussion you expect annual sales to be $15 million and net profit to be five percent or $750,000. Based upon the venture investor's knowledge of the market, your competitors, your product, and your management, as well as advice from consultants, he might decide that this is too optimistic. Let's say he cuts it back to $10 million in sales and $500,000 net profit.

Having determined what your company's sales and net profits might be five years in the future, he then tries to estimate what the value of your company will be at that time. He estimates what a reasonable price earnings ratio (P/E) for your stock is likely to be. Until recently, he would probably assume something in the range of 10 to one or less. Therefore, in the minds of the venture investor the value of your company five years from now is your net earnings times the P/E Ratio, $500,000 times 10, or $5 million.

Next, he will ask what is $5 million five years from now worth today, or its present value. To do this calculation you must assume a rate of return. Venture investors want a rate of return in the range of 25 percent to 50 percent, which is high because of the risk involved. For the sake of example, let us use 36 percent. The present value of $5 million five years from now at a 36 percent rate of return is a little over $1 million.

In the mind of the venture investor, your company is presently worth about $1 million. Therefore, if you are planning to raise $600,000 of capital, the venture investor will want to own 60 percent of your stock. Going through this process always shocks the entrepreneur by how low the valuation comes out to be.

In addition, many entrepreneurs in the early stages of their business make personal loans to their companies. When they work for less pay than ordinarily expected, they often show the differential on their balance sheet as deferred salaries. Their hope is that they will be reimbursed later from the capital they raise. However, I always advise against this practice. When an entrepreneur puts money into the company it should be an investment, not a loan. Working for a lower salary is just a way of life in a start up. Both of these practices are apt to make it much harder to raise capital because investors want their money used for future activities—not to pay for past obligations.

A business owner approached me several years ago trying to raise several hundred thousand dollars for his company. When I pressed him for the details, I learned that much of this money would be used to pay delinquent withholding tax obligations plus penalties. As you might guess, I let that one go by.

In the past few years, a number of new companies have come into existence that do business on the Internet. Frequently, they go public early in their corporate life, long before they have achieved profitability. In many cases, the stock price soars almost immediately after the initial public offering and the market value of the companies reach astronomical levels. Since they often do not have any earnings, their P/E ratio is infinity. So much for using P/E as an indication of the value of the business.

An interesting example of this is Amazon.com which sells books over the Internet. They are said to have over 1.5 million titles available which is more than can be found in even the largest bookstores such as Barnes & Nobles or Borders. I personally enjoy visiting bookstores but many people do not and prefer to shop at home. Also, Amazon.com sells at a substantial discount. The interesting part of this story is that even though Amazon.com is not profitable, its market value exceeds that of Barnes & Noble and Borders combined. There are many other examples of high market value for companies doing business on the Internet.

My personal belief is that this situation cannot last, and that sooner or later these Internet companies will have to develop profits comparable to other companies or the market value of their stock is sure to drop. In the long run, the best approach a new company can follow both to raise capital and to survive as a successful business is to develop a strategy by which their business can develop positive cash flow and a reasonable profit on a continuing basis.

Of the three type of investors, venture funds are likely to come up with the lowest valuation, corporate venture funds are likely to have somewhat higher valuation because they will attribute value to other factors than financial profit, and individual investors and informal venture groups will probably have the highest valuation.

Chapter 33

How to Get a Venture Investment: Improving the Odds

This chapter was written by Paul S. Brentlinger, partner in Morgenthaler Ventures, a venture capital firm with offices in Cleveland, Ohio and Menlo Park, California. The Morgenthaler firm manages approximately $425 million in venture capital assets, with a concentration in the information technology and health care fields. Earlier, Paul was senior vice president of finance at Harris Corporation. Paul has an M.B.A. from the University of Michigan and is a member of Phi Beta Kappa. He is a director of Allegheny Teledyne, Inc.; Wastequip, Inc.; and serves as chairman of Hypres, Inc.

There is a lot of money out there

If you believe the company you started can grow large, and if you are willing to work in partnership with investors who own a large share of your company's equity, you probably owe it to yourself to consider seeking capital from an institutional venture investor. Institutional venture capital comes from approximately 600 professionally-managed venture capital firms in the United States, as well as a few from abroad. They manage venture-type equity investments on behalf of pension funds, foundations, university endowment funds, among other institutional sources of money.

At the end of 1998, institutional venture capital firms in the United States were managing approximately $34 billion of equity capital. During 1998, these firms invested $13 billion in 1,800 different companies. More than 80 percent of this investment went into two industries—information technology and health care. This chapter focuses entirely on the investment process used by institutional venture capital firms, not individual investors.

Analyze your goals

The primary objective of some entrepreneurs is to build a comfortable, medium-sized company that is always subject to their personal control, that is designed to finance the family's yacht or the Florida condominium. They are also interested in providing jobs for children and relatives. These are legitimate objectives, but they are incompatible with the objectives of institutional venture capital firms.

To obtain money from institutional venture capitalists, it is important that you understand their goals. Pension funds, endowment funds, foundations, and other funds that entrust the investment of their money to venture capitalists expect a rate of return significantly higher than the return on investment attainable from buying publicly traded common stocks. To illustrate, if the Standard & Poor's stock average has produced an annual rate of return of 10 to 12 percent over the past five to 10 years, venture capital should produce a return in the 15- to 18-percent range.

Because some venture capital investments are total failures, and a number of others will produce minimal returns (these are called the "living dead"). The venture capitalist must see an opportunity for a very high rate of return, in the 30- to 40-percent range on any individual investment opportunity.

With this in mind, the venture capitalists are strictly equity-oriented investors. A share of the ownership of a company is what creates an opportunity for substantial capital gains. Venture capitalists do not lend money at six points over prime rate.

Entrepreneurs seeking institutional venture capital funding must be willing to share equity ownership and give up a significant degree of control of their enterprise.

Are you a candidate for a venture investment?

In general, venture capitalists prefer to invest in companies that plan on selling stock to the public within a five years period. This usually indicates the company should have the potential to generate annual sales revenue in the $50- to $100-million range within that time frame. It is also essential that the company's products or services address markets which investors believe to be large and rapidly growing—the kinds of markets which attract attention from professional securities analysts. You may have to be sensitive to investment fads, such as the current hot market for Internet-related stocks.

Working toward public ownership requires a professional approach to management. This probably means a willingness on the part of the entrepreneur to work with a board of directors comprised of a majority of outsiders, including venture capitalists. Also, the company must have the ability to generate financial statements prepared in accordance with generally accepted accounting practices and audited by one of the Big Five accounting firms, and the ability to develop an effective multilayer management team. This list is illustrative—it is by no means all-inclusive.

How to approach a venture capital firm

If you believe your objectives are consistent with those of institutional venture capitalists with all this in mind, how is the best way to approach a venture capital firm?

It is highly desirable to arrange an introduction through a mutual acquaintance. Lawyers, accountants, consultants, private investors, or friends who have a personal relationship with a venture capital firm represent ideal points of entry. Right or wrong, institutional venture capitalists rarely invest in companies that make a cold approach.

The business plan is crucial

Once the introduction has been made, the submission of a well thought out business plan is a key part of the process. For more information on this, turn back to Chapter 25 titled "What! Me Write A Business Plan?" on page 88—it is must reading.

In reviewing a business plan the venture capitalist probably will concentrate on the following issues:

- **The Business Concept:** What market is being addressed? Is a large and growing economic need being addressed?
- **Product or Service:** Does the product or service offer a genuine competitive advantage? Why will people buy your product as opposed to buying an alternative? Will customers pay a premium price? Is there patent protection? Are

there barriers to entry? Are there powerful competitors? Can the company be a low-cost producer?

- **Management Team:** Are members of management experienced in the market? Do they have a track record of success? Is the management team totally committed to the success of the enterprise? Are the team members capable of growth as the company grows?
- **Financial Aspects:** How much capital is needed? Is the business capital intensive? Will additional rounds of private venture capital investment be required? Are the financial projections realistic?
- **Valuation:** Will the venture capital investment buy enough shares in the company to produce the opportunity for at least a 30 to 40 percent return on investment described earlier? What is the probable exit strategy? Is the company a candidate for a public offering? And if so, when and at what multiple of sales or earnings? Is the company a candidate for acquisition at a high price by a larger company?

Why does the process take so long?

In a somewhat different vein, most venture capitalists like to co-invest in early stage companies with other strong venture capital firms. By doing so, they share the work load and financial burden. With this in mind, you must ask if your company is one that is likely to attract an investment from other well-financed venture capital firms capable of offering constructive collaboration. The individual venture capitalist will think about whether he or she would like to put his or her reputation on the line by introducing the deal to a friend in another venture capital firm.

Once an investment opportunity gets beyond the initial screening step, a series of meetings will take place between the venture capitalist and the company's management team. These meetings represent a critically important step. Venture capital investing involves a long-term partnership relationship with the management team. Before an investment is made, there must be sufficient personal interaction to ensure a mutual belief that the venture capitalist and the management have the same objectives. It is important that the people concerned will be comfortable working together over a period of several years to accomplish their mutual objectives.

If there appears to be a strong mutual interest regarding the investment, the venture capitalist can be expected to do a lot of reference checking regarding the management team. In many cases, the venture capitalist will also use outside consultants to advise on the technology and the market prospects. As an entrepreneur seeking venture capital funding, you have to be willing to share detailed information about your products and technology. You will also need to talk about yourself and your colleagues as part of this due diligence process.

You are entitled to receive assurances from the venture capitalist that proprietary information will be held in confidence.

Upon completion of the due diligence, the venture capitalist must make a yes/no decision. Most venture capital firms require that one of its partners recommend any specific investment—a partner must act as a sponsor or champion. Your personal relationship with the venture capital partner looking at your company is of vital importance—the partner is unlikely to champion an investment in your company unless he or she believes an effective relationship can be developed.

Reviewing the steps

To summarize, in order to attract an investment from an institutional venture capital firm the following conditions must exist:

1. Your objectives must be consistent with those of the venture capital firm.
2. You must be willing to share equity ownership and a degree of control with the venture capitalist.
3. You must submit a business plan that presents a compelling case for your business concept, products, management team, and probable financial results.
4. You must be prepared to have a lot of personal interaction with the venture capitalist in the course of an intense due diligence process. This will often require the sharing of your trade secrets.
5. You must be prepared to value your company at a level that satisfies the risk/reward criteria applied by the venture capitalist.

You get a lot of help beyond money

If your company receives funding from a group of strong venture investors, the ultimate benefits can be very rewarding. Good venture capitalists don't stop work after the investment is made—they contribute more than money. They can be helpful in such areas as arranging customer contacts, in executive recruiting, in shaping financial strategy, and in attracting strong underwriter support when the time comes for an initial public offering.

Although the venture capital process may appear to be long and arduous, enormous wealth has been created for entrepreneurs who have successfully traveled the path. Examples include companies such as Cisco Systems, Genentech, Sun Microsystems, VeriFone, and Premisys Communications.

Your challenge will be to add your company to this list of venture capital-backed winners—you may have a chance for personal immortality by being able to put your name on the newest building of your favorite university, or top Bill Gates in your contribution to a major library system. There is not much to lose if you try.

Chapter 34

Staying Private/ Going Public

Most financial experts advise new companies not to go public too soon. However, I'm not sure I agree with this conclusion so I will describe some of the benefits of going public, which can be considerable. But first, let me mention some of the disadvantages.

One of the major drawbacks of going public with a new venture is that you will bring in small investors. Even though your offering circular or prospectus will describe the risks in great detail and with great emphasis, the typical small investor may not fully understand them. The head of a start-up company has enough problems without having to worry about the "widows and orphans" among the shareholders who cannot afford to lose their investment.

A second frequently-cited drawback is that it puts unreasonable pressure on management to achieve short-term profitability in its desire to keep the price of the stock up. I see nothing wrong with management being under pressure to achieve profitable operations early. My experience is that most entrepreneurs have no trouble figuring out reasons to defer profits, and pressure in the other direction is likely to be good rather than bad.

A third disadvantage is the cost of going public. Legal fees and printing costs for a public stock offering will be considerable, and if you use an underwriter to sell the stock, commissions will also be considerable. This does not worry me too much either because it's an accepted fact that the cost of raising capital can be high.

A fourth disadvantage is the time required. In most cases you will need approval from the SEC, which can be a long and complicated process.

Finally, there is the possibility that the price of your stock will fall below the offering price, which may make it both difficult and costly to raise more capital at a later date. This should be a real concern, but it is somewhat offset by the possibility that the price of your stock may increase, making it easier and less costly to raise more capital at a later date. In recent years, the price of the stock increasing after a public offering is much more common than the price dropping.

The importance of this list may be serious or not serious at all. It obviously depends upon the specific situation. How about the advantages?

For one thing, going public is a way to avoid using venture investors. It usually results in at least several hundred small shareholders rather than a handful of very large ones. The public is likely to be easier to deal with.

A second advantage is that you are almost sure to get a higher price for your stock. As I discuss in another chapter, venture investors drive very hard financial deals. The public is likely to be much less demanding.

Another benefit is liquidity. Stock purchased in a public issue can be traded freely by outside investors. The people who help you get started are not forced to leave their money tied up for five years or more. The founders will also have greater liquidity...at least to a degree. There still remain substantial restrictions on when and under what circumstances the founders, officers, directors, and/or major shareholders can sell stock. Restrictions notwithstanding, stock in a publicly-owned company is somewhat easier to sell.

Still another benefit of public ownership is that the company becomes more visible. Among other things, this means that hiring new employees will be easier, and doing business with other companies will be easier. In a 1990 survey of about 100 companies that had recently gone public, more than 50 percent of the respondents listed such things as enhanced credibility with customers, suppliers, banks, and different sources as the most important benefit.

For senior people in the venture, increased public visibility can result in the job being more fun. Communicating with shareholders, having contact with them, and conducting annual meetings are all things that can make the job more interesting—especially when the company is doing well. These may not be so much fun when the company is doing poorly.

A final benefit of being publicly-owned will only be realized when the new venture decides to sell or merge with a larger company. It is my experience, both as a seller and a buyer of companies, that the price paid for a publicly-owned company is almost always higher than the price paid for a privately-owned company. In the case of a publicly-owned company, the price is normally the quoted price plus a premium. If the company has done well and can catch the fancy of the investing community, the price may indeed be high. I have seen fairly large transactions where the acquiring firm paid 40 or 50 times earnings and more. In negotiated deals for privately-held companies, the range may be as low as seven or 10 times earnings. If you are positioning your company to be acquired, going public can have considerable merit.

An interesting case

Let me tell you about my experience going public as a way to raise start-up capital. Rochester, during the 1960s, was a hotbed of new venture activity. I researched those years in some detail and learned that during the decade approximately 100 companies in the area had initial public stock offerings. The company I started, RF Communications, was one of the first.

RF came into existence during the summer of 1960. The four founders each invested $5,000 for a total of $20,000 of initial capital. We started as a partnership and incorporated several months later. Three of the four founders resigned their full-time jobs on February 1, 1961, and on March 1, 1961, RF became an independent company. The only problem was that we were still operating on the original $20,000 investment, which was being depleted in a hurry.

During the planning phase of our venture, we considered various financing alternatives. There were no venture capital funds at the time and we did not include many wealthy people among our acquaintances. Because of these factors, we decided to try to raise the bulk of our start-up capital through a public stock offering that we would do ourselves without an underwriter or a broker. Within two weeks after setting up shop we received SEC approval for a Regulation A Offering, which is a somewhat simplified way to sell stock to the public. Our goal was to raise $150,000 by selling 150,000 shares at $1 per share—a nice round number. These 150,000 shares represented one-third ownership in the company. The four founders retained the other two thirds. Considering inflation, this would be something like $500,000 or more today.

Upon receiving SEC authorization, we mailed about 600 offering circulars to a list of potential investors. We compiled a list of names of everyone we could think of who might be willing to invest a few hundred dollars in our risky little deal. To our amazement, the deal somehow caught the local investing community's fancy. Within a few days, the offering was heavily oversubscribed. We received about $500,000 from potential investors interested in purchasing shares of our stock. This was way above the $150,000 we were asking for and way above what we expected to be able to raise. Unfortunately, SEC rules permit you to keep only the amount of capital stated in the offering circular. We said we wanted to raise $150,000 and that was all we were permitted to retain. The oversubscription of about $350,000 had to be returned. We allocated the stock in a way we considered fair and sent back the oversubscribed amount.

Two small, local brokerage firms began making a market in the stock and the trading price jumped to two dollars a share within several days. When it was all done, RF Communications had raised $150,000 for one third ownership and the company was off and running.

We have often questioned whether the way we did this was smart or dumb. You could easily take the position that the mere fact that we raised so much money is evidence that we either priced the stock too low or sold too large a percentage of the company for $150,000. On the other hand, you could argue that our primary goal was to raise $150,000 so that we would have the chance to prove whether the group of four entrepreneurs had the necessary skills to create a business. This goal was achieved.

Years later my feelings are these:

* We felt we needed $150,000 to run the business and we raised that amount.
* The stock immediately began trading for $2 a share, so our initial investors had both liquidity and a good profit.
* Two years later, when we needed more capital, we raised another $270,000 through a second public offering at $5 per share. Not bad!
* The founders were all inexperienced at raising capital and selling stock, and we had absolutely no way of knowing whether the deal would fly. It flew. If we guessed wrong, we would have been out of business in a hurry.
* Finally, I am convinced that selling stock works like a step function. You are either a booming success or a disastrous failure. The offering will either be oversubscribed by a mile or left struggling. The least likely scenario is that the last interested investor will buy the last available share of stock.

To complete the story, RF Communications followed this second $270,000 public offering with a $450,000 private placement at about $10 per share. A short time later, we had a fourth financing, raising $1 million at $16 per share through a public offering using a New York underwriter. A year later, we were listed on the American Stock Exchange. A year after that, we had a final public offering at $36 per share—compared to the original $1 (taking splits into account).

And in 1969, eight years after the start up, RF Communications merged with Harris Corp. RF stock was exchanged for Harris stock at about $45 per share equivalent. At the time, this was approximately two and one-half times annual sales, five times net worth and 43 times earnings. Harris paid about a 3 percent annual dividend compared to no dividend at RF. You can see why I think that being publicly owned has merit.

During the late 1980s the government made available a faster and far less complex way for small companies to raise capital by going public. It is known as "SCOR," or Small Company Offering Registration. By early 1992, 21 states had adopted the SCOR registration process. I am not familiar with this type of offering, but I suggest you check whether your state is among these if you are seriously considering going public. Some of the restrictions in SCOR are that the maximum amount of money that can be raised is $1 million and the stock must be priced at five dollars per share or higher. This method of financing is not widely known but is likely to become more popular.

In 1992, the SEC introduced a new registration process known as "Regulation SB." To be eligible to use Regulation SB, the company must have revenues of less than $25 million. This and other changes in the securities regulations are intended to simplify and accelerate the registration process for going public and cut the cost of raising capital for small firms. Forms and instructions for using Regulation SB are available from the Securities and Exchange Commission.

In 1995, companies in the United States are estimated to have raised about $29 billion of new equity by going public for the first time. This is a huge amount of capital when compared to the $3 to $7 billion raised each year by several thousand companies from venture capital funds and the estimated $10 billion and more raised each year by about 30,000 ventures from individual investors. Even though 1995 may not have been a typical year for public offerings, the numbers are still mind boggling. Since then, the amount of money raised by entrepreneurial companies in public offerings has been even higher. These have often been Internet-related companies and I do not know the numbers.

And now, a word of caution. From recent articles I have read in business publications it seems that many companies going public during the past few years have been successfully sued for large sums by groups of their initial investors. The reason for these lawsuits is that the stock price dropped substantially a short time after the offering due to a downturn in business. The lawsuits claimed (and may well be right) that the companies should have known trouble was brewing and failed to disclose the possibility in its prospectus or offering circular at the time the stock was first sold.

The way to avoid this problem seems pretty clear to me. First, you must be absolutely and completely honest when you describe the business and financial situation of the company. In addition, you should only go public when you are virtually certain that the business is on an upward path that will last for a while. Try to be as sure as you possibly can that sales and earnings will continue to increase for a fairly extended time following the offering.

Congress recently passed a law making it harder to sue companies for faulty projections. However, even with this new law in effect, my advice is for a publicly-owned company to be extremely cautious when making public projections of future sales and earnings.

Estimating future sales and earnings is very difficult to do with any degree of confidence for a new company raising capital for the first time by going public. If you estimate too conservatively, it will be more difficult to sell the stock. If you estimate too optimistically, you may be in for trouble if you miss your goals and the stock price drops sharply soon after the offering.

Shareholder lawsuits sometimes involve large financial judgments against the officers and directors...as well as the company. It is obviously desirable to have officers' and directors' liability insurance as a way to give you some degree of protection, but this type of insurance is apt to be expensive and possibly not even available.

Chapter 35

Will the Government Really Give Me Money?

To the complete surprise of many entrepreneurs, there are numerous sources of financial and other types of support available to small businesses from the federal government, most state governments, and many county and municipal governments. These include grants that support research and development, loan guarantees, low-interest loans and, in some states, even direct investment. Many of these programs are new in the past 10 or 15 years and many entrepreneurs know almost nothing about them.

As you are probably already aware, dealing with the government, at any level, is often time-consuming and frustrating. A lot of paperwork is almost always required. Also, when you begin you have no assurance of a successful conclusion. It may well be worth the trouble because for many companies, these sources of financial aid have meant the difference between success and failure.

The following will describe several federal programs in some detail. Also, I will mention some of the programs available in New York State, as these are the ones I know most about. However, almost every state has programs of some sort but they may be entirely different. Some effort will be required to learn what is available in your area.

For starters, I suggest you telephone the National Technical Information Service (NTIS) at 800-553-6847, and purchase a copy of a Small Business Administration booklet entitled, *The States and Small Business—A Directory of Programs and Activities*. (The document ID number for this publication is PB 93-186-427.) NTIS is part of the Department of Commerce and has almost 3 million reports available describing a huge number of research programs. The latest edition that I am aware of is dated 1993, but there may be later editions by now. This booklet has a vast amount of useful information for anyone starting a business.

Another report they have that is of particular interest to entrepreneurs is the *Directory of Federal and State Business Assistance, 1988-1989: A Guide for New and Growing Businesses* (document ID number PB 88-101-977). Again, this report is fairly old, but there may be a later edition available. A description of NTIS services is also available through the Internet at www.fedworld.gov.

At the state and local level, almost every state, county, and city has an economic development agency of some sort, which can give you guidance as to the types of programs that are available and where to look. Also, your local chamber of commerce will be able to help you in your search.

Federal programs

Small Business Innovation Research Program

This program, which came into existence in 1982, makes financial grants known as SBIRs, to small businesses to support research and development activities.

In this program, 11 large government departments that sponsor research and development must set aside a small percentage of their external R&D budgets for companies with fewer than 500 employees. To qualify for an SBIR, the company must be U.S. owned and independently operated.

The agencies that participate in the SBIR program and their Internet home page addresses are the following:

- Department of Agriculture
  www.reeusda.gov/sbir/sbir.htm
- Department of Commerce
  www.oar.noaa.gov/ORTA/SBIR
- Department of Defense
  www.acq.osd.mil/sadbu/sbir/
  Within DOD, there are at least seven sub groups with Internet sites, such as the U.S. Army, U.S. Navy, etc.
- Department of Education
  www.ed.gov
- Department of Energy
  www.sbir.er.doc.gov/sbir.htm
- Department of Health and Human Services
  www.nih.gov/grants/funding/sbir.htm
- Department of Transportation
  www.volpe.dot.gov/sbir.htm
- Environmental Protectiom Agency
  www.epa.gov/ncerqa/
- National Aeronautices and Space Administration
  www.nctn.hq.nasa.gov/nctn/SBIR/SBIR.htm
- National Science Foundation
  www.eng.nsf.gov/dmii/sbir
- Nuclear Regulatory Commission
  www.nrc.gov

Because some of the agencies involved (especially the Department of Defense) have very large external research and development programs, this very small percentage adds up to a large amount of money.

Topics of interest are determined by the individual agency. These are generally quite broad, and, with so many agencies involved, if you look hard enough you should be able to find one that fits your needs.

The Internet addresses of several supporting agencies are these:

1. SBA Home Page:
   www.sbaonline.sba.gov
   Go to "Expanding Your Business" which covers Small Business Innovative Research opportunities (SBIRs).
2. The National Technology Transfer Center Home Page is www.nttc.edu

If you are not familiar with the use of the Internet as a means to obtain information, I strongly urge you to get help from someone who is. The amount of information that is available is simply immense. The use of the Internet as a selling tool is covered in another chapter and may be of help.

The SBIR program is intended to support R&D that will later benefit the sponsoring agency, the company, and the country.

I know of one company that received a grant for research in the use of laser devices to weld bowel tissue during surgery, another company that had a grant to develop techniques for ruggedized hand-held personal computers, and another that received several grants for the development of three dimensional imaging for use on a personal computer without the need for colored glasses. The list and variety of projects is endless.

SBIR awards are made on a competitive basis. The program has several phases. Phase One can be a six-month grant of up to $100,000 to determine the feasibility of the idea. This may then be followed by a Phase Two grant extending over a period of up to two years with awards of up to $750,000 for further work refining the ideas and developing prototypes.

These numbers vary from agency to agency. However, in most cases the question of when the program being funded will be commercialized is receiving more emphasis than in the past. The SBIR program does not provide funds to bring a product to market.

Another resource is a publication entitled *Writing SBIR Proposals,* which is available from Sandra Cohn Associates at 312-648-0082. An update was planned to be published about the end of 1996 and should be available by now. The price of earlier editions was about $75 (I do not know the price of the latest edition).

To give you an idea of the scope of the SBIR program, in 1991 there were about 3,800 Phase One Awards (about 12 percent of those that applied) and more than 1,025 Phase Two Awards (about one third of those that applied).

Small Business Technology Transfer Program

This is a more recent program (similar to the SBIR program) in which the small company is required to work in partnership with a public sector nonprofit research institution. These programs are known as STTR's and are funded at a level of between five and 10 percent of the money available in the SBIR programs. The purpose is to encourage small businesses to work jointly with various types of research institutions for the purpose of developing commercially viable products from earlier stage research programs.

The requirements for a small company to participate in the STTR program are about the same as in the SBIR program. For the nonprofit research institution there is no size limit, but it must be located in the United States and be either a college or university, a domestic nonprofit research organization, or a federally funded R&D Center.

A number of federal agencies reserve a portion of their R&D funds for STTR programs including the following:

* Department of Defense.
* Department of Energy.
* National Aeronautics and Space Administration.
* National Science Foundation.

Their Internet addresses are the same as noted under SBIRs.

Small Business Administration, 7(a) loan guarantees

In this program, the SBA provides guarantees to banks making loans to small businesses. This is intended for use by companies unable to obtain loans on their own. Funds may be used to establish a new business, enlarge an existing business, acquire machinery or equipment, or finance inventory or working capital. In its 40-year existence, the SBA loan programs have helped over one million small business owners. SBA guaranteed loans vary in size from $20,000 to $750,000 with most in the $150,000 range. A formal application to SBA for a 7(a) guarantee can be made by the bank that declined to make your business a conventional loan.

Banks unwilling to lend to a small business because it is unable to cover the entire loan with personal guarantees and liens on personal assets are frequently willing to lend with a partial SBA guarantee. In 1995, the SBA guaranteed a total of over 55,000 loans with a value of about $7.8 billion. However, the agency is in the process of reducing the percentage of the loan that it will guarantee and is raising fees to the borrowers in order to increase the dollar value of loans. According to the SBA, women, minorities, and veterans especially benefit from this program.

State programs

The financial aid and assistance programs of states are more diverse than the federal programs. These are usually intended to create or maintain jobs within the state, to attract companies to move to the state or to keep companies from relocating out of the state. For New York, where taxes are high, keeping companies from moving elsewhere is an important priority.

I cannot possibly cover all programs available in all states. Instead I will describe some that are available in New York to give you an idea of the scope of these programs. In 1994 George Pataki defeated Democrat Mario Cuomo as Governor and was re-elected in 1998. New York State has a Republican governor for the first time in many years. It is my understanding that since this change in administration occurred, some of the New York State programs have been consolidated and the application process simplified, but the level of spending is about the same as in the past. Listed here are some programs that are available:

Corporation for Innovation Development

The CID program is administered by the New York State Science and Technology Foundation and provides debt and equity capital to new technology-based businesses with fewer than 100 employees. CID operates in a way similar to a private venture capital fund but is willing to take greater risk. Its telephone number is 518-473-9741.

Empire State Development Corporation

This agency is new in New York State and it has combined a number of smaller programs, including the Urban Development Corporation and the Job Development Authority. More details are available from the agency headquarters in New York City at 212-803-3100.

When I called this number, the people I spoke to were very helpful and I was told the best way to proceed is to contact one of the 10 regional offices in or near the area in which you are located. The people in the regional offices will help determine whether there are any programs that might meet your needs. If you have trouble locating the local office for your area, check with your chamber of commerce for help, or call their headquarters number in New York City shown above.

Some of the programs of the Empire State Development Corporation can assist small businesses in obtaining loans for various purposes at favorable rates (under certain circumstances, this can provide significant tax benefits), can help train new employees in certain skill areas needed by the company, can advise and assist in gaining access to various Federal Assistance Programs, and so forth.

New York Business Development Corporation (NYBDC)

The NYBDC is a quasi-public agency that makes term loans to small businesses with varied collateral requirements. It offers the flexibility to collaborate with or complement loans from conventional lenders. Interest rates are competitive. Its telephone number is 518-463-2268.

In addition to this list of New York State programs, there are others administered by local governments, both county and city, either alone or in cooperation with the state, for the benefit of new or small businesses.

When you check into the availability of programs such as these in your area, be sure to remember that all involve dealing with a government bureaucracy of some sort. They are often slow, cumbersome, and involve too much red tape. Under no circumstances can you expect action that will help you meet next week's payroll. Get started early and you may be able to get financial assistance that is not available from any other source.

Chapter 36

Working With Public Accountants, Bankers, and Lawyers

Companies and organizations have personalities just as people do. The personality of the firm is generally determined by the personal style and values of the senior management. I do not suggest that this is either good or bad. It simply is a condition that prevails and should be recognized.

What does this have to do with public accountants, bankers, and lawyers? Well, public accounting firms, banks, and law firms also have personalities. Some are aggressive, others are conservative and cautious. Some are people-oriented, others are stuffy and formal. Some are willing to work with small, new companies, others consider them a nuisance. Since you will undoubtedly want a close working relationship with your public accountant, banker, and lawyer, it's important that you're comfortable with the personality of the organization you select.

Determining the personality of a public accounting firm, bank, or law firm is not easy. One way to start is to talk to present and former clients. Another way is to interview a number of firms, being very candid in the process. By doing this you are more likely to be satisfied with your choice.

In addition, you must recognize that even though these organizations have unique personalities, the day-to-day relationship in all cases is based upon working with one person or a small group of individuals within the larger unit. You must decide whether you are comfortable with the person assigned to your account. If you are not, talk to the head of the organization and ask that someone else be assigned. If for some reason your request is refused, change firms.

The cost of these services is another complex issue. All are expensive—accountants and lawyers in the form of fees, banks in the form of interest and/or fees. In your effort to keep your expenses down, I suggest you deal with the question of the cost of these services in an open and aggressive manner. Ask for a list of hours spent, rates charged, services provided, and fees charged to other clients. Do not hesitate to challenge any items you consider unreasonable. Very few people do this. The minimum benefit is that they will be more careful in the future, and the likelihood is that they will simply reduce the charge. In all cases, removing the irritant will lead to a better relationship.

Finally, I am frequently asked whether it is wise to ask public accountants, bankers, or lawyers to serve as directors of a company. Public accountants are not permitted by their professional code of ethics to serve on the board of directors of a client firm. It is a conflict that interferes with their objectivity. Both bankers and lawyers are hired by the firm to provide specialized services. You want directors who are objective and can represent your shareholders without conflicting demands on their loyalty. No person can be expected to be a paid provider of services and an independent director at the same time. A banker on the board is unlikely to advise you to change banks. A lawyer on the board is unlikely to advise you to change law firms.

In addition to the conflict issue, you should not waste a board position by adding expertise that you're already buying. Fill your board with experts in marketing, engineering, distribution, finance, and so forth, areas mainstream to your business. Now let's get specific.

Public accountants

The relationship between a company and its public accountant is an unusual one. Even though the accountants are selected by the management and paid by the company, they really represent the shareholders. In addition, they are required to act in accordance with well defined professional accounting standards because their opinions are used by outside agencies—such as banks and the IRS—to make judgments about the firm. They have responsibilities to others as well as to their client. They are, and must remain, independent. As a result, they do not push easily.

In practice, the public accountant reviews the financial data of the firm—profit and loss statements, balance sheets, and use of funds—and certifies that they have been prepared in accordance with accepted accounting standards. They check inventories and accounts receivable and generally mess around in the company's books.

In addition, each year they give their clients what is called a management letter, which comments on internal procedures and controls.

One decision an entrepreneur must make is whether to use a major national accounting firm, a large regional firm or a small firm with just a few professionals. The big firms are likely to offer expertise in more specialized areas of accounting and have larger support staffs. They also provide substantial financial credibility, which new companies often need badly. With a smaller firm, you are likely to get more attention from the senior professionals. They are likely to be more responsive and have lower hourly rates.

As I mentioned, good public accounting firms are expensive. However, because many understand the cash flow problems of a new company, they are often willing to work at reduced fees for the first year or so.

Some companies I know put their auditing work out to bid among several public accounting firms with the intention of picking the lowest bidder. I advise against this. Instead, pick the firm you want for reasons other than price, then negotiate fees.

There are several other cautions in dealing with public accountants. Your main contact is apt to be at least a manager and probably a partner. However, the person they send to your office or plant to do the work may be their most recent hire with a bachelor's degree in accounting. And worse yet, every year it is a different person. This is a tough one to deal with and if it bothers you, complain.

Keep in mind that your public accounting firm may intimidate your internal controller, if you have one. However, the role of the public accountant is not to tell you what you should or should not do but rather to tell you whether what you decided to do is acceptable. As a matter of principle, you should have a relationship in which you make the decisions, and then they determine their acceptability.

Finally, in dealing with public accountants, when the chips are down, they have the last say. If you cannot reach agreement with them on how some financial matter should be handled, they will simply either refuse to give you an unqualified opinion or describe their position on the issue under the dispute in a note to the financial statement. Since it is important for a company to have an unqualified opinion, your only alternative will be either to accept their position or try another public accountant.

I do not want to make it sound as if the relationship between a company and its public accountant must be adversarial. In fact, when your new company grows enough to need a controller, you will probably hire the person managing your account at your public accounting firm.

Bankers

You deal with banks in a number of ways. First, you will surely need many of the services they provide, such as a payroll account or as registrar and transfer agent for your stock. These are services for which, in some form or other, you pay a fee. Then, sooner or later, you are likely to need to borrow from your bank for working capital, inventory, or a mortgage on a building. The service part of the relationship is simple. It becomes more complex when you start to borrow.

Early in my adult life I had a hard time overcoming the attitude that a bank was doing me a favor when it loaned me money. Banks are in business to lend and unless they can find good borrowers, they will not be successful. Shake the attitude that banks are doing the borrower a favor, but remember that many bankers feel that way.

Also, remember the underlying philosophy of most banks when lending. They do not make loans when they think there may be any significant risk. Some people think that banks adjust the interest rates up and down to compensate for risk. That is not the case. If they think there is significant risk—no loan. I discussed this question recently with two bank presidents. One said I was entirely right, the other said it was not true. Test it yourself.

The next thing banks worry about is how they will be paid back. They want to see their interest covered by earnings and the principal covered by liquidation of whatever the money was used for. For example, if the loan is to finance a capital purchase, it must be paid back from depreciation. If the loan was to finance receivables, it must be paid back when the receivables are collected.

As a practical matter, you will have no trouble borrowing from most banks, provided you do not need the money very badly. In this way, the bank can be pretty sure the loan is safe and will be paid promptly. Establish your line of credit and perhaps even borrow when you do not need a loan, and repay promptly. Sounds silly, doesn't it? But believe me, this is good advice. There is nothing like a history of good credit to make you attractive to a banker.

I recently spoke to a woman who consults with several government agencies that make loans to small businesses. She said that many small business people are extremely naive when applying and do not present a very attractive deal to the lender. She wrote one of the other chapters of this book that covers the question of how a small business person should apply for a loan.

When lending to small companies, most banks demand the personal guarantees of the officers of the firms. This means that you must pledge as security all your savings, the equity in your home, and everything else of value that you own. Their logic is that if the officers do not have enough confidence in the company to personally guarantee the loans, it is too risky a deal for them. I feel very uncomfortable guaranteeing loans and have always refused to do so. My guess is that until your company has substantial sales and earnings, personal guarantees might be necessary.

It seems that new bank customers almost always get better deals than present customers, so shopping around is often a good practice. Obviously, it is not acceptable to change banks every six months. However, you can change once in a while. Let your current bank know that it is a possibility, and you might even do business routinely with more than one bank.

Finally, I have found it very difficult to determine with any degree of certainty what banks charge for their services. For instance, you borrow money at an agreed upon interest rate and then learn that you are expected to keep a sizable balance in your account at zero interest. We all know about mortgage loans where, in addition to interest, you must pay several points of closing costs, plus the cost for the bank's attorney to protect the bank against you.

Lawyers

No doubt about it—in the United States, we have more than five times as many lawyers as we need. They are all struggling to make a decent living and we have become a litigious society in which everyone seems to be suing each other.

But, be that as it may, in starting and running a business, you have no alternative but to use a lawyer—and clearly it is desirable to use a good one. The services they provide include setting up the corporation, advising you on securities regulations, assisting you in negotiations, preparing various types of contracts, counseling you on how to handle complex employee issues, and patent and copyright issues.

However, what constitutes a good lawyer from a business person's viewpoint is not entirely clear. Lawyers tend to be very conservative, and many are inclined to tell you that everything you want to do is a bad idea because of the risk involved. In the company I started, we were fortunate to have as one of the founders a young attorney who had a lot of entrepreneurial qualities. He was creative and imaginative in handling the raising of capital. And, during all the years that RF Communications was an independent company, he was always thinking ahead and prodding us to be more aggressive.

A lawyer may talk to you about justice, and that the practice of law involves trying to find just and fair solutions to disagreements and disputes. This is complete nonsense! Most lawyers have no interest whatever in justice. All they want to do is to win, and that's the way it should be! If you ever hear your lawyer begin talking about justice, find yourself another lawyer. You want a lawyer who works for you!

In most business situations, I suggest that you use your lawyer as much as possible for review of your work rather than as an originator of work. You prepare the agreements and ask for their review and comments, rather than having them prepare the agreements for your comments. This will keep your costs down.

Finally, law is a very complex field. Most attorneys concentrate in fairly narrow specialties. One of these specialties is corporate or business law. By all means, use an attorney who specializes in business law rather than divorce or real estate litigation. Business law is complex and your needs will only be satisfied by an attorney who is expert in this field.

These three professional groups, public accountants, bankers, and lawyers, are all very important to a start up business. Their value will be much greater if the entrepreneur understands the relationship and deals with it in an aggressive manner.

Chapter 37

Staffing Up, Staffing Down

The ability to hire people fast when they are required—and fire people fast when they aren't—is an important skill the head of any company must have. A new firm cannot afford the luxury of putting people on staff in anticipation of need, or keeping them when orders and cash flow say they cannot be afforded. Many entrepreneurs share a common fault—they are either unwilling or emotionally unable to make decisive hiring and firing decisions.

Hiring is essentially a random process, while firing is very selective. Consider for a moment that most hiring is done with very little information. It is often based upon reading a resume, several hours of interviews, and the checking of references. All of these are suspect. The resume can be exaggerated, most references are innocuous, and the interview is at best marginal, especially if the candidate has a lot of charm and personal presence.

You do the best you can in finding and evaluating the candidate. You try to be thorough in checking credentials. But when all is said and done, hiring decisions are largely intuitive. If your intuition is particularly good, you may have a good hiring record.

On the other hand, when you decide to terminate an employee, it is usually after working with them for several years. You have had a chance to examine their skills first-hand and compare his or her performance to others. You usually fire only after an agonizing period of evaluation and review and several personal interviews with the person. The process is very selective. Almost everyone does a better job in picking people to fire than they do in picking people to hire. Unfortunately, carrying out the decision to fire is as unpleasant as it is necessary.

I have heard, but never put in practice, the suggestion that the bottom 10 percent of staff should be terminated once a year. Start by ranking everyone who works for you. Rank highest those you would least like to lose. Then fire the bottom 10 percent. It sounds heartless, but the reality is that most organizations would benefit from this practice. Because of the random nature of hiring and the selective nature of firing, the overall quality of your staff would be certain to improve. The ability to staff up and down in a timely and decisive manner is an important personal quality in an entrepreneur.

The rest of this chapter will discuss a number of other staffing issues that new companies almost always face.

Relationships with former employers

When individuals quit a job in a big firm to start a new company, it is common for them to look upon the past employer as a source of business. Often, entrepreneurs are successful in obtaining orders from their former employers. Once a firm gets some business, the new company faces the problem of hiring people to do the work. Where is the natural place to look? To the same former employer, of course!

Obviously, this is a conflict. You cannot use the same source for both orders and new employees. I tell the start-up companies I am involved with that they must decide which is more important.

When my associates and I left General Dynamics to form RF Communications, we immediately hired a few people from them but also embarked on an aggressive effort to secure business as well. Since we had left on relatively friendly terms, this looked feasible. Within a few months we negotiated a fairly large contract for some product development work. The final step was for a General Dynamics attorney to send us a proposed contract. Included in the conditions was an acknowledgment that when we left we took proprietary information and trade secrets with us. Apparently, he thought we were naive. We did not accept it, negotiations bogged down, and we did not get the order.

In retrospect, he did us a favor. Over the next few years we recruited many skilled people from General Dynamics and we did this at very low cost because we had virtually no hiring or relocation expense. It was not a conscious decision at the time, but in effect, we had decided to use them as a source of employees rather than as a source of business.

Compaq Computer, one of the fastest-growing companies in U.S. history, was founded in 1982 by Rod Canion, its first president, and two other engineers from Texas Instruments. By mid-1987 Compaq had a total of 27 vice presidents, 17 of whom were also from TI. Because TI sued Compaq shortly after it started, the question of getting business from their former employer obviously was not an issue.

Salary policy

During our early staffing of RF, we did run into one hitch. When interviewing professional people from General Dynamics, we came to the question of salary. Our policy was to offer a 10 percent increase over their current salary. At the time, 20 to 25 percent was customary for people changing jobs, but since relocation was not required, we thought 10 percent was sufficient and for a while this policy worked.

Then one day, we had a call from a young engineer who had been offered and accepted a position with us. When he went to his supervisor to resign he was offered a 25 percent pay increase to stay. He asked whether we proposed to match it. We said, "No, thank you." and wished him luck. The last thing we wanted was a bidding war we could not afford. From then on we told people we were trying to hire that they would have to come to work for us at the same pay they had been earning—no raise. How strange! Yet it worked.

It put us under great pressure to make working for RF attractive and to identify benefits we could offer that General Dynamics could not. This was almost like a pricing decision. We had one benefit: the stock option. Almost every professional at RF Communications received a stock option, a perk that General Dynamics was not allowed to match. So when the young engineers were offered 25 percent raises to stay, they could say no. They were not leaving because of salary, so they would not stay because of salary. This is a good example of how a small company can innovate in the area of hiring policy.

Union problems

After RF was in business for several years, we sensed rumblings among our hourly employees that some might be interested in a union. The last thing a new company (or any company for that matter) needs is a union. I had no experience or any meaningful knowledge on how to deal with the situation.

At the time, I was teaching an evening business strategy course in a local M.B.A. program that involved inviting senior executives from local firms to speak to the class. I decided to invite the president of a labor union. During the discussion I had a student ask the union president the following question: "If you were the head of a company and did not want a union, what would you do?" His response, almost without thinking, was: "Provide a grievance path without fear of retribution and adhere strictly to seniority, especially in firing."

Boy, was that good advice! Both are complex issues. I will discuss only the seniority question here. Whenever a company faces cutbacks because of bad business, the temptation is to use it as an opportunity to clean house—get rid of the poor performers. Just a few paragraphs earlier I told you the benefits of this practice. However, the time that you make layoffs for financial reasons is not the time to clean house. You should, instead, lay off poor performers when business is good. Everyone in your organization knows the poor performers. The boss is the last to know. If you terminate poor performers during good times, your people will applaud the move. Then if you must lay off because of bad business you have at least a chance of honoring seniority.

Contract employees

Over the past few years, many companies have begun using contract employees rather than hiring full-time regular employees. This is something you might consider since it has a number of important benefits. Usually this is done through a contract company. The people are assigned to you to perform whatever work you give them under your supervision. Officially, they are employees of the contract firm and receive their paychecks from that firm. Their employer is responsible for income tax withholding, Social Security payments, and other mandated expenses. You are then billed by the contract firm for the services provided.

At the end of 1995, it was estimated that there were about 2.2 million people in the temporary work force, most in the categories of secretarial and blue collar workers. But this is changing fast. In the past few years a greater number of professionals have lost jobs than hourly workers. Companies are now beginning to fill more professional and management positions with temporaries.

The advantage of using contract people is that it does not require you to make a permanent commitment. If you only need people for a short-term assignment or to carry you through a peak workload you can arrange the contract accordingly. When the contract ends, the services end and it is not necessary for you to terminate the people involved.

In addition, if you eventually end up hiring the contract employee you have in effect found a way to learn how good they are before you make the hiring decision. The short-term costs may be somewhat higher but the long-term benefits can be great.

A word of caution is in order. You may at some time retain people as independent contractors without going through an intermediary. In many circumstances, the Internal Revenue Service frowns on this practice as it may be an attempt on the company's part to avoid the cost of Social Security, the necessity of withholding income tax, and so forth. The IRS has established some very specific guidelines that define when someone qualifies as an independent contractor. Be sure you become familiar with these guidelines since you could be subject to pretty severe penalties if you end up in the wrong. If you are in doubt about this question be sure to contact your lawyer for advice.

Less painful firing

Finally, on the subject of firing, I recognize that this is an agonizing process for many. Of all the things about being a boss that I do not like, firing ranks in first place.

After RF Communications became part of Harris, my new boss, Dr. Joseph Boyd, gave me some advice I have never forgotten. It is the kind of advice I should have been smart enough to figure out for myself years earlier.

He suggested that firing should be the result of two decisions. First, decide whether the individual is good enough for the job he or she holds. If so, there is no problem. If not, the employee must be removed from that job.

After you have decided to remove the person, the second decision is how to treat that employee fairly. For a long-term employee, counseling or additional training may help or you might change his or her job. Large companies often sweeten the retirement benefits to encourage people to leave voluntarily. This may be too expensive for the small firm. Or, you might terminate the person with a generous severance allowance and help finding another job.

If you make the firing process two decisions instead of one decision, the job will be much easier. In this way, you are more likely to make a careful, fair decision. If you remember nothing else from this book other than this two part termination process, you will have been repaid its cost at least a thousand times over.

One caution is in order. It is usually smart to adhere to a formal procedure of informing individuals in advance in writing that their performance is not satisfactory. Explain why, and give them a specific timetable over which to improve. This may have to be done several times in order to avoid problems with unemployment benefits or being challenged about your treatment of minorities, women, and the handicapped.

Federal, state, and local laws governing interviewing, hiring, promoting, drug and HIV testing, firing, continuation of health benefits following termination, and so forth, are complex and change frequently. For example, the Civil Rights Act of 1991 extends the right to a jury trial and punitive and expanded compensatory damages to victims of intentional job discrimination. The Americans With Disabilities Act of 1990 extends employment protection to the disabled. More recently, a federal Family Leave Act was passed requiring companies to permit employees to take unpaid leave without penalty for various personal reasons. The courts must still resolve major questions on how these and other employment practice legislation apply in specific cases. Seek legal counsel if you have any questions about the laws relating to any of these issues.

In summary, the staffing up and staffing down of a new business is a very tough problem. It requires the vision to see when it is necessary and the courage to do it decisively. No one but the head of the company can decide. Of underlying importance here is the question of limited resources and the need to aggressively manage cash flow. You will get absolutely no credit for letting a company go bust because of your inability to make difficult hiring and firing decisions.

Chapter 38

Reviewing Performance and Setting Standards

When RF Communications became a division of Harris Corp., many people thought that we would be overwhelmed by the bureaucracy and red tape of a large corporation, that we would lose our ability to react fast to customer needs and the freedom to be innovative and imaginative in our management. I would not be telling the truth if I said the merger occurred without problems, and some of them are described later. But the relationship with Harris had many benefits for RF because they encouraged us to do things that we should have been doing years earlier as an independent company.

One of things Harris introduced at RF was the Management Manpower Development Program (MMP). This program provided me with a number of very powerful management tools. The MMP had several different elements described below:

- Appraise the performance of all managers at least annually using a standard form as a guide.
- Review the results of this appraisal with each person.
- Suggest to the employee how he or she can improve performance, and what the company is prepared to do to help.
- Agree on performance goals for the coming year.
- Identify and evaluate replacement candidates for key positions.

Later in this chapter is a form that can be used for the individual appraisals. This is not the same form that was used by Harris. Rather, it is somewhat simplified to better meet the needs of a smaller company. Notice that it starts with basic information about the employee. The heart of the appraisal, however, includes three sections—results, methods, and qualifications.

In the results section, the appraiser lists the accomplishments of the individual during the period covered by the appraisal. This includes quantitative measures where possible and applicable—such as growth in sales, inventory levels, profits, costs, and number of orders. It should also include qualitative accomplishments such as effective leadership or innovative ideas.

The next section, called methods, includes comments on how the employee achieved the results. This is important if the results were less than satisfactory, as the methods used may be the explanation for the poor results. Failures here might include the inability to get along with people, being overly aggressive (this has been a problem for me on more than one occasion) and failure to plan in an organized manner.

The third section, qualifications, is important if the employee rates poorly on both results and methods. It may indicate that the person is in the wrong job, or that specific job training is needed.

Then, the employee is given an overall performance rating of either above standard, standard, below standard, or critical. The appraisal should also include suggestions as to what the individual should do to improve his or her performance, their potential in the organization, possible backups, and goals for the coming year.

The first time I did an appraisal of the five senior managers reporting directly to me, it was an agonizing process on which I spent many hours. At the end, I met privately with each manager and explained how I rated their performance. Doing these appraisals was very hard for me. Learning the results was even harder for the five managers.

As I mentioned, RF Communications had very serious business problems for several years following the merger with Harris. These first appraisals were done during those difficult times.

I gave one individual an overall rating of standard, and I thought he was going to explode. He was one of the hardest working, most highly motivated and smartest people I have ever met, and he was very unhappy with any rating other than the highest. After a long session where we were unable to reach accord he finally said, "All right, I will accept this rating for now, but I want you to tell me what I have to do next year to be rated above standard." I answered, "That sounds reasonable but instead of me telling you what you have to do, why don't you tell me what you have to do to improve your rating." I added that he should give it to me in writing—one page maximum.

A week or so later, we met again and he handed me his list. I had no trouble accepting it because he set goals for himself that I do not think he would have ever accepted from me. They were very tough. In doing this I learned another management lesson—that people will usually set more difficult goals for themselves than they will accept from their supervisor.

This approach had another unexpected benefit. A year later when I evaluated this person the second time it was very easy. I pulled out the set of goals we had agreed on a year earlier and he either met them or did not meet them. What took me several hours the first time took about 15 minutes the second time. Obviously his rating went up.

I rated another one of my managers below standard. During the review, I let him know what I considered his shortcomings were and told him he better improve quite a bit in the coming year or his job would be in jeopardy. A week or so later, the man's wife called me on the telephone. The first thing I thought was, "What am I in for now?" To my complete surprise, she thanked me. I asked her why she was thanking me when I just gave her husband a bad review and told him his job was in jeopardy. Her answer was, "At last he knows how he is doing and what is expected of him. He is determined to show you how good he can be."

In a third case, where I also rated a manager below standard, the individual came into my office about six months later and asked me to do another review. I asked why he wanted this because it was not scheduled until the end of the year. His answer was that he was very anxious to know whether he was on the right track.

In all three of these examples, the appraisal process forced me through the discipline of reviewing employees in an organized manner and letting them know the results. Instead of turning the people off, it turned them on even though in two of the cases I rated their performance as below standard.

The last step of the process required me to meet at corporate headquarters with my boss, the president of Harris; his boss, the chairman; and an outside consultant to review my entire organization. They had each received advance copies of the appraisals covering two levels of management down from me, or a total of about 30 people. In the front of the meeting room there was a large board to which was attached a card for each employee summarizing his or her performance. The cards were arranged like an organizational chart. A sample of the card is included in this chapter. The cards were color coded, blue for above standard, green for standard, red for below standard and striped for critical. This gave the group a good overview of the strengths and weaknesses of my organization.

During several hours of discussion, I had a chance to identify problems and tell what I planned to do about them. We pinpointed those people with the greatest future potential, areas where a stronger back up manager was needed, and so forth. I had the benefit of the counsel and suggestions of three people for whom I had the greatest respect. Not mentioned, but obvious, was that during this meeting they were also rating me.

This process may sound complicated—and it is complicated the first time you go through it. But it is a powerful tool for running a business, and once the novelty wears off, the people involved accept it willingly—its purpose is to help them become better at their job.

The type of formal appraisal and review process described here, or some variation of this process, is necessary to efficiently manage any business with more than a handful of people. It gives you the information you need to be sure you are on the right track. And, it provides your people with helpful feedback on how you view their performance and what is expected of them to improve their career potential. How big should you be before you develop a formal appraisal and review process? It's not entirely clear, but better too soon than too late.

Management Appraisal (Confidential)

Name: Period covered:

Position: Department:

Previous position: Years with company:

Years in position:

Total number of employees supervised:

RESULTS: (Be as specific as possible. Give numerical data where possible [such as sales, profit, inventory level, orders, etc.]. Compare actual results to goals for the period.)

METHODS: (Be as specific as possible. Include factors such as ability to handle people, planning skills, leadership skills, willingness to tackle unpleasant tasks, etc. If results are less than satisfactory, try to determine whether methods may be a contributing factor.)

Management Appraisal (Page 2)

QUALIFICATIONS: (Describe educational background, experience, and performance in previous positions. If results are less than satisfactory and methods do not explain the problem, try to identify whether qualifications are adequate for the positions.)

RATING: **PREVIOUS RATING:**
(Above Standard, Standard, Below Standard, or Critical)

PLANS FOR IMPROVEMENT:

POTENTIAL IN ORGANIZATION:

POTENTIAL BACKUPS:

GOALS FOR COMING YEAR:

Date of appraisal: Appraiser's name:

Position: Signature:

Sample of card used in overall organizational review

```
Photo        Name:                          color
             Position:                      code
             Dept:
             Years in position:
             Number supervised:

Rating:                  Previous Rating:

Potential:


Backup:
```

Chapter 39

Who Needs a Mentor?

Almost every entrepreneur needs help of some sort. Few people starting a business have ever started a business before. Almost without exception, the process of planning, starting, and managing a business is a new experience for the entrepreneur. Virtually everything that they do, they do for the first time.

And where do you go for entrepreneurship training? Nowhere! I suggested earlier that entrepreneurship is a vocation for which there is no apprenticeship.

Because of this, it is important and extremely helpful for the new entrepreneur to have a mentor—an individual or small group—to turn to for advice and guidance. A mentor should be someone you trust, someone you can share confidential information with and who you can talk to openly and candidly. Ideally, you should choose someone who also started a company, hopefully in a business somewhat related to yours.

One way to accomplish this is through your board of directors (if you have one) or some type of advisory committee or advisory board if you do not. Directors tend to be more effective than advisers because they have power to make change, but either can be very helpful in the management of a company.

In establishing either a formal board or advisory group, pick people who bring functional experience and wisdom as well. In developing the basic strategy for your business, hopefully you will have tried to identify the key factors required for success. Is it mostly a marketing company or is your main thrust advanced technical products? If your board members have expertise in these key areas, you will have formed a powerful support group of immeasurable value.

How do you attract such people willing to spend time with you, and what compensation or reward should you offer them? One approach is to draw upon friendship. This may work for a short period or for occasional contact but is not a satisfactory long-term solution. Obviously you cannot be in the position of continually requesting favors.

Another approach is to turn to the investors in your company. This is perhaps the best way because you can be assured of their interest and, generally speaking, their incentive will be the same as yours. The bigger the investment, the more the interest. Or, if all else fails, you should compensate your board with either money or some type of equity arrangement.

I advise people starting a new business against asking the head of a large company to be on their board. Such a person would add respectability and probably wisdom but the likelihood is that they will be too busy to give you much time.

I have been a board member of a number of start-up companies. In each, I had either a very large cash investment, a sizable stock holding, or both. With one exception, where friendship was the main connection, I would not serve on a board unless I had a significant stake. I refused to be involved where my principal role was to attract investors.

In an earlier chapter I suggested that you avoid putting lawyers or bankers on your board, or for that matter, anyone whose services you are already buying, unless friendship is a strong factor. A number of years ago I was on the board of a large New York Stock Exchange company. As a result of several acquisitions the board included two lawyers and two bankers. When time came to vote on some important issue, several would almost always disqualify themselves because of conflicts. On one important decision as to whether to relocate the headquarters of a major division, all four disqualified themselves.

Finally, I usually advise the heads of companies not to put any of the employees of the company on either the formal or advisory board. Again the conflict will discourage them from making critical comments in front of outsiders because it might put their own position in jeopardy. An exception to this might be senior employees who were members of the founding team.

In dealing with directors and advisors, you must be honest and candid. Seek their counsel on major problems, especially where they may have faced similar problems. And listen more than you talk. Nothing turns a mentor off faster than being told why everything he or she suggests has already been tried or may not be a good idea. Establish a working relationship where you will seek advice on key issues, but you reserve the right to make your own decisions.

In the startups on whose boards I served, I always encouraged monthly meetings. This does not take up too much time for either management or board members, yet it's frequent enough that problems will not get out of hand between meetings. I have found that meeting every two months or quarterly does not seem quite often enough. Whenever the frequency was reduced something usually happened to make us regret it.

A board of directors or board of advisors can be a powerful asset to a new business, especially where a mentor relationship also exists. However, you should select the people for what they can contribute, not for show. Do not waste board positions on people whose services you are already buying.

Chapter 40

What Is Really Important? Operating Lean and Mean

One of the most difficult management challenges faced by the head of a new business is trying to identify those things that are critical to the success of the business and those factors that contribute little or nothing. By devoting all of your limited resources to the important factors and avoiding spending money on the unimportant things, you will be able to get much more mileage from your limited resources. Cutting back on or eliminating all unimportant expenditures is what I call running a lean and mean operation.

Unfortunately, many entrepreneurs trained in the culture of a large company, have a great deal of trouble separating the "wheat from the chaff." I could name many things that employees of big companies become accustomed to and just assume to be a way of life in the business world. These include things such as expensive stationery, paved parking lots, pictures on the wall, private telephone extensions, and numerous service and support functions. Three that I like to use as examples are the size and elegance of the facility the new business acquires, "make-or-buy" decisions, and staff support.

One of the early decisions in every startup is the selection of a physical place of business. Many entrepreneurs envision a facility far more elaborate than needed. Is a posh office important? Will customers visit very often, and to what extent will the elegance of the quarters contribute to getting orders? It may very well be that a fancy facility will turn off potential customers, because it raises the question of prudent use of capital and fundamental business judgment.

Another argument for modest quarters is that it sets the proper tone for the entire organization. If one person has a large office with elegant furniture, others expect the same. The approach I took as the head of a start-up company was to always have a small, very conservatively furnished office. Since everyone else had to be satisfied with offices a little smaller and a little more spartan than the president's, the office situation never became a problem. When shopping for a factory or office for your new business, remember that Apple Computer and Hewlett-Packard both started in garages. RF Communications started in a basement.

An exception to the above is a retail business where location may be the most important early decision the founder can make. However, this is also a matter of setting values consistent with the character of the business. In this case, the character and nature of the business may require a big investment in store location. If this is true you will have to identify other areas of lesser importance where you can economize.

Another important issue involves the purchase of capital equipment and the make-or-buy decisions. At RF Communications, our products were complex electronics devices. These needed fairly expensive metal cabinets and chassis—fabricated sheet metal parts. Should we purchase these from outside sources or set up a shop in house with the machinery necessary to make them ourselves? There were arguments on both sides.

Our decision was to purchase all fabricated metal parts from outside sources because we believed there were more important things to do with our very limited capital. We felt that investing in new products and greater marketing effort were more productive ways to use resources. Many new businesses get carried away trying to do everything themselves and lose sight of their true distinctive competence. In an electronics firm, it is unlikely that skill at fabricating metal parts will ever be an important strength.

If you should find you must make capital purchases consider leasing rather than outright purchase. Leasing can slow down cash expenditures in a meaningful way. A lease has several other advantages in that they are usually much easier to obtain than a bank loan and the value of the item being leased may not have to appear as a liability on your balance sheet.

A final example relates to staff support. When I see a company with five employees and a full-time financial manager, I am pretty sure they are doing something wrong. When I see a company with fewer than 30 or 40 employees with a full-time personnel manager, I am pretty sure they are doing something wrong. When I see a new company doing its own payroll rather than using an outside payroll service, such as Paychex, I am pretty sure they are doing something wrong.

People in large firms are accustomed to a lot of staff support. It is very easy to forget that many of these functions can either be taught to a secretary, combined in one individual, or simply ignored.

Sharpen your sense of values to isolate those functions that really contribute to the success of the business. Concentrate your resources and energy on these. Resist the pressure, which will be continuous and considerable, to spend much time and money on unnecessary trappings.

Chapter 41

Patents, Copyrights, Trademarks, and Trade Secrets

Mr. William R. Alexander, Esq., specializing in corporate and intellectual property law for new and emerging companies, and Ronald S. Kareken, Esq., of the law firm Jaeckle, Fleischmann & Mugel, specializing in patents and intellectual property law, both in Rochester, New York, provided considerable assistance and suggestions in the preparation of this chapter.

The problems associated with protecting an idea, invention, or other intellectual property should be discussed in a book about entrepreneurship and starting a business. Unfortunately, this is a subject about which I have little knowledge and almost no practical experience. There are numerous books on this subject at your local bookstore and library. I encourage you to read as many as you think you need in order to make an intelligent decision on whether you should secure patent, copyright, trademark, or trade secret protection or worry about the protection others may have.

Also, I encourage you to get advice from an attorney experienced in these areas. These are complex questions that require expert counsel. Sometimes the protections overlap and many are covered by both state and federal laws, making it even more difficult to be sure what you are doing is right. Also, if you do business overseas many countries have laws that are different than ours that should be considered. The following discussion is a brief review of the subject with comments on several related issues. The four separate areas in which protection should be considered are:

- **Patents:** A non-renewable right granted by the U.S. Patent Office to prevent others from making, using, or selling an idea covered by your invention.

- **Copyrights:** Protects the work of an author or the expression of an idea. It does not protect the idea itself.

- **Trademarks:** Words or designs that distinguish or differentiate a certain source of goods or services from the goods or services of others.

- **Trade secrets:** Includes unpatented technology or internal business information that may give your company a competitive advantage.

Here are several examples: Polaroid protected its inventions relative to instant photography with patents. Coca-Cola is one of the most famous trademarks of all times. The formula for Coca-Cola is a trade secret, access to which is carefully limited within the company. And, much of Coca-Cola's advertising and other public information about its products are protected by copyright.

Patents

Patenting an invention is a complex, time-consuming, and expensive legal procedure. It is possible but difficult for an individual to secure a patent without the services of an attorney. The protection you get from a patent is determined by what the patent examiner allows in your claims. The broader your claims, the better your protection—but the more difficult it is to get the patent.

Obtaining a patent can take several years and a lot of constant back-and-forth cor-respondance between the attorney and the patent examiner, but in certain cases this time period can be longer. The longest that I know of is the patent for the laser which was issued in 1989, thirty years and $6 million after the initial filing. An interesting twist to this situation was that at that time, the 17-year protection period began when the patent was issued—not when the application was filed. Had the patent for the laser been issued promptly it may well have expired long before the use of lasers in countless applications became as pervasive as it is today. The good news is that the delay may have made the patent much more valuable. The bad news is that the inventor was 68-years-old before the patent was issued.

In the United States, an inventor has one year to file an application following the first public disclosure or sale of the item or process being patented. For an individual or small company operating with limited resources, this gives them a chance to test the idea before going to the expense of trying to obtain a patent. Keep in mind though that in many other countries the patent must be filed before any public disclosure or sale of the invention in order to obtain protection. However, you can wait up to one year after filing in the United States to file in many other countries. This makes the timing issue much more complex.

Recently the United States agreed to the revisions in GATT (General Agreement on Tariffs and Trade) which changes our patent situation in several important ways. Now, if a patent issues the protection period will expire 20 years after the filing date instead of 17 years after the issue date.

Periodic fees are required to maintain a patent and the term "patent pending" generally has no legal significance other than to discourage copiers.

Another form of protection that I seldom hear discussed is market penetration and customer acceptance of a product. This important form of protection is unrelated to the patent. The difficulty and cost of taking a product to market may be as big a deterrent to a potential competitor as the existence of a patent.

I have seen one situation where the process of getting the maximum possible patent protection before taking any steps to commercialize the idea may have hurt the company more than it helped. In that case, the inventor spent several years and thousands of dollars getting patent coverage in many countries before deciding to build and sell the product. My personal belief is that he may have been better served filing a patent application in the United States and immediately taking the product to market rather than using so much of his limited resources trying to get worldwide protection. This is another complex question that has no right or wrong answer.

Also, be sure any patent you file is significant. I have seen one situation where an electronics company, after being informed that it was infringing a patent, spent about a day designing new circuitry. This avoided the infringement yet did not significantly change the final product in which the circuitry was used.

A serious difficulty the individual inventor faces is that if a large company takes the risk of infringing a patent, the only remedy the inventor has may be to sue for damages. For someone with limited financial resources, the problems associated with launching and winning a lawsuit against a giant infringer may not be very appealing.

Copyrights

A copyright protects the authorship or expression of an idea. The idea itself is not protected. Copyrights can be obtained for novels, business manuscripts, books about entrepreneurship, paintings, plays, works of art, computer software—and more! Protection begins as soon as the work is fixed in tangible form.

To provide notice of copyright all you have do is print the word Copyright near the beginning of the document or the letter C inside a circle (©), followed by the author's name and the date of first publication. However, registering your copyright with the Copyright Office is far better protection, and well worth the trouble. The address is Copyright Office, Library of Congress, Washington, DC 20559, 202-707-9100. The Copyright Office also has several circulars with basic information about copyrights. Unlike a patent, the job of registering a copyright is fairly simple and relatively inexpensive. I did it myself for the first edition of this book.

Interestingly, while the contents of a publication can be protected by a copyright, the title normally cannot. That is one reason you occasionally see several books with identical or near-identical titles. However, titles to some works, such as periodicals and computer software, can sometimes be protected as trademarks.

Trademarks

First, you want to protect the words or designs that distinguish your product or service. Second, you want to be sure that your trademark does not infringe upon or duplicate someone else's mark.

Trademark rights are generally established by use. However, for maximum protection it is better that they be registered. Trademarks used in interstate commerce can be registered with the Patent and Trademark Office, U.S. Department of Commerce, Washington, DC 20231. They have a pamphlet entitled *Basic Facts About Trademarks*. In some areas it may also be advisable to register a trademark at the state level especially if the mark is only used in one state.

Also, you may be able to file an application to register on the basis of a "bona fide" intent to use a mark in commerce.

In the one case that I registered a mark, I used an attorney. It was not very expensive and I saved myself the time and trouble of learning how it was done.

I often think about an amusing situation I encountered many years ago when I worked for the Radio Corporation of America as an engineer just out of college. Their trademark was the letters RCA and they protected it with a vengeance. As I recall, two organizations gave them fits because they apparently used the letters R, C, and A before the Radio Corporation of America even came into existence. One was the Radio Club of America and the other the Rodeo Cowboys Association.

Trade secrets

Consider for a moment the things that you believe may give your company a competitive advantage. This could include a secret formula, manufacturing techniques, customer lists, pricing information, and similar things that your competitors would like to know about. These are your trade secrets. Like any other secret, the best way to protect this material is to avoid disclosing it to anyone. However, that may not be a practical solution. Trade secrets can be protected by a variety of agreements between a company and its employees, customers, licensees, contractors, and others to whom the information is disclosed. Sometimes the law will help even if you do not have agreements, but don't count on it.

Most large companies have written agreements with their employees requiring them to assign their inventions to the company, preventing the employee from competing for a given period of time after they leave the company and requiring that the employee not divulge any confidential information to outsiders or make use of the information for their own benefit either during or following their employment. Anyone in a technical business or in a business where internal information may have value or may provide a competitive advantage should consider using such an agreement. Many companies learn too late that without an agreement they may have no protection or rights to inventions of employees who leave.

In addition, confidentiality agreements are usually required from anyone retained by the company as a consultant or independent contractor.

Also, when you divulge information to another company, such as a potential customer or possible strategic partner, it is worth trying to get them to sign a confidentiality agreement. However, this may not be possible in every situation. For instance, I spend a lot of time with entrepreneurs who are either thinking about or who have already started a business. They come to me for general advice, to review a business plan, or to just test an idea. Occasionally, they ask me to sign a confidentiality agreement and I always refuse. My reason is that I have a lot of involvement with new businesses and have no way of knowing whether someone was in to see me yesterday or may come in to see me tomorrow with exactly the same idea. Obviously, I am protecting myself even though I am extremely careful to treat everything I see or hear during these discussions as confidential even without an agreement.

Patents, copyrights, trademarks, and trade secrets are complex issues. They may or may not be important in your particular situation but in some cases they can be the most valuable asset a company has. As a minimum, early-stage companies should give serious consideration to implementing some type of intellectual property protection program covering all of the valuable information that may be important to their long-term competitive position.

Chapter 42

Two Plus Two Equals Five—No, Two Plus Two Equals Three: The Theory of Acquisitions

I mentioned earlier that the management skills needed in a small firm are substantially different from those needed in a large firm. Managing a small business is much more of a hands on proposition. Managers making the transition from a large organization to a start-up business often have a difficult time adjusting.

Similarly, the skills needed to manage an acquisition are also substantially different. Most business people do not give this issue sufficient consideration. This is one reason many acquisitions turn out badly. The risk, difficulty, and complexity associated with the acquisition process is widely underestimated.

If the company you start is successful, sooner or later you will be faced with the decision of whether to buy another firm in order to grow faster or improve your product and/or market position. My advice is to proceed with the utmost caution, because it may turn out to be a much harder process than you think.

The following discussion is entirely from the viewpoint of the acquirer, or purchasing company. The problems associated with selling a business, or being acquired, are entirely different. The four principal reasons why one company might acquire another are:

- The company wants to offer a new product line or enter a new business. Even though they may have the skills and resources to develop the product, the objective is to do it faster by acquisition. Buying another company, even though usually much more expensive, might save several years or more. An acquisition buys time.

- The company can reduce the risk of developing a new product or entering a new market by acquiring another business. The other company is already there. No matter what your skills, there is always more risk doing it from scratch.

- There is the hope that synergism will be achieved. Synergism suggests that the whole is greater than the sum of the parts. Two plus two equals five, so to speak.

- Finally, when a company acquires a much smaller firm they often believe that the hot new start up will give an infusion of entrepreneurial spirit.

Through the years I have been personally involved in the acquisition of four companies. They all turned out rather bad. In each case, within a few years, the acquired firm was either sold at a loss or permitted to disappear from sight. Here are a few of the factors that make the acquisition process so difficult:

- Managing a small acquisition is a very time-consuming proposition for the acquirer. It takes a disproportionate amount of effort and energy, especially if the new company is in a remote location or in a different line of business. The acquirer will often try to delegate responsibility to a staff group or lower level of management. This tends to flood the acquired firm with red tape and bureaucracy.

- Some people in the acquired company will either leave or completely lose interest. Recently I had a conversation with a senior manager of a company that had just paid a handsome price to acquire a successful small business. He said several unanticipated problems had developed. Both senior people and lower-level employees were leaving, creating big holes in the operation. I said that neither should have been a surprise.

  For the senior people, the acquisition in all likelihood made them rich and liquid. They do not have to work anymore. Sure, they all had contracts but a contract is usually more binding on the company than it is on the employee. You can require people to come to work every day but you cannot force them to do a good job.

  For lower-level employees, the situation was a bit different. If they wanted to work for a larger company they would have. So, after the acquisition, there was a drifting away as these people found other jobs more to their liking.

- What was previously a very profitable small company is likely to become less profitable after it is acquired by a larger firm. There are several reasons for this. First, the employees of the acquired company become uncertain about their future with the new owner. Work is no longer as much fun as it was before. The tendency is for everyone's commitment to decline.

- Another reason is that small companies tend to be lean while large firms are not. This may be the main reason the smaller company is profitable. In the acquiring company, offices are probably larger, support staffs larger, fringe benefits more generous, and on and on. The natural result is for the smaller unit to emulate its new owner and everything becomes more expensive. Also, there is an overhead administrative cost imposed on the small unit to pay for the management services the new owner provides. The acquired company has to absorb its share of the headquarters staff, the company plane, the president's salary, and other frills. This can be in the range of 5 to 10 percent of sales, a burden which could have a very detrimental effect on profits.

- Finally, and perhaps most importantly, there is the possibility that the only reason the owners of the acquired firm agreed to sell was that the future no longer looked so bright. Their products were no longer quite as competitive, they had lost some key players, their competitors were suddenly giving them more trouble, among other problems. The business looked like it was in for some serious problems and it was time to sell the store.

So it is my belief that two plus two seldom, if ever, equals five. You will be fortunate, indeed, if two plus two equals four, and the likelihood is that two plus two will equal three or less. Charles Exley, retired chairman and CEO of NCR, describes most acquisitions as being like, "Two manufacturers of left shoes getting together to build on their combined strengths."

Even very large companies who you would think would have the skills and resources to handle an acquisition in an area somewhat unrelated to their core business are often unsuccessful in the process. Many are forced to take immense write-offs in the process of withdrawing from those businesses.

A number of years back, Xerox, the world's leading company in high-end copiers, acquired Kohlberg, Kravis, Roberts & Co., a large casualty insurer. According to the business press, the cost was about $5 billion. I read that Xerox apparently decided that insurance was a business they should not be in and they put the company up for sale. It was reported that they were willing to take a billion dollar loss but were unable to find a buyer. They then divided it into smaller insurance business units which they put up for sale. I do not know how this ultimately worked out for Xerox but you can imagine the disruption it caused within the company.

There are, of course, exceptions. Gannett, one of the countries fastest growing newspaper chains, and Teledyne, a notable high-tech conglomerate, were built on a long series of successful acquisitions. My guess is that in both cases they organized their own firms so that the acquiring process became a distinctive competence to which they devoted major effort. Acquiring was an important strategic thrust. The following chapter, describing what might be done to improve the odds of an acquisition program succeeding, was written by Douglas McCorkindale, Vice Chairman and President of Gannett.

Another exception is when you purchase a separate, discrete product line rather than the entire business. It will be much easier to integrate the new activity into your operation, thereby minimizing many of the drawbacks of outright purchase of an entire company.

You will not get an idea of how difficult and risky the acquisition process is by reading annual corporate reports. All you seem to hear about are the acquisitions that work. The bad ones attract little attention and seem to just fade away with little or no fanfare.

Chapter 43

Making an Acquisition Work

This chapter was written by Douglas H. McCorkindale, vice chairman and president of Gannett. For over 28 years, he has been responsible for the very successful Gannett acquisition program. Before that he was a partner in the New York law firm of Thacher, Profitt & Wood. Doug is a director of Gannett and a number of other organizations and a graduate of Columbia Law School.

Bill Stolze suggests that most acquisitions do not work because the people acquiring do not know how to manage an acquisition. Or companies make acquisitions for the wrong reasons, or the sellers are selling for the wrong reasons, etc. Bill may be right about many companies but at Gannett acquisitions have been an important and successful part of our growth strategy. That's probably why he asked me to write this section of his book.

When Gannett went public in 1967, we had revenues of $110 million and owned 28 newspapers. At the end of 1998, we owned 75 daily newspapers, a variety of nondaily publications, 21 television stations, 515,000 cable subscribers, more than 60 Internet sites, and Internet businesses...as well as many other related businesses.

Have all of our acquisitions been successful? No. But it is not an exaggeration to say that over 90 percent of them have been.

It is Gannett's experience that an acquisition must be analyzed from several different viewpoints. First (and fundamental to the acquisition) is the question, "How do you get the seller to agree to sell?" Well, we spend a lot of time making sure the seller feels at home in Gannett, making sure the seller will stay to run the business (we do not have an excess of managers to run every acquisition). We work on making the seller's employees feel positive about their future, big company employer. If the seller wishes to talk about taking Gannett stock as part of the acquisition purchase price, we show them that the stock is a worthwhile investment.

Assuming the seller is ready, Gannett has developed an internal process for analyzing acquisitions and making them work. As we acquired more and more properties, we built a statistical database to compare the operations of the potential acquisition against our existing properties. We can quickly decide where expenses are too high, where revenues are too low, where the body count is high or low, where rates look out of line, and so on.

We combine that analysis with what we think we can bring to the property in terms of "help from corporate." Help from corporate includes purchasing equipment and supplies (mostly newsprint) at significant discounts.

Gannett does not have a planning department to review acquisitions. Rather, they are analyzed by the people who are on the firing line in operations, production, marketing, and finance, among other departments. It's part of their day-to-day job to look into the acquisitions being considered and decide where they fit and how much money they could make if they were part of Gannett. Each operating group gets a chance to provide input. Once we have the overall picture, the pricing decision comes into play.

For almost 35 years, Gannett has used a simple formula—the purchase price must be such that the acquisition should make a contribution to Gannett's operating profit within three or four years. We estimate the long-term cost of money and calculate what the operating profit must be to exceed the cost of money, plus any goodwill write off. If we can find a way to obtain the necessary operating profit in the required time frame, all the customary equations and calculations used to analyze financial performance generally fall into place.

Over the years, the formula has worked reasonably well in all lines of business, but some lines of business are less predictable than others. Newspapers have generally been the easiest to predict. Television is somewhat more risky. The game plan with a local station is to get to number 1 or 2 in local news (above all else) in the market. Local news is where success starts.

The cable business is generally easy to analyze, but the impact of technology has made it more risky and, maybe more rewarding, especially over the last few years. Although many of our Internet sites are profitable, the risk/reward ratio is very high in this developing business.

On the human resources front, once an acquisition is completed, the opportunity is almost unlimited within Gannett. If the employees (or even the seller) decide to stay on and desire to move up, the opportunity is there. A number of present Gannett senior executives came to the company as a result of such acquisitions.

An additional factor that has made Gannett's acquisition program successful is that we don't have many rules that "must be followed" concerning fringe benefits. We don't argue over such things that are important to sellers. In fact, we consider them part of the purchase price. We don't do a deal in one single form. We're flexible and try to meet all of the seller's needs. We'll use stock, cash, notes, or any combination thereof. Sellers generally sell only once—we buy often. It's a very difficult experience for the seller and we understand that. We do not nickle and dime the seller out of business.

However, having said all that, if the economics described above don't work, then we simply pass on the opportunity. We do not have any "need" to do an acquisition...just for the sake of doing one. As a result, we passed up many acquisition opportunities in the late 1980s when prices got out of control. Some of these properties were offered to us again by buyers who paid too much, who assumed the world would always be a profitable place and that inflation would cure their mistakes.

A similar culture seems to be in place in the late 1990s. As a result, we have not been willing to pay very high cash flow multiples for well run properties. We have used our excess cash to pay down debt or buy back stock.

At our corporate office, we always try to remain financially in order to take advantage of any acquisition opportunity whenever one becomes available. We have learned that we cannot plan for a certain number or certain size of acquisitions to happen every year. Instead, we have to be ready to act when the opportunity strikes. For example, in the mid-1980s, we completed $1.2 billion in acquisitions in approximately 18 months. A number of properties that we thought would never be available all came on the market at the same time. In December of 1995, we closed the $2.3 billion acquisition of Multimedia—a company we had been following since the early 1970s.

It is possible to succeed in the business of making acquisitions. But we have found that it is necessary for it to be part of the basic strategy of your company, to which you *will* commit considerable resources. You must be prepared to make a move when the opportunity occurs and you must understand that you cannot expect 100-percent success.

Chapter 44

Selling the Rest of the World: Exporting As an Opportunity

Very few start-up companies that I am acquainted with seem to put much effort into selling their product or service outside of the United States. One reason for this is that the process appears to be hopelessly complex and expensive to someone unfamiliar with exporting. By failing to pursue the international market, the entrepreneur may be missing an extremely valuable business opportunity.

Consider this: More than 30 percent of all goods manufactured in the United States are now sold outside of the country. In recent years, the political and economic changes that have taken place in Europe, the former Soviet Union, and the Far East have greatly increased the attractiveness of world markets.

At RF Communications, our main product line (long range radio equipment) had a natural market in lesser developed areas of the world. However, very few things in a start up happen easily. It took an aggressive and dedicated effort to capitalize fully on this opportunity—and what an opportunity it turned out to be!

Our first order two weeks after starting RF was a simple electronics assembly contract from the University of Rochester. Our second order three weeks later was a $50,000 order for 20 radios all the way from the government of Pakistan. Within a few years, we shipped equipment to over 100 different countries. (To give you a feel for this, try to list the names of 100 countries without referring to an atlas. My guess is that not one person in 1,000 can do it.) In some years, approximately 80 percent of RF Communications' sales were to customers outside of the United States. Had we not gone after this market as aggressively as we did, it would surely have become an entirely different and much less successful company.

RF Communications realized another important benefit from such strong participation in the international market. For us the international market seemed to be contracyclical in nature to the U.S. Government market (another important group of RF customers). When U.S. government sales were down, export sales usually increased, and vice versa. Through the years this helped RF avoid large swings in sales revenue as economic conditions changed.

Selling outside the United States is yet another subject to which we could devote an entire book. My goal here, however, is to cover some fundamentals and to give you enough information to encourage you to consider the international market more seriously.

There are two basic approaches to international business. One is to consider business outside of the U.S. as icing on the cake. Not much effort and very little risk would be involved but the result might be an increase in sales of five or 10 percent. Handled well, this approach should be profitable. The second approach is to make a genuine commitment with the goal that business outside the United States should become as important as domestic business. This is the strategy used by large companies such as Boeing, Kodak, and Xerox, among others. It was our strategy at RF.

Some of the alternative ways available to develop international business are shown in the chart below. The U.S. company is on the left, the overseas customer is on the right, the ocean in the middle. As we move from top to bottom, the investment required and accompanying risk increase, but the opportunity is correspondingly greater:

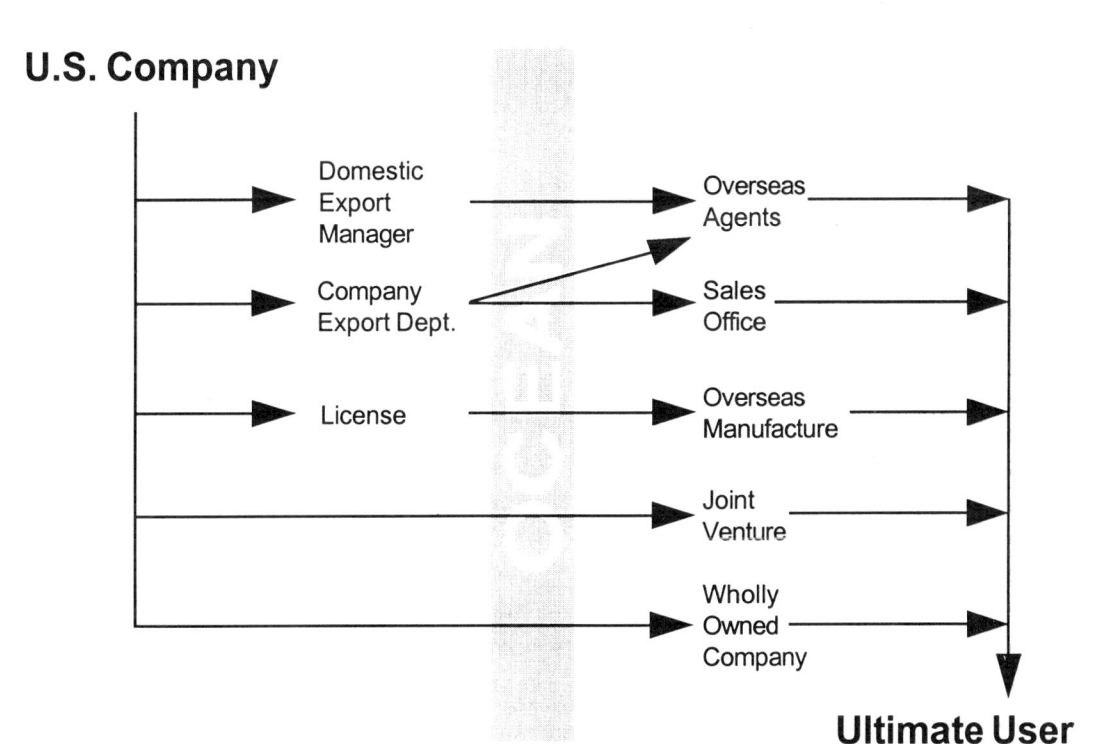

U.S. Company

```
U.S. Company                          Overseas
    ├──► Domestic Export Manager ──► Overseas Agents ──────►
    ├──► Company Export Dept. ─────► Sales Office ──────────►
    ├──► License ──────────────────► Overseas Manufacture ──►
    ├─────────────────────────────► Joint Venture ──────────►
    └─────────────────────────────► Wholly Owned Company ───►
                                                             ▼
                                                      Ultimate User
```

At the top, a company employs the services of an independent domestic exporter or consultant to handle its overseas sales. The exporter typically gets information about products from the company, and then offers them to the ultimate user through a network of independent "agents" located in various countries, with whom the exporter has a working relationship.

Incidentally, I use the term "agent" in the generic sense. Depending on the area of the world in which you do business and the nature of your product line, the term distributor, representative, dealer, or whatever else, may be more appropriate.

In an ideal situation, the exporter will handle a number of complementary lines that are combined into a more attractive offering to the end user. When orders are received, they normally come to the exporter who in turn, places them with supplier firms. Since your orders are from another U.S. firm, you are relieved of the problems of securing export licenses, arranging shipment, dealing in other currencies and the complications of collection. The credit risk is another U.S. company rather than an overseas buyer.

The exporter expects a fee of 5 to 15 percent of the purchase price, and the overseas agent or dealer also expects anywhere from 5 to 25 percent. Even though these markups appear high, if the exporter and its agents do a good job, this arrangement could, in fact, be a bargain.

A little further down on the graph, the next approach shows the U.S. firm doing its own exporting and dealing directly with the overseas agents. The markup of one middleman is eliminated, but the company assumes all of the exporter's functions and expenses, which are not trivial. However, neither are they burdonsome. This approach has many advantages for a small company trying to emphasize international business. An important benefit of doing your own exporting is that it speeds up communications between the company and its overseas agents and customers—a middleman has been eliminated from the process.

The major challenge is to find the best possible agents to represent you in as many countries as possible. As in using external channels for domestic sales, you must work hard at finding agents, training them and supporting them aggressively in every possible way. The selection of top quality agents is absolutely crucial if you want your export business to be a success. The qualities to look for are:

- Technically qualified to understand your product.
- Not already committed to a competitor.
- Financially strong.
- Politically well connected.
- Ambitious and motivated.
- Willing to set up service facilities if needed.
- Able to install your products and train the customer.

In addition to the above list of qualities what separates the "superagent" from a "good agent" is when someone in the organization is familiar with people at all levels in their customer's organization—from elevator operator to the most senior general. Their information-gathering potential will then be very great and your ability to make informed sales decisions will increase dramatically. Agents such as these are few and far between, but if you find one, they are worth their weight in gold.

For a highly technical product, how many people with these skills do you think can be found in places like Tanzania, Bahrain, Venezuela, Morocco, and Nigeria? Not many, you can be sure. In the beginning, we found that the better qualified agents were all committed to competitors. However, the combination of hustle and the strength of our product line soon permitted us to build an agent organization second to none.

Another way for a new company to build up its export business is to have a senior person visit each of its agents on their home turf. This will give you a better feeling for their skills and help develop a close personal relationship. Incidentally, whenever anyone from your company visits another country, it is a good idea to be sure to stop at the U.S. Embassy and get to know the Commercial Attaché. This is a person whose role is to help U.S. companies develop business in that country. In all likelihood, the Commercial Attaché will be able to help identify business opportunities and may be able to assist you in your search for a first-class agent.

In dealing with agents and customers from other countries, Americans often fail to realize how different the culture and customs are in other parts of the world. In order to develop strong, long-term relationships, it is important to be sensitive to these differences.

One piece of advice I always give business people is to be sure to treat their visitors to the U.S. the same way they are likely to be treated when visiting other countries. For example, some years ago I visited an agent in a Middle Eastern country where we had sold a large number of radios. I was going there from Stockholm and was scheduled to arrive around 8 p.m. Our agent, a man in his mid-70s, said he would meet my plane. Unfortunately, the flight was delayed and I arrived about six hours late at 2 a.m.

To my surprise as I walked off the plane, our agent and his wife were at the gate. They whisked me through customs and drove me to a downtown hotel. Earlier that day, the wife had inspected the room and registered me in advance. They saw that I was comfortable, arranged for pickup the next morning, and left me to catch up on my sleep.

They really knew how to welcome someone to a strange country. How many Americans would treat a business visitor in this way? (Also, you may have noticed that I never use the word "foreign" to refer to either people or places.)

The mechanics of handling export shipments also tend to intimidate U.S. business people. It is not quite as simple as calling UPS or FedEx, but neither is it all that complicated. Almost everyone I know who exports directly uses a forwarding agent of some sort. This is a service business located in most major U.S. cities, devoted entirely to handling the complexities of export shipment. It will often arrange for packaging and crating, schedule shipment via ship or plane as specified by the buyer, provide evidence of shipment for use in securing payment, and generally take over most of the onerous technicalities of exporting. The charge made by the forwarding agent may be as low as $25 or $50 per shipment. This is incredible, considering the problems it takes off your hands. You might ask how the agent can do so much for so little. They can't! In addition to the fee you pay, the forwarder covers some of its costs by commissions from the carriers that transport the shipment.

When a company acts as its own exporter, one area of risk it must manage is getting paid. In general, the lesser developed the country to which you are selling, the greater the risk. For RF Communications the best answer was to require payment by confirmed, irrevocable letter of credit (LC) through a major international bank whenever possible. LCs are the equivalent of a check, issued to you in advance by a bank, that can be cashed when you show evidence of shipment. They have become more difficult to obtain in recent years; however, other things you can do to minimize the risk are to require large downpayments or to ship C.O.D.

Another issue that has become more common in recent years is a thing called "offset." This is where the country buying your product requires that you offset part of the cost either by doing some local manufacturing or by unrelated purchases from sources within their country. This may involve things completely unrelated to what you are selling. For example, in order to sell radios you may have to buy apples. Offset usually applies only to very large purchases. When it does it is often possible to find another U.S. company willing to work with you to take the offset material off your hands.

The U.S. exporting firm can also consider putting its own employees overseas to either sell direct, manage the agent relationship, or both. As your export business grows, this is something you will almost surely consider doing in regions where your market is strongest. I am not sure it is always a good idea.

Take this example. We, at one time, had a company-employed salesman residing in his native Portugal, whose territory was southern Europe and Africa. Two problems developed: A field salesperson simply will not travel 100 percent of the time. Anyone with a family will always figure out how to be at home at least half the time. Travel time from Rochester to most of Africa was not much longer than from Portugal. This being the case, home should be the company's headquarters where the individual can interface with the organization during these periods.

A second problem (which we did not realize until later) was that Portugal is a former colonial country and its citizens were not especially welcome in many parts of Africa.

Today, the increased business sophistication that exists in many areas of the world is such that this situation has changed. I am told that in many countries, the chances of doing much business are small unless the company has a corporate presence in the country. In some countries, such as India and China, it may even be necessary to manufacture at least some of the product locally in order to generate significant sales.

Another arrangement to consider involves the U.S. firm licensing one or more overseas companies to build and sell its products in return for upfront licensing fees plus royalties. These are fairly low risk approaches, but hard to control.

The final example concerns the U.S. firm establishing an overseas manufacturing and marketing subsidiary either alone or as a joint venture with a non-U.S. partner. I have been involved in several such overseas manufacturing arrangements. The results ranged from mediocre to bad. It was our good fortune that all the deals were small. Take the following as an example of how naive we were in one undertaking.

We were asked by our distributor in Mexico City to set up a joint venture to manufacture one of our products for sale in Mexico. They had represented us for a number of years, importing from the United States and reselling. The relationship was generally good. The arrangement they suggested was to set up a jointly-owned company with the ownership and investment divided 51 percent for them and 49 percent for us—a requirement of Mexican law. The first signal of future problems developed when they wanted to borrow their part of the investment from us, secured by a commission that would be due them on an order expected to ship several months in the future. Unwisely, we agreed.

Shortly after the business was set up, we learned that one of their first purchases was a company car and that the president of the new company was a son of one of our Mexican partners. The son had no experience in the radio business...or any business for that matter. From there, the relationship deteriorated. Considerable fault lies on both sides, but the result was that we both lost our investment, and our business in Mexico went from a modest amount of exporting to nothing.

Manufacturing in another country under any arrangement is more difficult than exporting and should be approached with caution. This may be an area where large firms have a natural advantage and it may represent excessive risk for a small enterprise.

As I mentioned, the further down on the graph you move, the greater the opportunity and the greater the risk. A young company would be well-advised to achieve at least some success in exporting before it spends very much time worrying about overseas manufacture.

The most important advice I can give the entrepreneur entering the international market is to do it with a high degree of commitment. Don't just dabble. In the changing world we now live in, the international market cannot be ignored. In many situations, business outside of the United States can be an immense opportunity.

Chapter 45

Help! Help! Where Do I Go for Help?

When I started a company in 1961, there were very few places I could go to for help. Today there are countless places and people that offer help, counsel and guidance. It is no longer a question of whether there is help available but more a question of which sources of help to use. This chapter lists some that I consider to be of potential value. They are almost certain to be able to give you answers to many questions—and give you greater confidence in your program for becoming an entrepreneur.

Other entrepreneurs

Perhaps the most valuable help you can get in planning, raising capital, or managing a new business is from someone who has already started a business. I am approached constantly by entrepreneurs and potential entrepreneurs to discuss every imaginable problem related to going out on their own. I seldom refuse to see them and rarely charge a fee. In almost every case, I can help them in some way.

You may wonder why I do this. I often ask myself the same question. At one time I was actively seeking investment opportunities and did, in fact, invest in about a half dozen of these situations. But today, I no longer make venture investments and still see about 100 entrepreneurs every year. It is something that I enjoy and I guess it provides me satisfaction in being able to help others.

What I am suggesting is that you should get to know a few successful entrepreneurs in your area and try to spend time with them. Make it clear that you are seeking advice, not trying to raise money or sell them anything. You'll be surprised at how often they are willing to see you. Almost invariably, they will be able to help you in some way and not expect to be paid. And, if you can generate enough interest you may even attract an investment.

The Internet

An earlier chapter of this book describes the Internet in some detail, mostly from the viewpoint of how it might be used to sell whatever product or service your new business is offering. The information in that chapter will not be repeated here.

This section covers how the Internet can be used as a source of information that might be of help in starting and managing a new business. The following list of Web sites does not pretend to be complete. By the time this book reaches the shelves of bookstores there will undoubtedly be many additional sources of information and some of the sources presently available will have disappeared.

Several interesting Web sites are mentioned in other chapters of this book. The following is a list of a quite a few that would be well worth for someone starting a business:

- www.sbaonline.sba.gov
  This Web site includes literally hundreds of SBA publications on every subject imaginable.
- www.inc.com
  This is *Inc* magazine's Web site and includes articles on many subjects.
- www.entrepreneurmag.com
  The Web site of *Entrepreneur* magazine includes many articles from past issues.
- www.ideacafe.com
  This is the Web site of an organization devoted to entrepreneurship and small business.
- www.amazon.com
  This is an Internet book store that lists the availability of well over a million books, including many on the subject of entrepreneurship.
- www.sec.gov
  Includes reports filed with the Securities Exchange Commission by almost every company in the United States that has issued stock to the public. This is all public information—under normal circumstances, it is hard to obtain in printed form.
- www.thebcnnetwork.com
  This Web site lists thousands of business cards.
- www.village.com
  It is possible to incorporate over the telephone by using this Web site.
- www.jm-publ.com
  This Web site has information about venture capital.
- www.aboutwork.com
  This Web site has many elements, one being entrepreneurship.
- www.businessfinance.com
  This is a Web site devoted to raising money for a business.
- www.sba.gov.inv
  This is a Web site that lists all Small Business Investment Companies.
- www.scor-net.com
  This Web site is almost entirely devoted to problems companies may face when going public.

As you start using the Internet for help in running your business—including the raising of capital—you are sure to learn about other sites that may be useful.

Books, tapes, and videos

Books, audio tapes, and videos on the subject of entrepreneurship and the financing of a new business have become very popular in recent years. For example, sales of the first four editions of this book are approaching 100,000 copies and it is used as a text or in small business programs at more than 50 colleges and universities.

I read, listen to, and watch many of these aides on starting a business. Some I find to be extremely informative. Others are interesting but a little short on useful advice. In any case, I advise you to go to your bookstore or library and use as many as you can find. At the least, you will end up a little smarter...and you may garner some advice and suggestions that will be of great value.

College courses

Few colleges and universities offered formal courses in entrepreneurship and small business management as part of their curriculum 15 to 20 years ago. Today, there are about 1,400 schools in the United States that offer such classes. In some schools, entrepreneurship and small business management are major concentrations. Some universities have large entrepreneurial centers devoted to teaching and academic research in the field. A number have endowed chairs in entrepreneurship. Some of these courses are taught by successful entrepreneurs who are involved on a part-time basis. These entrepreneurs are willing to devote considerable effort for small compensation to help students along the road to starting and financing a business.

In almost all of these courses, the term project is the preparation of a business plan. I taught entrepreneurship in M.B.A. programs for about 10 years. Most of my students were young people with little or no business experience, individuals who did not yet know whether they wanted to go out on their own. However, when a student either had already started his or her own business, seriously planned to do so or was employed by a small company, I strongly encouraged him or her to write a plan about their own business.

You should consider taking one of these courses. In doing so, you will probably be forced through the discipline of writing a real life business plan and, in all likelihood, get a formal, detailed critique of the plan either from the faculty or other students.

In many of these courses, entrepreneurs are invited to address the classes. This is a good way to establish contact with a business owner you can network with later on your own.

Small Business Administration (SBA)

SBA offices are spread all across the country. They have countless publications available and many programs in which you may have an interest. The SBA has a Small Business Answer Desk (800-827-5722) and a Web site (www.sba.gov) that can answer many general business questions, including the location of the SBA office nearest to you. They can also provide a list of the many publications and videos available to small businesses at very low-cost that may be of value to an entrepreneur.

Small Business Development Centers (SBDCs)

This is another program of great value to small business owners that is supported by the Small Business Administration. SBDCs are usually associated with a community college or a state university. They each have a small group of business specialists who will counsel and advise you on a one-on-one basis, and who conduct seminars, programs, and courses for entrepreneurs. Often the SBDCs have a library of books, pamphlets, and other material. In some cases they publish newsletters with articles of interest to entrepreneurs. There are approximately 800 of these centers around the country. You can contact the Association of Small Business Development Centers in Washington, D.C. at 703-448-6124, or your local chamber of commerce for the location of the SBDC in your area.

Business incubators

A business incubator is an organization that provides low-cost space to new companies on a leased basis. This usually includes modest rental charges, small units of space when necessary, short leases, and the availability of shared services that most new businesses cannot justify having on their own.

Sometimes business incubators are publicly supported and sometimes privately financed. The types of shared services available will vary but are likely to include a conference room, copier, fax machine, and secretarial services. I have seen one where a law firm and public accountant were among the tenants.

Finally, the sponsors of the incubator may also be able to provide the new companies with general business guidance and counseling.

A list of incubators can be obtained from the National Business Incubation Assoc., 20 East Circle Drive, Ste. 190, Athens, OH, 45701, 614-593-4331. Also, your local chamber of commerce will probably be able to guide you to the location of business incubators in your area that are not associated with the above association.

Service Corps of Retired Executives (SCORE)

This is a free program sponsored by the Small Business Administration in which retired business people agree to devote time counseling small business owners. In many cases, SCORE chapters are associated with a local chamber of commerce. You cannot always choose your advisor, but in almost every case, you will benefit from the opportunity to discuss your problems with a knowledgeable person.

Small Business Councils

Many chambers of commerce have subgroups called councils. In Rochester, the chamber has an international business council, a sales executives council, a minority business owners council, a small business council (SBC), among others.

The SBC in Rochester has more than 250 members who are mostly owners of small and not-so-small businesses. The council runs seminars on entrepreneurship, occasional breakfast meetings devoted to specific problems faced by small firms, and monthly evening meetings where extensive networking is encouraged. Also, they organize small groups of owners of non-competing businesses into advisory boards that meet monthly to discuss mutual problems.

These SBCs can be a valuable resource for an entrepreneur. Check your nearest chamber of commerce to see what is available in your area.

Small business seminars

Seminars are available on almost every imaginable subject of interest to a small business owner. Check the events list in the business section of your local newspaper for information about what is happening in your area. Sometimes these cost hundreds of dollars, and sometimes they cost little or nothing, depending on who organizes and runs the seminar.

Several years ago, a woman business owner and I organized and conducted a seminar for women entrepreneurs. It drew about 100 attendees. The fee was $75 and a local bank and public accounting firm provided some financial support. We ended up with a $5,000 profit that we used to set up a small scholarship fund for women business owners in an area business school. Seminars of this type can be a valuable source of information and networking for an entrepreneur.

Entrepreneurial magazines

There are number of specialty magazines devoted to entrepreneurship and small business management. Some have huge circulations, such as *Inc.*, *Entrepreneur*, and *Home Office Computing*, while others are smaller and more focused, such as *Midnight Engineering* and *InBusiness*. These magazines try to include articles, book reviews, case histories, and other material of interest to entrepreneurs.

I make a habit of reading as many as I can and almost always find information that is both interesting and useful. Almost all of these have Web Sites.

General business publications

Publications such as *BusinessWeek*, *Forbes*, *Fortune*, *The Wall Street Journal*, and others are devoted almost entirely to business subjects of every kind imaginable. There are articles of interest to small businesses in almost every issue. Most of these publications also have Web sites.

Professional service organizations

Many public accounting firms, law firms, and banks have various kinds of written information and publications that they make available to entrepreneurs and small business owners. Those that I have seen are mostly in the form of pamphlets and small booklets. I know they give them to clients free and charge little or nothing to others. Most of this material is very good.

Venture capital clubs

These groups provide a forum to which entrepreneurs can present an outline of their business plans, usually for the purpose of raising outside capital. In Rochester, we have a group which meets 10 times a year. Typically there are one or two presentations at each meeting. Sometimes the entrepreneur is successful in raising money, other times not. Recently, it has become more difficult. At worst, these groups can be the source of contacts. At best, these groups are a source of interested investors.

The best way to determine whether there is such a club in your area is through your local chamber of commerce, or to simply ask around. A good source would be other entrepreneurs or bankers, lawyers, and accountants with small business clients.

Networking

How do you find people with whom you can share problems and gain useful advice and counsel? Take seminars, attend association meetings, take advantage of everything mentioned here and make a habit of asking for one or two more names of other possible sources of help whenever you talk to anyone about a business problem. Doing this may get you a personal introduction that will make it easier to gain an audience with your next contact. The value of networking will be increased if you are well prepared in advance. Be sure to have at least a good outline of a business plan available and a list of questions or problems you would like to discuss.

Professional associations for small businesses

Finally, there are a number of national associations whose main purpose is to help various categories of small business people. Several are:

- **National Association of the Self-Employed.** This group represents about 320,000 entrepreneurs, most of whom have only a handful of employees. It has a number of publications including the *Small Business Resource Guide*. Their telephone number is 800-232-6273, and their address is 2121 Precinct Line Rd., Hurst, TX, 76054. Their Web address is www.nase.org.
- **National Federation of Independent Businesses.** This organization has about 600,000 members and in addition to lobbying in Washington on small business issues they have a monthly publication. Their telephone number is 800-634-2669, and their address is 600 Maryland Ave., SW, Washington, DC, 20024. Their Web address is www.nfibonline.com.

- **The Council of Growing Companies.** This is an organization of the heads of small and medium sized companies that provides lobbying, seminars, and conferences for its members. Its telephone number is 301-951-1138; its address is 7910 Woodmont Ave., Ste. 1206, Bethesda, MD, 20814.

Summary

When I first began writing this chapter and began putting words on paper, I was surprised at the long list of people and places an entrepreneur can go to for help. I suspect your problem will not be finding sources of help, but deciding how many you should take the trouble to use, while sorting out the contradictory advice you are sure to get. Most are available at little or no cost and most can help you identify and solve problems that would have been much more difficult on your own. Gaining access to some of these sources may require you to be pushy and aggressive from time to time, but the benefits are almost sure to justify the effort.

Chapter 46

Entrepreneurship for Women! Is It Different Than for Men?

Up until 15 or 20 years ago, there were not many women entrepreneurs. Those who did manage to start a business often started either service businesses, such as bookkeeping firms, or small local retailers, such as gift shops. This is definitely no longer true. Today in the United States, women are starting businesses at a much higher rate than men. Near the beginning of this book I mentioned that the 1990s are the "age of the entrepreneur." The 1990s might as well also be described as the "age of the woman entrepreneur."

Evidence confirming this fact is clear. According to the National Foundation for Women Business Owners, their analysis has shown that:

- There were nearly 8 million women-owned enterprises as of 1996 (36 percent of all U.S. firms).
- These firms employed 18.5 million people (one out of every four company workers). Women-owned firms generated close to $2.3 trillion in sales (up 236 percent from 1987 to 1996).
- Women-owned businesses represent from one-quarter to one-third of businesses internationally.

Is this progress for women? You better believe it is!

To achieve this growth, woman-owned businesses are hiring new employees at a much higher rate than larger companies, many of which are going through extended periods of massive down sizing. Many analysts consider woman-owned businesses as one of the hottest growth sectors of the U.S. economy.

Why has this happened?

First, I want to mention a few of the reasons why I think this dramatic change has taken place. There are still a number of obstacles faced by women who start businesses that men do not face.

Back in the 1970s, when I first began teaching in a prominent graduate business school, there was almost never a woman student in any of my classes. This is no longer the case.

In entrepreneurship-based M.B.A. classes that I recently lectured in, anywhere from a quarter to one half of the students were women. This means that women entering the business world over the past few years are as well trained in business skills as men and, in general, are able to compete effectively.

Even in spite of the "glass ceiling" that still exists in some large organizations, women are holding much more responsible positions today than in the past. When they make the decision to go out on their own, they are more knowledgeable, more experienced, and much more likely to succeed.

A second factor that I also think drives many women into the business world is the need for two incomes in many families. The Bureau of Labor Statistics estimates that almost 50 percent of all workers now come from married, dual-income couples. Because of this large increase in the number of married women entering the work force, many decide the best way to increase the family income is to start their own business.

Third, the trend in the United States is for better-educated married couples to have fewer children. This makes it possible for women to take jobs at a younger age than in the past and with fewer family responsibilities. Because the willingness to work long and hard hours is an important personal quality of successful entrepreneurs, fewer family responsibilities may also be a positive factor.

Finally, once having decided to go into the work force, the flexibility a woman has in setting working hours is much better for an entrepreneur than it is at a company with a time clock. Women entrepreneurs are better able to match the demands of their business with the responsibilities of home and family than would be possible in a "normal" work situation.

This category should probably also include divorced women who must support themselves and their children and are unable to get enough financial assistance from their ex-husbands. They sometimes have to enter the work force for the simple purpose of survival. Some of these women will decide to start their own businesses and time flexibility could be an important factor.

For these reasons (and probably others of which I am not aware) we are in the midst of great change in the U.S. business world.

What are the differences?

Over the years, a woman entrepreneur faced a much tougher road in many ways than a man. There were probably a few things in which women had the advantage, but not many. Today, many of these bumps in the road for women have disappeared. I think some still exist because some men simply are still uncomfortable working with or working for women.

Knowing from teaching and counseling many women business owners, they tend to be much more fiscally conservative than men. For example, over the years I have gotten to know about 100 women business owners and until a few years ago only one of these has taken outside equity investors (this comment does not include assistance from husbands). This kind of fiscal conservatism has some benefits in that there have been many fewer failures among women business owners in recent years than among men. Women's financial obligations to outsiders are much lower—they have fewer loan obligations, less commitment to equity investors, and so forth.

One of the reasons for this fiscal conservatism, I believe, is the fact that it was probably much harder to get the business underway in the first place. Therefore women, in general, are more reluctant to share the ownership in their enterprise with others. I also think they tend to have a greater fear that outside investors may try to take over their business if it ever became possible.

Regardless of these fears, I think this is an unwise attitude for several reasons. First, by having outside investors and sharing the ownership of the business, the risk of entrepreneurship can be greatly reduced. Starting a business using other peoples' money clearly has less risk than putting everything you own on the line.

Another reason why I think it is desirable for women to have outside investors is that it gives them access to much more capital with which to run the business. This probably means greater opportunity to grow a larger and more successful business than would be the case using only one's own limited personal resources.

A final reason is that many outside investors are willing and anxious to serve as directors of or advisors to the companies in which they invest. These investors provide an excellent and knowledgeable source of guidance and advice.

The question of control is also one that I believe many women consider to be far too important an issue. The compulsion to own 51 percent of the business forever will also limit growth opportunity and make it much harder to find outside equity investors.

I should also mention the difficulty many women business owners still face getting bank loans. This situation is changing but has by no means been completely eliminated. In discussing this problem with one woman entrepreneur, she said, "Were you ever asked by a bank loan officer, does your wife know you're here?"

On the positive side, I read an article in *The Wall Street Journal* that described an interview with the head of the Small Business Administration. He stated that the number of SBA guaranteed loans to women business owners was more than $1.4 billion in fiscal 1995, an increase of over 84 percent from the prior period.

In mid-1995, I discussed the difficulty women entrepreneurs have had raising equity capital with two friends who manage venture capital funds—one a very large fund, the other a medium-sized fund. They both said they were just about to make their first equity investment in women-controlled businesses. This trend has become more prevalent in the recent years, much to the benefit of the more aggressive woman entrepreneur.

How about preferences?

"Affirmative Action" preferences are a complex issue. In the past few years, both the federal and many state governments have started to eliminate or reduce preferences of all sorts for many minority groups.

I must mention that I personally oppose business preferences. There are several reasons for this, but the most important is this: If the business you start depends on a preference in securing orders for what you are selling, there is a good chance that your idea for the business and/or the strategy you are following may not strong enough to stand alone. Sooner or later, most preferences will probably disappear and without them your business could be in big trouble.

However, if you ask me whether or not people should take advantage of any preferences that are available, my answer would be, "Of course!" This position goes back to the time I read of an interview with Milton Freidman, one of our country's best known free-market economists. He was asked how he could, with a clear conscience, possibly live in a rent controlled apartment. His response was that people should make decisions that maximize their own personal well-being. If any local government is dumb enough to institute rent control, anyone who can benefit from living in a rent controlled unit should do so.

My counsel to women entrepreneurs is to take advantage of every preference you can find. But don't forget that sooner or later your business will probably have to operate without these. Your fundamental strategy must be good enough to accomplish this—to stand on its own feet.

How about some examples?

Throughout other chapters of this book I include a number of examples of what I view as very successful woman-owned businesses. Here are a few more.

Mary Kay Ash, a great-grandmother and founder of Mary Kay Cosmetics, started her business after a successful career in real estate sales. At first, she planned to operate her business with her husband, but he died just before it started in 1963. She went ahead on her own and in 1984, when Mary Kay went from a publicly owned company to a privately owned company, their annual sales were more than $280 million.

Louise Woerner is an early graduate of the Business School at the University of Chicago. Initially she worked as a management consultant. Later, she founded HCR Rochester, which provides home health care in competition with Visiting Nurses. HCR is a privately owned, for profit company competing with a nonprofit and doing it very well. Louise now has about 700 employees and has achieved national recognition as an entrepreneur.

At the other end of the size spectrum, I am acquainted with a woman named Nancy Carlson who purchased a small toy shop named "Kaleidoscope" located in a suburb of Rochester. The store was in a poor location and was not very successful. Nancy came to me for advice on raising outside equity capital and I suggested that in her situation it would be difficult if not impossible.

I asked her how she was doing with the Nintendo video game system, which she displayed prominently in her store. At the time, this was a very popular game. Her answer was that it was a terrible product for her because her cost was very close to the selling price at major toy retail chains—which meant she could not make a profit.

I then asked her what products she had that the larger toy stores might not have. Her answer was christening dresses. This surprised me. She pointed out that christening dresses were bought mostly by grandparents, they were not widely available, and price was not an important part of the purchase decision.

Focusing on this, Kaleidoscope soon moved to a new location, introduced an extensive line of children's wear for ages zero to five or six and children's toys and books for ages zero to nine or ten. She provides very attractive gift wrapping at no extra charge.

I saw her again recently and asked her how business was going. She answered, "Very good." Then, I asked how she was doing with Nintendo sales, and she said they no longer carried it. In addition to being an excellent example of a successful woman-owned business, Kaleidoscope is also an excellent example of finding a unique niche and sticking to it.

Interestingly, Nancy recently liquidated her business. Her two children are now adults, and she and her husband both decided they were ready for a major change in lifestyle. They have moved to another state, where he has a job opportunity with great potential.

I asked about her future plans and she said her first goal was to relax for six months or so. Then, she added that owning her own business is probably in her blood, and that within a year or so, she will probably become an entrepreneur again.

Home offices

Because many businesses started by women are still small service type businesses, it is sometimes possible to operate the business from the entrepreneur's home. Rhonda Abrams, an independent consultant based in Palo Alto, California, said in a

Gannett news article that 12 years ago, when she started her own home-based business, people generally believed it was because she could not afford an office. Now, she says, people envy home-based workers.

However, before doing this, be sure to determine whether zoning codes in your neighborhood permit home-operated businesses, and whether you can have other employees of the business also work from your home. Some of the reasons home-based businesses have become more prevalent in recent years are the availability of fax machines, cellular telephones, inexpensive copiers, the Internet, e-mail, and personal computers. These technologies have made operating from one's home a reality.

If you decide to operate your business from your home or simply have a home office, there are a few guidelines you should remember. These are very important, especially if customers are likely to go there to carry out their business.

First, and perhaps most important, be sure your office is isolated from the rest of your home and, if possible, has an entrance from the outside so that visitors do not have to go through your living room or kitchen. Also, be sure it is used exclusively for business purposes.

Recently, three of my six children operated all or part of their business activities from their homes. One daughter is a tax accountant, another daughter worked for a large health care company, and one son is a salesman for major instrument company. Nowadays, large companies are either permitting or requiring that their employees operate from home offices.

In summary, it is important that the office in your home be just as professional as any other place of business.

Where do women look for help?

Another chapter of this book lists many sources of help available to all entrepreneurs and small business owners. Those listed below are a few of the others that are of specific interest to women:

- The Spring, 1995 issue of *Small Business Forum*, the former national publication of Small Business Development Centers, published a very interesting article entitled "What Is the Most Important Difference in Management Styles Between Men and Women?" The article describes a research study conducted by the National Foundation For Women Business Owners. Included in the same issue were the reactions of eight business specialists to the conclusions of the study. Even though this publication no longer exists, this issue may still be available from the SBDC at 608-263-7843.

- National Association of Women Business Owners (NAWBO). NAWBO is a national organization that represents women business owners of all kinds in all fields of endeavor (1100 Wayne Ave., Suite 830, Silver Springs, MD, 20190, 301-608-2590). Their Web site is www.nawbo.org.

- National Foundation of Women Business Owners. This group has approximately 7,000 members, publishes a monthly magazine, and holds management retreats, among other things (1100 Wayne Ave., Suite 830, Silver Springs, MD, 20910-5603, 301-495- 4975). Their Web site is www.nfwbo.org.

- Office of Women's Business Ownership (WBO). This office provides information to women regarding federally-funded programs for small business owners. They can be reached through your Small Business Administration District Office.

- The complete Census Bureau report on women-owned businesses ("1987 Women-Owned Businesses") may be obtained from the Superintendent of Documents, 202-783-3238. The document number is 033-024-06949-1.

What does all this mean?

The path women entrepreneurs should travel is not entirely clear and depends upon the nature of the business they are trying to start along with their personal goals. For women today, the opportunity to own one's own business is greater than ever before in history.

Chapter 47

This Is How It Should Be Done!

Valerie Mannix and Mercury Print Productions, Inc.

Mercury Print Productions is a woman-owned, full-service printing company located in Rochester, New York. It was founded by Valerie Mannix in 1968 in the basement of her home in order to support herself and her two small children following a divorce. Today, Mercury Print Productions occupies a number of plants, has about 200 employees, and has annual sales of $20 million.

Mannix is a graduate of a Rochester High School but does not have a college degree. Before starting Mercury, she worked in various jobs, starting as a comptometer operator up to managing a small print shop for a local manufacturing company.

The following is a transcript of an interview and discussions I had with Valerie Mannix in early 1996 following her selection as the winner of the prestigious Vanden Brul Entrepreneur of the Year Award by Rochester Institute of Technology (RIT).

As you read this section, think about the strategies Mercury followed and the problems she faced as a female entrepreneur and how they compare to the strategies and operating principles suggested in earlier chapters of this book.

Q: What is your educational background and how come you did not get a college degree?

A: As a high school student, I wanted to become a lab technician, but I hated math. My school counselor said I wouldn't really need it so I didn't take any math classes. Well, you can imagine what happened when I came to take the entrance exam at RIT. The first page, and most of the rest, was all math. I closed the exam book and left.

Q: What did you do then?

A: After leaving RIT that day, I came home and found a flyer in my mailbox for a training course on a comptometer machine. It said I would be guaranteed a job when I finished so off I went. Now, if many of your readers know what a comptometer is I would be amazed. It was a machine that performed calculations in such a round-about way that it soon became obsolete.

Q: Did you get a job as a comptometer operator?

A: I did get a job as promised...a job I couldn't wait to get out of! If my story so far doesn't sound much like "How to become an Entrepreneur for Fun and Profit," you're right. I never started out planning to one day own a multi-million-dollar business. But I did have determination, the ability to work hard, and I did have confidence in myself.

To my dismay, that first job landed me in the payroll department of a small company. Needless to say, I hated it. I went to the personnel department and said, "I'll do anything else, anything." They told me they were buying a printing press and would train me to run it. I learned how to operate that press, often came home covered with ink, and loved it.

Q: Did that job change your goals?
A: I loved finding ways to do the impossible on that small press, like a nine color printing job on a machine that could only print one color at a time. I have always loved the adventure of a new challenge.

Q: How long did that job last?
A: A few years, but when that company left Rochester, I started a new job and became assistant to the manager of an in-house printing operation at a much larger company. After just three months, the manager left and I was given his position. Now a woman printer was definitely not the norm then. It's still not common now, but I didn't worry about whether being a printer was a "right" career choice. I just knew it was something I wanted to do.

Q: How did you handle the new job?
A: I developed more work for the in-plant print shop by talking with people throughout the company about the forms they used in their departments. I created enough work for two shifts in the print room while saving the company a lot of money in the process. Then in the early 1960s, I became pregnant and had to take a maternity leave. It may sound cliched, but the company put a man into my position who knew nothing about printing. They knew, of course, that if a woman could do a job then certainly any man could do it just as well.

Q: What happened when you returned from your maternity leave?
A: When I returned, I was told that he would stay in charge of the print room. Working under someone who knew nothing about a job I knew well was just not possible for me. I resigned knowing it was time to start my own company.

Q: Did you have the financial resources to take such a step?
A: You won't be surprised to hear that not a single bank would lend me the $800 I needed back in 1969 to buy my first printing press and supplies. I had to ask my ex-husband to co-sign a loan for the money I needed to get started. But finally, my basement business was born and I named it Mercury Forms. I chose the name Mercury because it represented someone who was very fast and very efficient...and for the practical reason that I already had a piece of artwork to serve as my logo!

Q: How did you sell your services in what was a very competitive business?
A: I began to build my business by making sales calls during the day, printing the jobs I got at night, and saving every penny I could. Thanks to my replacement, my former employer closed its print shop. I bought all their equipment for $3,000, paid in cash from the money I had been saving. At this point, my basement was full but I was still just learning.

Q: Learning? What do you mean by that?
A: There are many ways to get an education. Formal training and college courses

are certainly two good routes to take, but my own road to success was to learn by doing and by listening to others who knew more than I did. My business continued to grow and in 1979, I moved out of my basement and into a building near my home.

Q: How did that work out?

A: New challenges, overhead, and more employees! My next major obstacle was learning that one of my major clients, Xerox Corp., would no longer be available to me. My ex-husband had begun to work in the department that bought their printing services from me and my company was now perceived as having a "conflict of interest."

Not wanting to lose this important client, I gambled by investing in some typesetting equipment. This meant I would still be able to get Xerox business through another department, while diversifying my business at the same time. My strategy worked, and the gamble paid off. In fact, I soon had three typesetters and several artists working for me as my company continued to grow in this new direction. Printing actually became a smaller percentage of our workload.

Q: So you still had Xerox as a major client?

A: Then as fate would have it, my former husband was moved to the typesetting department at Xerox and my company again faced a conflict of interest problem! Determined to keep doing work for this major customer, I rented more space and bought a bigger press. I was soon calling on their print buyers again. But now my growing business wouldn't fit in that new building so it was time to buy one where it would fit!

Q: Things were going well again?

A: Yes. We moved to another plant in the city and Mercury Forms was really on its way. But we also had an identity problem now. We weren't doing mostly forms any longer. We were doing a variety of printing jobs for a wide range of customers. My company became Mercury Print Productions.

Within just six years, this plant couldn't hold us any longer and I sold it. I bought another building three times bigger and I was sure we would have plenty of room, which we did for about a year. Two years later I was looking for a larger facility again. Rather than trying to find an existing building I decided to build one.

Q: How did you manage this and was being a woman a factor?

A: I applied for and received financial assistance from the City of Rochester and the County of Monroe partly because I was a woman in addition to having a successful business track record. I didn't need a man to co-sign for me this time and the amount far exceeded that first $800 loan by a few million dollars.

My company continued to grow. We added more shifts, more equipment, and more staff. However, at this point, I could see that new technology for high-volume copiers would soon replace most of our black and white printing.

Q: Did this mean you had to shift your strategy?

A: If you look in *Webster's Dictionary*, an entrepreneur is defined as "a person who organizes and manages a business undertaking, assuming the risk for the sake of the profit."

To fit this definition, I started thinking color. My strategy was to quote four-color work as if we had a four-color press. But we had to run it on a two-color press twice. Not too profitable. When 25 percent of our workload was color, it was time to look for a full-color press. I finally bought a used five-color press from England, because European printers run fewer shifts and work their equipment less than here in the United States. On December 1, 1994, our huge Heidelberg press arrived, a machine that wouldn't fit in my entire house when I started, let alone the basement.

Q: **This really represented a major step forward, didn't it?**
A: It certainly did. Over the past 27 years, the small company I started so that I could make enough money to support myself and my two children had moved four times to larger quarters that could hold more equipment and a growing staff.

Mercury Print Productions now occupies 30,000 square feet in a custom-designed facility. Our previous building is also still in use—as a satellite facility for our high-speed copier division. Now I'm looking to add on to our current building sometime in 1996.

Q: **Have these moves and rapid growth affected the quality of your work?**
A: No, rapid growth has never resulted in reducing the quality of our work. We met quality control standards to become an approved printer for Xerox Corporation in 1988—we were certified by Xerox in 1995. In fact, Mercury is the only printing company certified worldwide. We're now working to achieve the international ISO 9000 standard; our goal is five years.

Q: **Your record as an entrepreneur has been outstanding. How do you feel when you think about these accomplishments?**
A: At a recent quality control meeting for our staff, I stood at the podium and looked out over 87 employees gathered in a hotel conference room and couldn't believe it. Where did all these people come from? I now employ 113 people full-time and another 23 part-time. In 1994 we did about $5 million in sales. In 1995 we reached $10 million—three years sooner than our business plan had projected!

Over the years, rapidly changing technology in the printing industry has kept me challenged. There are so many more choices to make when doing a print job now and the needs of our customers have certainly changed over this past quarter of a century.

Q: **Please comment on what you think it requires to be a successful entrepreneur.**
A: I think that I have always been able to spot an entrepreneur. There are certain qualities that just give them away. For example, an entrepreneur is willing to take a calculated risk. You have to know how to focus on a long-range goal and to envision the steps needed to get there. But most important of all is to really love what you're doing.

You must be passionate about your business, and know that the first success is never the end of the road. An entrepreneur is always driven to accomplish something more. To be successful, you must be willing to dream, but not be satisfied with just generating ideas. You must plan and organize for the future as well. The entrepreneurs working for me all have initiative, dedication to a goal, and the drive to achieve.

Q: **Is that all?**
A: Loving your business is not enough. You must know every aspect of it. Get to know your competitors. Know where their weaknesses are. Get to know their business strategies, their customers, the niches they succeed in. Know where to

look for opportunities for your own business and learn from others how to spot problems you may face yourself one day.

Very often, I find college students expect to go right into a job that pays them 40 to 60 thousand dollars a year. That may lead to a comfortable lifestyle, but if you are an entrepreneur at heart, it won't be enough

Q: Thinking back, what were the most important factors that drove you to go out on your own?

A: I didn't get into business to get rich, I just needed to support myself and my children. But believe it or not, running your own business can almost be compared to being on vacation. There are always new adventures and interesting people to meet. Also, there are bonuses, the excitement of success, and the satisfaction of overcoming failure. Don't get me wrong, I have bad days just like everyone else. But as I look back on my career, I realize that the moments when I had butterflies in my stomach taking a chance on something were the most rewarding and exciting times in my life.

Q: How has all this affected your personal life?

A: On the personal side, we entrepreneurs are not easy to live with. There were times when personal relationships kept me from growing. And, I have learned that the significant people in your life can't be threatened by your success. I was never in a hurry to reap rewards from my earliest business efforts. I put every penny I made back into my company. It was 15 years before I allowed myself the luxury of taking more than just a wage to live on.

Q: Do you have any advice for people thinking about starting a business?

A: To all entrepreneurs out there today, I urge you to do the same things I did. Take only a small salary at first, and invest your profits in your own business dream. The rewards will be much greater in the long run. Take small steps but always move forward. And don't be afraid of failure—welcome it! If you fail at something along the way, okay it happens. Do everything you can to correct the situation and learn from it. Learn the lessons that no one, not your parents or not your most respected professors can teach you.

Just know you won't make the same mistake again and you have a lifetime to get it right! To me, retiring may mean cutting back to just three days eventually, maybe taking a month off to travel once in a while. I don't think I could do it "cold turkey." If I did, I'd probably go out and start something else, but I still love what I'm doing now.

Q: Do you have any final comments?

A: Yes, I want to thank my family and friends for their support over the years, especially my mother, my husband Jim, and my son John, who is my vice president and right hand man, and my daughter Jackie. Both of my children work at Mercury. I also thank all the employees who have helped my company to grow. While I provided the vision and the leadership, they became the ones to help carry it out.

Finally, I want to challenge all of the readers of your book, Bill. They should never settle for a job well done, They should always look for the next challenge, and if it doesn't already exist, go out and create it!

The previous interview took place in 1996. In 1999, I asked Valerie for any additional comments she had for this fifth edition of Start Up. *She sent me the following:*

It's 1999, and at Mercury we are busily preparing to enter the year 2000 on the right foot. We've nearly doubled the size of our plant, having recently completed a 33,000 square foot addition. Our newest endeavor, compact disc duplication, is housed in a separate 30,000 square foot building. (If anyone had told me 30 years ago that we'd be printing on little round disks I never would have believed it!) We've purchased the latest in prepress technology, including a Creo (direct to plate) system, and have a print management software system up and running throughout the entire plant.

Employment is at an all time high of 200 people, and 1998 sales hit $20 million. Just three years prior, when I won the Vanden Brul Award, sales were only $10 million.

Mercury is a dynamic place, always moving forward. I don't look back too often. But if I do, and if I think too long about how it was, and how I thought it would be compared to how it is, I just have to shake my head in amazement. But I wouldn't have it any other way. The changes we've made over time and the growth we've experienced are testimony to the fact that we continuously meet the challenges presented by our customers, our competition, and by the ever changing industry. I can't say it enough: Always move forward. Don't be afraid of failure. Just go for it and someday maybe you too can say "only $10 million."

Chapter 48

Managing a Turnaround

There are a number of reasons why managing a turnaround situation may be important to an entrepreneur. The first reason is that sometimes during the life of your business, you may face a situation where everything seems to go bad for any number of reasons.

A second reason is that companies go through stages of growth. Sooner or later, they reach the point where they must make the transition from a founder-dominated operation to one that is more professionally managed. As was discussed in an earlier chapter, failure to do this can cause very serious business problems.

A third reason is that buying a business is one way to become an entrepreneur. Buying a business in trouble, or even in bankruptcy, that needs a turnaround, is a way to buy a business at a bargain price.

When RF Communications was about seven years old, I left to take a faculty position at an area business school. About a year later RF merged with Harris Corp. At that time the services of the lawyer, who was our vice president of finance, were no longer needed by Harris and he left.

During the next two and a half years, the business situation at RF Communications deteriorated badly. Sales dropped by about one-third, there had been large staff reductions, and they were experiencing substantial losses.

One of the other founders, who succeeded me as president, did not get along with Harris. About a year after the merger he left the company. A year or so after that, the fourth founder, who had succeeded him, also announced his desire to leave. This left Harris with a serious problem. They had paid a very high price for RF Communications, all of the founders had left the company, and everything seemed to be going wrong.

Harris invited me to return full-time to head up the company again and I accepted...with many reservations. I no longer had any financial need to take such a demanding job, and I was uncertain whether I had the skills to turn the situation around. Managing a turnaround turned out to be the most difficult and challenging business experience I ever had.

I spent much time thinking about why things went so bad. It was in the early 1970s and the United States was in a modest recession. Additionally, defense spending, which represented an important part of our business, had been reduced. RF had also just gone through two and a half years of becoming part of a much larger company. This was a very disruptive process. Perhaps more important though, RF never made the complete transition from a founder-dominated company, where the four founders made all the important decisions, to a professionally managed company with more structure and more formal control and review procedures.

After returning and spending the first few weeks looking around and talking to people, this is what I found:

- Many employees felt demoralized. There had been a number of substantial staff reductions and everyone was worried about his or her job.
- Orders were drastically down.
- There were two product lines unrelated to the core business that were a financial drain on the company.
- A former vice president of marketing and several other employees had left to form their own company in direct competition with RF.
- There were poor controls throughout the organization. Inventory levels were skyrocketing. Even though orders were down, most shipments were late because of parts shortages.
- The company seemed unable to make a decent sales forecast as little as one month in advance. Yet, a senior member of management spent almost a third of his time doing the forecasting.

There were many other problems, but these give you an idea of what I faced. Anyone who has managed a company during a turnaround is certainly familiar with this list. It is a perfect example of a situation where if anything goes bad, everything goes bad. Here are some of the things I did:

One of the first problems I tackled was improving morale. I decided to visit every department in the company and speak to every employee. RF had about 600 employees. I met with groups of 15 or 20 people at a time, right in their workplace, and spoke for 15 or 20 minutes. It took two whole days.

The approach I used was to simply tell the truth. I told them exactly what I had concluded about the problems we faced and asked for their help. I said business was bad, there would be no salary raises for the foreseeable future, and that in all likelihood, there would be further staff reductions. When I finished my short speech in most cases the people applauded. I was astonished. When I asked why they were applauding when all I told them was bad news, their answer was, "At last somebody understands the problem." This was a real lesson for me. Communicating honestly with your employees almost always pays handsome dividends.

I addressed the orders problem by making myself the head of marketing. Almost every problem we had would have been less of a problem if we had more orders. For almost a year, I spent half to three quarters of my time working on the problem of getting orders. As mentioned many times in this book, the head of the company is almost always a most effective salesperson.

I immediately did many things to cut expenses, such as banning first class air travel, eliminating raises, walking around in the evening turning off lights and pulling out soldering irons, and ending all charitable contributions. But the fact is, while these efforts were highly visible and may have looked good, they had little effect on profits. In most situations the only meaningful way to cut expenses is to reduce the number of employees. This I also did quite aggressively, mostly at the managerial level.

I reorganized operations and within six months had reduced the rate of annual expenses by about $400,000, which was almost enough to reach break even.

We had two products outside of our main line of business that seemed to be going nowhere. Even though each had taken a sizable investment, I decided the best approach was to terminate them and concentrate on what we knew best. One product I sold to another company for about half our investment and the other we transferred to another division of Harris at no loss.

Another major problem resulted from the fact that we had always been founder dominated, and never took the trouble to introduce formal management review and control procedures. I knew this was a problem but did not know how to deal with it. So, I visited two of the people I considered the most effective division managers in the entire Harris organization. I spent a day with each observing how they ran their operations. I learned a lot and put much of what I learned into place at RF.

The most important step I took was to establish formal, monthly review meetings. During one week in the middle of the month, we spent a day going over every active program, a day reviewing marketing opportunities, a half day on financial review and sales forecasting, and a day on ad hoc, in-depth review of new research and development projects. At first many of the people reporting to me complained that they could not afford the time. However, it soon became apparent that these meetings were an invaluable aid for us in keeping on top of what was going on and learning about problems before they became serious.

I remember one situation vividly. During a review meeting I learned that we were getting back about half as many units as we shipped each month on an especially complex product. I discovered that the units were being shipped to customers without instruction manuals. I blew my stack. I was told the publications department was busy and the manual would be ready soon. My reply was, "All right, no more shipments until an instruction manual was ready." The answer I got was, "You can't do that, our customers will get mad." My reply was, "I certainly can do that and our customers will not get half as mad as they will if they have a problem with the equipment with no instruction manual to help fix it."

I am almost embarrassed to tell this story because it sounds so ridiculous. How long this situation would have lasted without the benefit of the formal review meetings, I have no way of knowing. This same disciplined review process also helped correct the problems of accurate sales forecasting and excessive inventory.

How did all these changes work out? Just great! The first quarter after my return we had another huge loss, the second quarter we cut the loss almost in half, the third quarter we broke even and the fourth quarter we had enough of a profit to almost break even for the year. The following year, RF ended up in a tie for the award as the best performing division within the entire company.

I mentioned earlier that buying a bankrupt company is one way for an entrepreneur to go into business at a bargain price. In preparing to write this chapter, I came across the January, 1992 issue of *Inc.* magazine, which had an article about another interesting turnaround. It describes the situation at Elyria Foundry, in Lorain County, Ohio, where in 1983, a man named Greg Foster purchased the company from the former owners at a very attractive price. Since then, he turned a bad situation completely around and the company is profitable again and successful in a very tough industry. The article describes a long list of problems generally similar to mine. But in addition to these, Foster also had to deal with a union. Eventually the employees decertified the union, which helped him immensely. But boy, did he have his hands full for a while! Anyone facing a turnaround situation would do well to read that issue of *Inc*.

Chapter 49

When Should the Entrepreneur Step Aside?

The goal of almost every entrepreneur is both to get their new business successfully off the ground and to make the new business grow into a large business. However, I have tried to emphasize many times in this book that the skills needed to manage a start-up company are substantially different then the skills needed to manage a large company. Herein lies a dilemma. If the entrepreneur succeeds in getting their start-up company off the ground, the entrepreneur must then decide whether he or she still has the skills needed to continue as head of the company, or should he or she step aside and let someone else takeover? Some entrepreneurs have the skills but many do not, and should not try.

Starting the business has probably been an exciting and challenging experience loaded with "fun." Managing a large business will probably not be nearly as exciting for them and, almost surely, not as much fun.

Ideally, the founder and his or her board of directors or board of advisors should try to make the change with as little disruption as possible. An important decision is whether to select someone to head up the company who already works there and seems to have the necessary skills, or to recruit someone from a larger outside company.

Several years ago, I read an interesting example on how one company resolved this problem as the company grew. John Walker, founder of Autodesk, Inc. (the very successful producer of AutoCad drafting software sold to architects and engineers), stepped out as president on his own initiative to return full-time to programming. He apparently concluded that his programming skills would be of greater value to the company than his administrative skills.

Perhaps the management transition that was done with the most fanfare and most publicity in recent years happened at Apple Computer. A little over a decade ago Steve Jobs, one of the founders of Apple, was replaced as CEO by John Scully, who was recruited from Pepsi Co. Jobs continued with the company as chairman of the board.

All I know about the situation at Apple is what I read in the business press but it seems that they did not get along very well. A short time later Jobs left to form NeXT, another start-up computer company.

In early 1993, Scully stepped down as head of Apple and, since then, there have been several other CEO changes and much turmoil among its senior management.

Whether Apple was better off under Scully's leadership than it would have been under Jobs's leadership is impossible to say. Even though the Macintosh personal computer that Jobs helped create before he left the company has been quite successful, conventional wisdom in the investment community is that Apple now faces some very challenging problems over the next few years.

Recently, Jobs returned to head up Apple on an interim basis and introduced several new and exciting products. The company is growing and is profitable again.

I have been personally involved in several management transitions where the board of directors took the initiative for the change. All were difficult to handle. In one situation the company was doing poorly. A person already employed there was promoted. The company continued to face hard times and soon after went bust. In the other, a new CEO was hired from the outside. Here, the company survived the change, but there was a fairly long period of adjustment for everyone involved.

Obviously, it is better for the entrepreneur to accept the necessity for a move such as this and actively participate in making it work. An entrepreneur who successfully started a business and built that business to a substantial size, should not be embarrassed to step aside to make room for someone with skills they do not have—they will be doing themselves a favor. It is likely that much of their personal net worth is still in the form of stock in the company they started. Doing the things needed to help that company continue to thrive can only be good.

The main message I wish to make is this: Everyone involved—the entrepreneur, the board, the shareholders, and the other managers of the company—should address the situation well before it becomes a serious problem.

Chapter 50

Cashing Some Chips or Getting Out

This chapter is about the problems entrepreneurs face in converting their ownership in a business into liquid (or cash) form. The business that you own, in all or in part, may be the most valuable asset you have—but it is probably a paper asset. Sooner or later, you surely will want to use some of that asset for things such as buying a more expensive home or for paying college tuition. Or it may be that your interests have changed and you just decided to withdraw entirely from the business and move on to other things.

Your goal will be to convert "worth on paper" to a more liquid, spendable form known as "worth in the bank." Unfortunately, this is a difficult subject to discuss because so much is affected by your specific situation. As I mentioned so many times, it all depends.

My goal in this chapter is modest. I will describe the process of "cashing some chips" in general terms and then describe some of my personal experiences. Hopefully, it will give entrepreneurs an idea of some of the possibilities available and some of the obstacles they may encounter.

But first let's set the stage. Assume, for the sake of discussion, your venture is five to 10 years old, had substantial growth in sales during that period, and in recent years, had achieved an acceptable level of earnings. Chances are you will find yourself in the following situation:

- You are no longer working 80 hours a week (probably only 60 hours).
- Your salary has reached a level that is about proper for the job.
- Your share of ownership in the business has achieved value but remains almost completely nonliquid.
- You are becoming nervous about having all your eggs in one basket and, as a result, are more cautious in running the business.
- The personal interests of the team of people who started the business with you are changing.
- Your family is becoming restless.
- Your children have reached college age.
- For the first time in your life you have written a will and have started doing estate planning.
- You are becoming bored. The excitement and thrill of running the business is beginning to wear thin.
- The business has reached the stage where it must make the transition from being founder-dominated to one that utilizes more formal and more disciplined

management practices. (This, incidentally, is a very difficult hurdle for many entrepreneurs.)

Which of these applied to my situation after starting and running a company for seven years? All of them applied—where else would I have gotten the list?

Your ownership situation is the most important factor in how you approach achieving liquidity. Three possibilities are:

* You own the business yourself, or have one or several partners active in the operation of the business.
* You have a number of passive shareholders, probably as a result of raising capital through private sale of stock. However, these shares are restricted, and there is no public market.
* The company has gone public and the stock is openly traded, probably in the over-the-counter market.

Before suggesting how you can sell all or part of your share of the business, I advise you to seek counsel from experienced securities and tax lawyers. Securities laws are complex—especially regarding the sale of stock by officers, directors, or principal owners of a business. They change from time to time and at best are confusing, and hard to interpret or understand. In addition, these types of transactions can have serious tax implications, and the tax laws are also complex and continually changing. Some main alternatives are:

* Going public if you are not already.
* Selling all or part of your ownership to one of your partners or an outside investor.
* Selling the entire business.

Depending on whether you use an underwriter and the specific circumstances of the offering, you may be able to sell some of your own stock as part of an initial public offering. When the company sells stock, it has the purpose of raising money for the business. However, if you include some of your personal stock in this offering, it has the purpose of raising money for you. These are conflicting goals that make some investors nervous.

When founder stock is sold as part of a general offering it is called either a "secondary" or a "bail out," depending on how kind your underwriter wants to be. Frequently, underwriters will refuse to include founder stock in a public offering. Even so, going public may be your best approach because it sets the stage for you to sell your founder stock more readily at a later date.

In closely-held companies, selling all or part of your share of the business to one of your partners is a way to cash some chips. It is fairly simple legally, but it has the drawback that you may have to take much of your money on an installment plan. There are also tax implications you should look into.

Selling all or part of your share of the business to an individual or investor not already associated with the company may be more difficult to arrange. In addition to the financial aspects of the transaction, you must find an investor who is acceptable to the other owners.

If your company is not publicly held but already has a number of outside investors, the sale of all or part of your stock to another outsider can also be a fairly simple transaction, provided the buyer is willing to accept the same restrictions that you have. But under any circumstances, restrictions tend to make for a lower price.

Bartering, or trading stock for other things of value, may be a legal way to achieve some degree of liquidity. I know of one entrepreneur who used restricted stock to pay an orthodontist to straighten the teeth of two of his children. I have used restricted stock as security on loans for fairly large real estate transactions.

A common way to cash all of your chips is to sell the entire business. This can be done either for cash or in exchange for stock in the acquiring company. Each has advantages and disadvantages. If you sell for cash, all the uncertainty of the transaction is removed...but your profit may be taxable immediately. If you take stock in the acquiring firm it may be possible to defer taxes on the gain, sometimes permanently. But the long-term value of the deal will vary depending on the performance of the acquiring company.

One way to look at a stock-for-stock transaction is that it is simply another way to go public. Whether you keep the new stock becomes an investment or a tax decision, rather than a business decision.

Finally, if you decide to sell your business, you have the difficult task of determining its value. This is another issue that could be the subject of an entire book. Sales, net worth, or earnings are often used as a guide or market value, if the company is already publicly owned. As I mentioned earlier, my experience as both a buyer and seller of companies is that the price is almost always higher with a publicly owned company than when negotiating a private sale.

Which way or combination of ways you use to achieve liquidity depends on the specific situation. The best advice I can give is to plan for it well in advance and then get expert advice. You want at least a fair chance of maximizing your return—and minimizing your taxes.

Chapter 51

This Is How It Should Be Done!

Tom Golisano and Paychex, Inc.

Paychex, Inc., is a payroll service company specializing in providing services to companies with between one and 200 employees. It was founded in 1970 by B. Thomas Golisano and has since grown to become a company with over 5,000 employees. Paychex has processing branches in 103 of the largest metropolitan areas of the country and the District of Columbia. Its sales exceed $600 million and it serves over 320,000 clients. As part of their service, Paychex prints paychecks for their clients and they now print well over two million checks a week.

Golisano is a graduate of Alfred Tech. with a degree in business. Before starting Paychex, he was sales manager for a payroll service provider, selling mostly to larger clients. The rest of this section is in the words of Tom Golisano describing the process he went through creating an extremely successful business that required using almost every type of financing available.

I think the most important thing that drove me to start Paychex was the nature of my prior job. At the time, I was sales manager for a payroll processing firm called Electronic Accounting Systems (EAS). Like the traditional payroll processing providers during the mid-60s and early 70s, most of EAS's marketing and sales effort was directed at companies with between 50 and 500 employees. I think their rationale was this: The larger the client, the better the revenue and profit potential for the company.

However, it seemed to me that if you drive down any street in the United States today and look at the businesses out there you certainly get the impression that most of them have less than 50 employees. One day, I went to the library and found a publication called *County Business Patterns*. It was put out by the federal government based upon payroll tax returns. I learned that about 98 percent of all American businesses have fewer than 100 employees and 93 percent have fewer than 50.

From this, I concluded that there was a market niche out there in which no one had an interest. However, I also concluded that in order to be successful addressing this small company market you had to do three things differently.

First, make it very easy for small companies to transmit their payroll data to the processor each pay period. Up until that time, it was customary to have the client fill out a complex computer input sheet. It was an error-prone procedure that required skills most small businesses did not have. Instead of having the client fill out the complex computer input sheet I decided that it would be great if they could just

Start Up

call in the information on the telephone. A payroll specialist would read the name of each employee and the client would tell them how to process that person's payroll. Any changes in wage rates or exemptions, marital status, or address could also be verbalized over the telephone.

A typical client with 20 employees can complete this chore in three or four minutes. It is very simple for the client; it can be done from anywhere.

Next, provide the client with payroll tax returns. Only one company in the country provided that service at the time. In the United States, employers are unpaid tax collectors. They are required to collect taxes from their employees and remit the funds to federal, state, and local governments on a timely basis. The fines and penalties for nonpayment are severe. So, I concluded that this could be an important adjunct, or addition, to the preparation of paychecks. To give you an idea of what a difficult chore this is remember that in New York State a company with five employees must file a minimum of 42 payroll tax returns each year. This is a very onerous task for small firms.

Finally costs had to be controlled. Payroll processors at the time had a very high minimum processing charge. For example, if you had five people on your payroll the minimum charge was something like $24 a pay period. This was a large burden for a very small company. My belief was that we could substantially reduce the minimum processing charge and sell our service to many more very small companies. In fact when Paychex started our minimum charge was $5 for the first five employees. Today it is still less than $10.

I put these three ideas together and went to the management of Electronic Accounting Systems with a proposal to go after this low-end market. They rejected my idea. I think they were concerned that certified public accountants, the CPA community, would look unfavorably upon a payroll processing firm that prepared payroll tax returns.

My intuition was that they were wrong and that CPAs would look favorably on our doing payroll tax returns. This assumption proved to be correct and CPAs have become an important source of new client referrals for Paychex.

Well, when Electronic Accounting Systems told me they were not interested in this concept I left my job there to start Paychex. When I started Paychex I only had a total of $3,000. Starting a business with only $3,000 was probably impossible—even in 1971. If I had to do it over again, I probably would not do it. At the time, I felt so secure in what I was doing that even though I did not have enough money I started anyway. The $3,000 lasted about 30 days. Then, I found myself in a situation where I was borrowing money using consumer installment loans from several banks. I borrowed money from relatives, I even used my credit card to meet our payroll on a few occasions. I did all the things undercapitalized companies must do to survive. I was not able to get out of debt until 1977 or 1978.

It only took me a couple weeks to get my first customer. Getting customers was not as big an issue with me as it might be in other cases. I had two years' experience in selling payroll service and I knew the market was there. The credibility issue was a bigger problem because here I was starting out as the new payroll processing company in town with zero clients. That was an issue during the first few months but after we had 30 or 40 clients it became much easier.

Establishing Paychex offices in other cities did not start until 1974. It started when a friend of mine who worked at Electronic

Accounting Systems with me walked into my office one day and said, "Tom, it looks like this Paychex is going to be successful. How can I get involved?" I came up with the idea that we could each put in some money and start a corporation in which we each had 50 percent ownership. It was to be located in Syracuse, New York, and patterned after Paychex. It was a joint venture partnership—a separate company.

A few months later, an employee of one of our clients walked into my office and said to me, "This service is terrific—it can be sold in other cities. I want to go down to Miami, Florida, and start a Paychex office there." I said "That's great, I would like to be partners with you." He said, "No, I don't want to be your partner, but I will be your franchisee." So we put together a very loose franchise agreement and he moved to Miami and started a Paychex operation down there. After these two offices got going I could see that it could be done and represented a major opportunity. I began the process of going out and finding people to start Paychex offices in other parts of the country.

Over the next four years, this approach evolved into 11 joint ventures and six franchise operations. The total cost on the average to get a new Paychex office to the point of breaking even was somewhere between $35,000 and $50,000. If it was a franchise the franchisee had to pay all of it. In the case of a joint venture we split whatever amount it turned out to be. The people in Washington, D.C., got it going for $22,000, that was the lowest. I think the highest was over $100,000. It was a matter of the capability of the person and how fast they could build sales volume.

Before long, I decided that it would be very desirable to have a single integrated company and bring the joint ventures and franchises back into the parent. There were a number of factors for this decision. Firstly, I began to realize was that even though these people that I got involved with were very entrepreneurial and very aggressive, I started to notice a difference in their ambition level. Some of the people were very aggressive in opening multiple office locations and others only wanted to open one and rest on those laurels. That began to bother me because I started to see some undeveloped territory.

The second thing that I realized was some of the people were very good in the sales side of our business but not very good operationally and vice versa. We were not doing a very good job of skill matching.

The third reason was that these individual corporations, even though they were working, were very weak. It was very difficult for them to buy computers and to upgrade offices; it was just a weak environment in which to operate.

And fourth, no one had given any thought to how they would cash out when the appropriate time came. I think many entrepreneurs never think about this when they start their venture.

The way I went about the job of integrating these independent business units was to write a business plan and send it out to the group in early December of 1978. It was an outline for a consolidation of the 18 separate Paychex operations. It included spending three years building the sales organization to open new markets and the next two years concentrating on building profitability. The end goal was to either become a publicly owned corporation or to merge.

Of course, when I presented this plan, it created a lot of consternation and generated many telephone calls; most of the people really did not understand my rationale. Just a year or two earlier, I had encouraged them to become entrepreneurs and now I was suddenly telling them we should consolidate. I was suggesting we should combine into one larger company and that we should all be shareholders and employees of that company.

In February 1979, we all met around a big table down in the Bahamas and spent an entire day discussing the pros and cons of this kind of consolidation. The next morning we sat around the big table again and I went around the room asking each person whether or not they would agree to this consolidation. They all agreed to it.

One key question they all had was how much stock each one of them would receive for their contribution to the new corporation. That was done by formula by myself and two others. The final point we reached in the consolidation was when we announced how much stock each one of the individuals were going to get in this new corporation. We did not allow any negotiation. I knew as soon as I allowed one person to negotiate and change their stock allocation, every one of them would be standing outside the door and nothing would have been accomplished. I just decided I was going to stand firm and it was going to be take it or leave it.

One thing I did was to give the people the option of continuing on their own if they chose. If a person decided they did not want to become part of this new venture, we guaranteed them we would not open a Paychex branch in their city. Fortunately, none of the group decided to continue on their own.

While Paychex was growing, there were several people outside the company who we leaned on for advice and counsel. In 1981, the University of Rochester and the Hambrecht & Quist Venture Capital Fund bought substantial equity stakes in Paychex. This was before we became a public company. Those two organizations had people in them, namely Phil Horsley at the U of R and Grant Inman at H&Q, who became members of our board of directors.

They are both still on our board and in addition to their expertise in the area of general management they had great expertise in the area of finance and going public. Their relationship with Wall Street and stock analysts has been extremely helpful to us.

It is interesting to note that money the U of R and H&Q invested to get a stake in Paychex did not go to the corporation. It went to existing shareholders. The real benefit was that it gave some of our shareholders liquidity before we had a public offering. That was very important because many of us had gone for many years without any way to cash in.

We never brought in any additional equity capital before we went public. We borrowed money from banks and at one point our loans were even classified. We used every method available to raise capital. Everything from home equity loans to family borrowing to borrowing from banks to borrowing larger amounts from banks to venture capital to going public. I think we used them all.

In 1983, Paychex became a publicly owned company. We did this for a number of reasons. Obviously most important was to provide liquidity for our shareholders. By then we had approximately 85 or 90 shareholders with varying stakes in the company. This included the original joint venture people and franchisees who each owned from two to six percent of the company. The other shareholders had been very patient and very supportive, but it was time to do something to give them their rewards.

Another reason we went public was that we were able to raise about $7 million for the company, which we immediately spent in developing a greatly-improved online computer system. This system gave us a great economic advantage in offering our payroll services. Also, it gave us more visibility and more credibility with our customers.

Finally, being a public corporation made it much easier to recruit key employees. A publicly-owned company gives the perception that you are more stable and will probably have a longer existence. You also have the additional benefit that you can give employees more visible incentives such as stock options.

To this day, I never regretted the decision to go public. Some people say that dealing with the Securities Exchange Commission is a problem. Fortunately, we had a Chief Financial Officer, Tom Clark, who was responsible for maintaining a good relationship with the SEC and making sure we are always in complete compliance.

In addition, we always looked at the Wall Street community as providing us with a sense of discipline. You hear a lot of CEOs tell how burdensome it is to run their company on a year-to-year, quarter-to-quarter basis. We have never looked at it that way. We think the outside investor market gives us a structure and discipline and makes us focus better on our responsibilities. Quite frankly, I have never felt that being a public corporation had any negatives.

It is of interest that the market we serve is not becoming saturated even though we have many new competitors. If you add up all the companies doing payroll processing in the United States combined they have less than 14 or 15 percent of the total market. The rest of the market is either still doing their payroll manually or have some sort of in house system.

Ours remains a near virgin territory. Paychex, with 320,000 clients, still has about three percent of the total market, and about six percent of the market that we serve. Remember that many Fortune 500 companies are downsizing. People are starting small companies today who would not have considered it 10 or 15 years ago. Even though Paychex has a great track record of client growth over the last 10 years we are only growing at about the same rate that the market is growing.

I view Paychex as being a niche-based company—we concentrate on our offering and we concentrate on our target market. I think if you analyze all the great companies of the world, you will find a similar quality. We made the decision years ago, as we consolidated the franchisees and joint ventures, that we would focus on geography with current payroll products. Rather than diversifying into other services, we knew we could establish more branch offices selling the same product and make money at it. We wanted to do it in as many geographic areas as possible and build the distribution network. Then we would have a client base that we could sell additional products and services to. The ability to sell additional products to existing customers is a lot easier than selling new products to new customers but we tried to find the right time to make that move.

In recent years, we have expanded the services we offer our clients. We now offer employee handbooks, Section 125 Cafeteria Plans, 401(k) recordkeeping, as well as administration of health, workman's compensation, and disability insurances. We also offer other employee-based products even as basic as writing job descriptions and the posters that go on the company billboards regarding state labor laws.

Of course, Paychex no longer has any trouble borrowing and the banks are seeking us rather than chasing us away. With the rapid growth and good profit that we have had recently, cash flow from operations covers much of our capital needs.

Chapter 52

This Is How It Should Be Done!

Paul Orfalea and Kinko's, Inc.

This is the third detailed description of a very successful start-up company that has grown to be a very successful large company. As I write this, it has become apparent that all three examples, Mercury Print Productions, Paychex, and Kinko's, have a number of qualities in common. They exhibit many of the important qualities and have followed strategies I described earlier in the book as being crucial to the success of a new business.

1. Because they all started on a financial shoestring, in each of the three cases the founders had to struggle to raise the money needed to get the business off the ground. They used all of their personal savings, borrowed from friends and family, used credit cards, and other primative ways of raising capital.
2. In all three cases, the founders can be described as very intelligent and very imaginative entrepreneurs, but none can be described as technological or academic geniuses.
3. All three companies were based upon the intuitive judgment and imagination of the founders, not on formal market research or unique technology. They all succeeded in businesses that have few barriers to entry.
4. In all three cases the companies are in markets that have changed rapidly with the times. But the founders had the imagination and judgment to modify the strategy of their companies to match the changing times, thereby staying in the forefront of the industries in which they participate. Yet none abandoned the niche in which they had established themselves and been so successful.
5. I do not like to use the term "born entrepreneurs" but if that description ever applied to people who started their own businesses it applies to Valerie Mannix, Tom Golisano, and Paul Orfalea, founder of Kinko's, whose market is now the world.

Having set the stage, let me tell you about the third company of this group, a company which is the leader in its industry and which achieved this position through the incredibly good judgment and business skills of its founder. That company is Kinko's.

My guess is that 99 percent of the people reading this chapter have used the services of Kinko's at one time or another, but I also guess that very few have any idea of the variety of services that Kinko's offers its customers and the unique strategy they follow.

This Is How It Should Be Done!

Kinko's was founded by Paul Orfalea (pronounced Orfala) in 1970. He has kinky red curly hair and while he was in college his friends called him Kinko—which he decided to use as the name of his company.

The average person, unfamiliar with Kinko's, would describe it as a place where the customers can make copies. That is what it was back in 1970 when it first came into existence. But this does not describe Kinko's as it is today. The list on the following page, which I found displayed at the Kinko's store in Melbourne, Florida, shows most of the services offered at most of their locations. As you can see, this list includes many things in addition to making copies.

But many Kinko's stores can do other things not shown on this list. For example, they have personal computers at their facilities (both IBM and Mac) and printers which can be used by their customers. These computers include a variety of popular software programs. They also have computer stations where their customers can bring their own portable computer and connect it to a high quality printer. It is my understanding that computer services now represent approximately one third of Kinko's sales.

Most Kinko's locations are open 24 hours a day, seven days a week. The people who work at Kinko's are not known as employees but are known as co-workers. When they are hired, they receive intensive training in the use of the equipment in their stores so they can answer almost any questions their customers may have and assist them in the use of the equipment.

A new service they provide is video-conferencing, which makes it possible for their customers to communicate visually over long distances for business meetings, job interviews, and so forth. For example, a face-to-face interview is much more effective then a telephone interview. This process saves the companies large amounts of money in reduced travel expense.

Quite unusual for a company in a service business is that many branches provide free pickup and delivery, and have the capability of copying documents in reasonably large quantities and delivering them in a matter of hours, rather than days or weeks. Each store has Federal Express and U.S. Mail pickup service.

At a small number of stores in southern California, a local bank has established mini-branches for the use of its customers. And, at least one large national bank has indicated an interest in putting mini-branches in many other Kinko's locations nationwide. While the customers are waiting for their other work to be completed they can visit the bank in the store.

Many locations have telephones where their customers can make local calls at no charge, and many stores have a conference room available for the use of their customers. They sell books and other published material that may be of interest to a small business owner, as well as every imaginable kind of paper and copier supplies.

And all of the above services are provided by people who are anxious to help their customers—services that are available at surprisingly reasonable cost.

Kinko's is no longer just a place to make a few copies of a term paper or birth certificate. They serve as the sophisticated, well-equipped publications department for thousands of small businesses—departments that provide services these businesses need, but could not possibly afford with their own limited resources. Because Kinko's co-workers are so sensitive to the needs and requirements of the people who use their services, it is the opinion of many people who go into a Kinko's store that they are more like partners than suppliers.

Start Up

kinko's

2700 W. New Haven Ave. • Melbourne, Florida 32904 • TEL (407)725-7556 • FAX (407)725-7569

- Full & Self-Service Copying
- Color Copying
- Posters
- Banners
- Oversize Copies
- Oversize Digital Printing
- Binding
- Transparencies
- T-Shirt Transfers
- Booklet Making
- Laminating
- Foam Core Mounting
- In-Store Computer Rental
- Faxing
- Passport Photos
- Business Cards
- Rubber Stamps
- Resumes
- Flyer Design
- Announcements
- Custom Stationery
- Ad Specialties
- Photo Scanning
- Text Scanning
- Logo Design
- Photo Editing
- Photo Restoration
- Newsletter Design
- Brochure Design
- Labels

For more information, please see a co-worker at the front counter.

This Is How It Should Be Done!

When Kinko's came into existence in 1970, Orfalea was a student at the University of Southern California. At that time and through most of his childhood, he suffered from dyslexia. While at USC he graduated with a "C" grade point average, which, for someone suffering from dyslexia, was quite an achievement.

The idea he had for a business was to provide copier service for students. This service was available at the university library but at a cost of 10 cents a copy. Orfalea felt that this was a valuable service for the students but that the cost per copy was much too high. His belief was that he could sell copies for less than half that price and still make a profit.

He decided to open a copy business adjacent to the campus of the University of California at Santa Barbara near where he planned to live when he finished at USC. The store he rented was located in a former hamburger stand and occupied about 80 square feet. Rent was $100 per month. In addition to a copier, it also included binding equipment and sold paper and other copier supplies. Sometimes the store was so crowded that they had to wheel the copier to the sidewalk outside the store for their customers to make copies.

Orfalea's original capital to start this store was a $5,000 loan he secured from a local bank. I understand Orfalea's father co-signed the note which probably made it possible for him to get the loan.

However, it soon became very obvious that Orfalea's business acumen should not be underestimated. By 1980, Kinko's had expanded to about 80 stores, all located near college campuses and offering primarily copier services. The average size of these was about 400 square feet.

It was pretty clear by then that Orfalea's business strategy was a good one. But through this period of expansion, he needed a source of capital because the equipment in each location was fairly expensive. He decided to start each additional store as a joint venture together with local investors, with Orfalea retaining a majority interest. Each new location was independently-owned by Orfalea and his local partners but operated under the Kinko's name, providing generally similar services.

I have not been privy to the financial performance of Kinko's through this period of expansion, but my guess is that it was quite good and Orfalea had the option of continuing down the same path and having a comfortable life.

However, it was during the 1980s that the business environment in this country went through some dramatic changes. Orfalea had the business foresight to sense these changes and the effect they would have on his business. He recognized that the customers using his stores would be different, and he recognized the new business services these new customers would need and be willing to buy from an outside supplier.

The change I refer to is that many large companies began going through massive downsizing—reduction in the number of people they employed. These downsizings cut jobs by the tens of thousands. Hardly a day went by that you would not read in *The Wall Street Journal* that company "X" was planning a 10-percent staff reduction or 15,000 people, and company "Y" was planning a cutback of 10,000 people over the coming year, and so on and so forth. How did this affect Kinko's? In a number of ways.

First, many of the people who suddenly were unemployed became disillusioned with working for big companies and decided to go out on their own. They started small entrepreneurial businesses, often working from their homes, and needed many services other than simply making copies. These people required equipment that they could not afford to buy on their own. Yes, they had personal computers, fax machines, cellular telephones, and access to the Internet and e-mail, but if you look again at the list of services Kinko's now provides you will see what I mean.

Second, many of the large companies going through this downsizing eliminated some functions previously provided by internal departments. They would now outsource—meaning buying from outside suppliers.

Third, many young people entering the job market from high school or college decided the future in large companies no longer looked like heaven and perhaps they should give it a try on their own. The average age of people becoming entrepreneurs dropped significantly through this period. Obviously, most had to get their business going with very limited capital.

Finally, in many households where the wife entered the job market, they found that having their own business and working from their home gave them much more time flexibility in matching their business and family responsibilities. At the present time, it is estimated that there are about 40 million people in the United States who work from their homes.

All of these things represented opportunity for Kinko's to expand the services they provided, and what an opportunity it turned out to be. In effect, Kinko's became the reproduction department of thousands of small, one or two person businesses all over the United States and in many foreign countries.

Today Kinko's has more than 24,000 co-workers, over 950 locations in the United States, and a growing number outside of the country. Their average store size is about 7,000 square feet. While Kinko's does not make their annual sales public, some people in the media estimate it to be in the range of $1 billion. It is estimated that they make over 12 billion copies a year, more than two copies for every person in the world. Wow.

To accomplish this transition, Kinko's obviously needed a substantial increase in capital. In early 1997, the firm of Clayton, Dubilier & Rice invested $219 million in Kinko's, for about a one-third ownership in the company. At about that time, each of the semi-independent Kinko's units were consolidated into the parent company, headquartered in Ventura, California. Currently, this outside investor owns about one-third of Kinko's stock, Mr. Orfalea owns about one-third and the rest is owned by his former joint venture partners and current co-workers.

According to articles in several business publications, there is a good likelihood that Kinko's will attempt a public stock offering within the next year or so. This added capital will be used to finance expansion—especially outside the country.

Before finishing this story I would like to mention some of the other unique contributions Orfalea made during the rapid growth of Kinko's. Apparently he disliked office work intensely and spent a minimum amount of time sitting behind his desk. He spends an immense amount of time visiting Kinko's locations all over the world meeting with his co-workers and, more importantly, keeping close contact with and understanding of the needs of their customers.

He is very concerned that people who work at Kinko's consider themselves to be co-owners rather than simply employees, and that they try to do everything they possibly can to improve their service to their customers. Kinko's has an extremely generous and flexible benefit program. Their pay scale is generous and the company frequently rewards their co-workers for exceptional service.

As I wrote this chapter, I visited a number of Kinko's stores in upstate New York and Florida. The atmosphere in their stores is similar, even though the services they offer vary somewhat from store to store. The people skills, knowledge, and attitude of all co-workers is consistently very high.

Several years ago, during an acceptance speech for an award he received from USC, Orfalea quoted his wife as saying the best definition of management that she knows is, "To remove obstacles." This pretty accurately describes his management style. He is described by some people in the financial community as a "Business genius."

In mid-1997 the management of Kinko's went through a major reorganization. As he passed his 50th birthday, Orfalea left the Kinko's president/CEO position but remained chairperson of the board of directors. His job now is to spend most of his time identifying new market opportunities for Kinko's, both in the United States and overseas, and trying to determine how the company will fit into these new markets five years in the future.

They hired as his successor Joseph Hardin, Jr., who had been president and chief executive of Wal-Mart's Sam's Club during a decade of rapid growth. It seems to me that Kinko's is entering a new period of growth and that by stepping aside, Orfalea is doing exactly the right thing at exactly the right time. And, it appears that he has had no problem adjusting to this new role, which is much to his credit.

Earlier in this book, I suggest that three important qualities that an entrepreneurial company should have are the ability to differentiate, lead and do not follow competitors; concentrate, find a niche and stick to it; and try to innovate in every aspect of the business. Kinko's has done all of these with exceptional skill.

Chapter 53

25 Entrepreneurial Death Traps: Avoid the Classic Entrepreneurial Mistakes

This chapter was written by Frederick J. Beste, CEO of the General Partners of the Midatlantic Venture Fund based in Bethlehem, Pennsylvania, with a branch in northern Virginia. They specialize in seed and start up stage venture capital investing. Beste has seen many successes and many failures among start up companies. These death traps are the things he considers the most important common mistakes made by entrepreneurs. Previously he was CEO of Kentucky Highlands Investment Corp., a venture development firm in London, Kentucky, and vice president of Greater Washington Investors, Inc., a venture capital firm in Washington, D.C. He has been a venture capitalist since 1968.

Entrepreneurs face all kinds of potential adversity—some can kill them, some merely set them back a little. The saddest failures I have seen are those that should have been so predictable that they should have been avoided. As senseless as some of these death traps seem, they can be very difficult to avoid. Some of them appear in the form of well-worn paths which logic, greed, and even common sense might suggest taking. How tragic it is that some take entrepreneurs over the cliff time and time again.

Even though none of these traps are certain to be fatal, they have been for many new companies. Each should be avoided or tempered if possible. In my opinion, the following are the most serious hazards faced by new and small businesses (not necessarily in any order of importance whatsoever):

1. Overreliance on one or two customers

Getting a telephone call from a very large customer telling you that they are planning to bring the work you have been doing back in-house can be a devastating experience. Suddenly you find yourself running a $1 million business that has a $3 million break even. I strongly recommend that you do everything possible to build up other parts of your business to reduce your dependence on a single large customer.

2. Three (Four?) (Five?) musketeers

Three friends start a business. They split the ownership absolutely equally, they draw identical salaries, and they plan to make decisions by "consensus." One, perhaps the oldest, reluctantly becomes president.

This arrangement has three drawbacks. First, the company has no leader, no one with ultimate responsibility for its success or failure. Second, sooner or later there is sure to be an honest disagreement among the principals with no one to resolve the impasse. And third, the president will almost inevitably see himself or herself as "a little more than equal." The others will resent it.

The solution? Pick a leader from the start and treat that person as the leader. He or she should have the largest equity position and the largest salary. Somebody has to sit where the buck stops.

3. 50-50 partnerships

This is similar to the "Three Musketeers" with all the same problems plus one—a stalemate of power. It implies distrust. These marriages almost always turn sour or end in divorce.

4. "Mousetrap" teams

A handful of brilliant engineers spend six months in the basement designing an absolutely amazing prototype that should set the world on fire. They have created a "better mousetrap," however the world does not beat a path to their door. No one on the team has ever commercialized a technology. Doing it is as hard or harder than creating the product. It is imperative that at least one member of the team has been down this road before.

5. Underpricing

A startup which adopts a lowest price market strategy is roughly analogous to Lichtenstein insisting on settling a dispute with the United States with ICBMs. I would add that the statement that causes me to want to lose my last meal fastest is this: "We're going to have the best product at the lowest price."

6. Insufficient start-up capital

Even though detailed cash flow projections have been made, the reality is that sales and margins do not meet expectations in 90-plus percent of new businesses for many different reasons. If each founder initially chipped in the limit of his or her resources, it may already be time for the fat lady to sing. Do not start a business if you can't come up with more capital than you think you might need.

7. Failure to consider the downside

Three critical factors drive the cash needs of a business—product development time, sales, and gross margins. Most entrepreneurs are too optimistic on all three. Look at the downside in advance. Developing fallback plans is the only effective medicine for failed initial assumptions.

8. Failure to look at industry norms

Most entrepreneurs who fail blame "undercapitalization" as the culprit. Once again, overoptimism is the real villain. Do not project margins of 30 percent in an industry where 10 percent is considered as doing well.

9. Lack of focus

A new venture's most precious resource is talent. Doing one thing well from scratch is an enormous challenge. Tackling three or four is inviting disaster. Sort out the opportunities before you start to determine the best market and product opportunity. Pursue the daylights out of the best.

10. Bringing on the vulture

The bad news is that while all money is green, it is not all equal. There really are vulture capitalists out there and they do not all work for venture capital firms. They are obstructive, controlling, heavy-handed, and mistrustful. The good news is that there are also investors out there who are gems—experienced, constructive, supportive—and they all don't work for venture capital firms.

How can you tell a jerk from a gem, before the fact? Do two things. First, ask around among the service providers—the lawyers, the accountants, the bankers. They know who the good guys are and who the bad guys are. Second, ask for a comprehensive list of phone numbers of CEOs of companies the firm or individual has backed, after which call them and grill them mercilessly as to what kind of partner the investor has been.

11. First class from the start

Show me a start-up in fancy quarters with elegant furniture and management salaries matching their last position and I will show you a prescription for failure. Most of the successful entrepreneurs I have seen have an uncanny ability to spend a nickel in six places.

12. Diversification into the unknown

There are many reasons why this is done: an initial failure in one field, "the grass is greener" syndrome, whatever. If you do not know the marketplace—not the technology, the *marketplace*—and the competition, you are asking for trouble.

13. Emotional litigation

I am virtually allergic to litigation for small businesses. Justice is all too often not achieved. Lawsuits are expensive, outrageously distracting, emotionally stressful, and often end up with all parties ultimately agreeing to drop the action. There are some circumstances where such action is needed, but most of the time, entrepreneurs should bite their tongues and get on with the business. Talk to your peers who have been down this road—horror stories are in abundance.

14. Product never ready for market

Many engineers simply will not show their baby to the world until they achieve perfection. This is an unattainable goal. When you have your product to the point that it represents a clearly superior choice, freeze the design and hand it over to the sales force.

15. Low barrier to entry growth industry

Video retailing, oversized chocolate chip cookies, and quick change oil franchises burst unto the scene virtually overnight. In many of these, there is has been a tremendous shakeout of the Johnny-come-slightly-latelies. If industry visibility is high and the barriers to entry low, the growth rate of supply will, in all probably, exceed the growth rate of demand all too quickly.

16. Inadequate market research

A book could be written on this phenomenon alone. Suffice it to say that failure of the entrepreneur to get out there and research the marketplace and talk to at least a dozen prime potential customers before committing to a product is asking for trouble.

17. Failure to segment the market

The U.S. tent market is $100 million. Your product is a high-end backpacking tent and you hope to sell $5 million annually in five years. All you need is five percent of the market—right? No sweat, a piece of cake.

Wrong! Circus, funeral, and special events tents take 20 percent of the market, the military represents 20 percent, and backyard family tents are 20 percent. And the two largest backpack retailers controlling 20 percent of the market own captive suppliers. That leaves 10 percent as your opportunity...so you really need 50 percent to achieve your goal.

18. No reason for the customer to change

The best entrepreneurial efforts I have seen have flowed from the development of a competitive matrix, such as a comparison by vendor (competitors) of all factors influencing the purchase decision. If you cannot find good reason for potential customers to switch to your product, they probably won't.

19. Payback can't be calculated

If you intend to sell your product based upon saving your customers money, make sure the savings are easily calculable. A claim that you save on scrap is easy to demonstrate, a claim that your product will cut down on back injuries is not. The latter is a much tougher sale than the former.

20. Failure to admit a mistake

Psychologically, one of the most insidious death traps is the one entitled "We have too much invested in this to walk away now." Do not hesitate to admit a mistake. The right question to ask is "Would we invest in this, knowing what we know now, if it were presented as a new opportunity?"

21. Step function growth

Every once in a while, a venture grows by leaps and bounds. When such a happy event occurs, be sure you don't succeed yourself into bankruptcy. Some pitfalls include failure to check credit, poor quality control, hiring unqualified people and bad customer service. Keep a careful eye on the business and adjust to your success accordingly.

22. Betting the ranch

Contrary to legend, entrepreneurs are not high-rollers. They are not afraid to take moderate risk that is largely under their control, but they would never bet the ranch, whether on an acquisition, a new product, or anything else. They will not risk all that they have, even on a "sure thing."

23. Ignoring the handwriting on the wall

Holding on to old ways, continuing to rely on original, bedrock assumptions in the face of mounting evidence to the contrary, can take even a healthy company down in an amazingly short time.

Several years ago, the stuffed toy industry began to shift to offshore production to reap the benefits of lower wage rates. One domestic manufacturer reacted to an eroding market share by cheapening its line and offering lower quality. Obviously, this did not work. The firm ultimately abandoned stuffed toys entirely and redirected its efforts into other businesses.

24. Spiraling costs

As you expand from your garage into an industrial park, hire a chief financial officer, or install a new computer system, your break even point will creep—maybe even gallop—up and up. Before you increase expenses by these kinds of moves, plan carefully and develop fallback positions before going ahead.

25. Silliness phase

This does not need to be a company jet; lesser gluttonies can have the same effect. "If they can have a leased car, why can't I?," "Maybe I have earned a country club membership," and other such extravagances can inflict major damage to work force morale, and divert management energy, sharpness, and desire.

As you build your business, keep this list in mind. It may sound strange, but you cannot succeed if you do not avoid failure. Entrepreneurial human nature is to just be on the offensive; but even in building a business defense is critically important. Avoid making these classic mistakes and you can be sure that you have substantially increased your chances of winning the game.

Chapter 54

The Personal Computer and the Entrepreneur

Without question, the introduction of the personal computer over 20 years ago caused a revolution in entrepreneurial activity. A number of today's finest companies started because of the popularity of the PC. Who would ever have predicted companies like Microsoft, Compaq Computer, Dell Computer, Amazon.com, Intel, and hundreds of others coming into existence and thriving over such a short period of time?

This chapter is about the PC—not about starting a business based upon some hardware or software concept, but the idea of using the PC as a tool to help you in the management of your business.

Anyone starting or managing a new business would be well advised to become skilled in the use of a personal computer. You do not have to be a programmer or hardware expert, but by learning and using some inexpensive, readily available, off-the-shelf programs you can save many, many hours in the operation of your business and probably do a better job as well. The following discussion covers both software and hardware questions as well as several recent new capabilities.

Software

Described below are a number of software applications that will almost surely make your job easier. I mention, as examples, several popular programs that you might consider in these applications. Even though most of these programs are good, this chapter is not intended to be a quality rating of PC software.

I believe it is more important to use programs with which you are familiar than more modern programs, loaded with features you are unlikely to ever need. Several of the more important programs I use have been around for five or six years. I am completely familiar with their operation and can almost run them with my eyes closed. I believe this is much more desirable than changing to more modern programs that are much more complex and must be learned over from scratch—especially when many of the new features in these are features that I neither need nor are apt to use.

A second issue is the subject of upgrades. Selling upgrades is an important source of revenue for software companies. They come out almost once a year and the temptation to upgrade is frequently very persuasive. My policy is to buy the first one or two upgrades. In addition to offering new features, they often correct errors and bugs inherent in the original version. After that, I usually no longer purchase the upgrades because they are frequently more complex, have features I will not use and often take much more memory.

Spreadsheets

Programs such as Excel, QuattroPro, or Lotus 1-2-3 can be of immense value in doing financial projections, cash management, scheduling, and other similar tasks. A spreadsheet helps you organize your thoughts in a sensible way and performs arithmetic and mathematical calculations automatically as you change the data in the model.

Word processors

These programs let you compose and print letters, reports, memos, and so forth. They check spelling and grammar and let you modify and change sections without retyping the entire document. In the United States, it is very difficult to buy a manual typewriter.

The high-end word processors include Microsoft Word and WordPerfect. They are both extremely versatile. If you do not need the power of these programs there are others with somewhat less capability but that are less expensive and easier to learn and use. I mostly use an old version of a program that completely meets my needs. You can get advice from a computer-skilled friend or a local dealer on which will be best for you.

Databases

I used a database to maintain lists of thousands of potential and actual buyers of the first edition of this book, which I published myself. It helped me do many focused mailings based on these lists. The names and addresses were mostly obtained from the membership directories of various professional associations. Many of these people included the teachers of courses in entrepreneurship at over 500 colleges and universities, several hundred business incubators, about 800 Small Business Development Centers in all 50 states, and so forth. These were very productive mailings.

When you buy your word processor and database programs, be sure they include a capability known as "mailmerge." This is a system for writing a single letter and sending it to all of the names you select from your database. The final document will have the recipient's name and address printed on the top of the sheet, which makes the letter appear personally typed. There are a number of excellent, high quality database programs available that include mailmerge.

Checkbook management

For many years I have used a checkbook program named Quicken from Intuit. It keeps a list of the names and addresses of frequent payees and maintains records of everyone to whom you send a check, sorted into categories that you define. It greatly simplifies the tedious chore of writing checks and balancing your account. It is also a big help in doing year-end tax summaries. There are several other checkbook programs that I hear are also quite good.

Financial accounting

I have not personally used any of these programs, but I am told that several low-end, inexpensive accounting programs can be of great value to the small business owner. Your accountant may be able to advise you on which program is best for your particular situation.

Telephone/address lists

This is the program you will probably use more than any other. It keeps a file of names, addresses, and telephone numbers similar to a Rolodex. It will also automatically dial numbers if you use a modem. Some of these also provide a calendar and have the capability to organize your daily appointment schedule and keep track of "to-do" lists.

Desktop publishing

This is somewhat similar to a word processor but is designed specifically for the preparation of brochures, catalogs, promotional material, and other printed products. Most have the capability to print in color. There are a few available that cost about $100 that do a very good job. Using such a program can substantially reduce your publication costs.

Presentation programs

If you do many presentations in the course of managing your business, you might consider a presentation program. This can be used to develop overheads and slides which combine words with icons and graphics. I use one of these frequently to prepare overheads. However, I urge caution when you use a presentation program so that the graphics and icons are not so elaborate that they detract from the message.

Utility programs

If you use a PC very much you will soon find the need for a utility program to use in managing files, making backups, searching for viruses, cleaning up your hard drive, and other tasks. There are a number of excellent programs available. However, be sure the utility program you choose is compatible with the operating system you use.

Information services

If you need information about almost any imaginable subject you might want to subscribe to a service such as America Online (AOL). In the past few years, AOL has become the leading online information service and I understand they now have many million subscribers.

These information services can help you with information searches, e-mail, airline schedules, stock quotes, weather forecasts, and countless other tasks. The cost is only a few dollars a month and the value can be great.

Some have a service called forums which are groups of people interested in a particular specialized subject. I use a number of these, including Entrepreneurs Forum (for my business) and Photoforum (for my hobby). I have sold a fair number of books through contacts made on these services. A woman I know who started a successful business plan writing business gets many of her clients through these forums.

Integrated software

There are also programs available that combine a number of the above functions (such as Microsoft Works). Some include a word processor, data base, spreadsheet, and communications capability...in a single package. These might be applicable in your situation, cost less, and have the benefit of a common feel. For a beginner, the advantage of using integrated programs is that they should shorten the learning process and assure compatibility between functions.

Focused software

Depending on the business you are in, there may be programs available that are designed for your specific situation that will be directly applicable. I know of programs for retail stores, automobile service stations, restaurants, dry cleaning businesses, doctors, dentists, lawyers, consultants, and many others. These may be worth looking into.

Other

As your company grows you should consider using a computer for things such as production control, inventory management, employee records, and so forth. I am not personally acquainted with these, so I cannot offer much advice. However, one place to look is in the publications of the professional societies related to the subject of interest.

Hardware

The following are some suggestions about hardware:

Desktop PCs

Here you have almost an infinite number of choices—personal computers are now almost a commodity. I use IBM clones at my office and at home that have Intel Pentium III microprocessors and large hard drives.

So far, these have served me well. But with software programs becoming more complex and more demanding of memory, I am beginning to feel the need for more powerful machines. If you are planning to purchase a new computer, it is almost surely appropriate to go upscale. Prices are now low enough that a machine with greater capability may be well worth the investment. As I write this, it is now possible to purchase powerful personal computers with about all of the features a new business might need at prices under $1,000.

Apple now has a line of new computers that provide capabilities superior to the IBM PCs, and most of the programs mentioned above, or their equivalent, are also available in versions that work on Apple Computers.

Another fairly recent addition to the list of PC capabilities that is now almost a standard feature is the CD-ROM. Many CD-ROMs are now available to help in any task an entrepreneur faces. CD-ROMs usually have sound capability but to date I have not found any particular need for this feature.

Several CD-ROM programs that I use regularly are an encyclopedia and two programs that sell for under $20 each. These list 100 million individual telephone numbers and 10 million business telephone numbers. Sometimes a name is missing or a telephone number has changed, but over 90 percent of the time what I am looking for is there. It is much faster and less expensive than using an information operator.

Other examples of the impact of CD-ROMs are in accounting, law, and any other activity that requires frequent updating of complex rules and regulations. My daughter, a CPA, specializes in taxes for small businesses and individuals. Up until a few years ago, she had to have about 20 volumes of tax regulations. They were updated monthly with supplements of about 100 pages that had to be inserted into the correct volume.

Now she has all of this information on four CD-ROMs, one updated annually, two quarterly, and one monthly. In addition to the space savings in her office she has much, much better search capability and saves a lot of time. The cost is about the same as the printed volumes.

Laptop PCs

These have capabilities generally similar to a desktop machine with very few limitations, that they weigh only a few pounds, operate from batteries, and are small enough to be easily carried on business trips or back-and-forth between office and home.

When equipped with a modem, messages and files can usually be sent from a hotel room, your car, or over a cellular telephone back to your office, and sometimes from your office to your hotel room or car. I have used laptop machines extensively on airplanes during business trips. Be sure the machine you buy has a floppy disk drive and, if possible, CD-ROM capability as well.

Printers

By all means, use a laser or ink jet printer. They provide high-quality output that looks almost as if it were typed on an IBM executive typewriter with proportional spacing. The cost of good printers of this type now starts at a few hundred dollars. They can print graphics and give you a choice of fonts and type sizes, as well as other features. Typically they print at four pages and more a minute—faster than the world's fastest typist. For professional looking printed documents, one of these printers is a must. For special applications many of them also have color capability.

These printers can usually print names and addresses on envelopes and can be used with the mailmerge programs described earlier to give your mass mailings a personalized look.

Scanners

With a scanner, you can feed in a printed document and convert it to a computer file without the need for retyping. Obviously, this can be a valuable feature. Recently, I read that at least two major computer manufacturers are offering a scanner as an integral part of the keyboard. I have used scanners from time to time but would undoubtedly use one more frequently if it were right in front of me as part of the machine.

Special applications

The Internet and e-mail

These are computer resources that have become incredibly popular in a very short period of time. They are described in detail in an earlier chapter.

Networks

As the PC use in your company increases, you are almost sure, at some point, to consider using a network of some sort. By using a network system that ties PCs together, people in your organization can share data and communicate with each other. I have not used networks and am not familiar with the details of their use. Here I recommend you consult a computer professional to get expert advice and counsel.

Other things you decide to do with your PC will depend on your specific needs and skills. However, using a computer for many day-to-day applications can save the new business much time and money—and probably do the jobs better as well.

As I wrote this chapter, it occurred to me that by the time you read it, the information will almost surely be at least partly out of date. I have purchased new PCs on about eight different occasions over the years and in each case six months or so later I concluded that perhaps I should have waited. There was either a drastic drop in prices, an increase in features, or both, that I would have liked to have had. Nothing you can do will change this. I recommend you get the machine that best meets your needs at the time and accept the fact that a few years from now you may want to upgrade to a more powerful machine.

Chapter 55

In Search of Excellence and the New Venture

In 1982, a book titled *In Search of Excellence* (by Thomas J. Peters and Robert H. Waterman, Jr., published by Harper & Row) hit the bookstores. Since then, more than 5 million copies have been sold, making it one of the best selling books ever published on the subject of management.

In examining more than 300 U.S. companies—mostly large firms—Peters and Waterman identified eight qualities, which they call "findings," that seem to be present in the excellent companies. The eight attributes that seem to characterize most excellent large companies are these:

1. A bias for action.
2. Close to the customer.
3. Autonomy and entrepreneurship.
4. Productivity through people.
5. Hands-on, value-driven management.
6. Sticking to the knitting.
7. Simple form, lean staff.
8. Simultaneous loose-tight properties. The excellent companies are both centralized and decentralized.

However, I look at this differently. I suggest that these eight qualities also accurately describe the situation that exists in most successful entrepreneurial start up companies. If you carefully examine successful new ventures and try to identify the qualities that most contribute to their success, I believe you could end up with an almost identical list.

I urge the readers of this book, who are individuals thinking about starting a new business or who have recently started a new business, to race to your local bookstore and buy a copy of *In Search of Excellence*. Read it carefully from cover to cover. If you already own the book, read it again.

But do not read it from the viewpoint of the manager of a large company who wishes to do things to improve the performance of his organization compared to other large companies. Read it from the viewpoint of an entrepreneur whose organization may already have most of these eight qualities. Try to think of things that you can do to consciously incorporate these eight principles as key parts of your basic business strategy. Try to think of things you can do to avoid losing them as your company grows.

Epilogue

In writing this book, I have tried to include as much of my personal knowledge and experience as possible to help those among the readers who are really interested in becoming entrepreneurs and having a business of their own. The information here is generally of a very practical nature and includes example after example to illustrate the points I am trying to make.

My goal was to identify and discuss the key issues that will help improve the chances of your business being a success. Some things I did not include I considered as being too elementary and obvious. If I guessed wrong, refer to other sources to get more information.

This fifth edition includes two new sample business plans, several new chapters on subjects that have become more important since the fourth edition was written, and the updating of all chapters and the expansion of many.

It also includes a number of chapters written by others. I did this for two reasons. First, some of the new material covers issues on which I do not have too much personal experience. The people who contributed are all more expert than I and their comments more valuable. The second reason is to present the other side of certain issues where I have a strong bias that is sometimes in conflict with conventional wisdom. This, I believe, makes *Start Up* a better book.

Remember that there are very few right or wrong answers to the problems of starting a business. The best you can hope for are answers that work, and you will never know whether another approach would have had a better result.

Hard work and persistence are important qualities in almost every successful entrepreneur I know. Somehow or other they find ways to meet and overcome adversity. No one in their right mind will suggest that starting a business is easy. It's not easy—it's hard. But it can be the most exciting business experience of a lifetime and, when and if you succeed, it can have rewards beyond belief. These rewards can be professional, emotional, and financial. Also, being an entrepreneur gives you infinitely more freedom to control your own life and your own destiny.

If you found this book helpful, please tell your entrepreneurial friends to read a copy if you think it will be of value to them.

In closing, I wish all of you who start a business of your own the best possible success. I hope this book has helped. Please contact me if you have suggestions to make future editions more valuable. I can be reached by e-mail at wjs896@aol.com or through the publisher. Good luck to all of you.

Appendix 1

Sample Business Plan: LawTech, L.L.C.

The following business plan was developed as a course project in the M.B.A. class in Entrepreneurship and New Venture Formation, taught by Dr. Charles Hofer, Regent's Professor of Strategy and Entrepreneurship, Terry College of Business, at the University of Georgia.

This is a very well-written and well-organized business plan for a unique service business. LawTech is a company already in existence and as a result, the company requested that forecasts of future sales and earnings be included only by reference, but not in detail.

The plan was prepared by:
Robert J. Motyka
Amanda J. Pullen
Cavit Yantac
Ricky Ryssel

For further information please contact:
Dr. Charles Hofer
University of Georgia
Terry College of Business
Brooks Hall
Athens, GA 30602
706-542-3724

Copyright © 1999 by Robert J. Motyka and printed by permission.
Please note that there may be omissions in the plan due to space limitations

LawTech LLC

Optimizing Legal Productivity

Robert J. Motyka, Esq.
195 Highland Avenue
Athens, GA 30606
706-546-1411

March 31, 1999

Key Milestones

Activity	Date
LawTech, L.L.C. founded	July 1998
First sale	July 1998
$25,000 in sales	August 1998
Athens office started	August 1998
Contract for project management consulting	August 1998
Added Worldox® to Product Line	September 1998
Savannah office opened	October 1998
Sales topped $100,000	October 1998
1998 sales: $170,000	December 1998
1998 profits: $20,000	December 1998
Sales reach: $250,000	March 1999

Table of Contents

Executive Summary
Company Overview
Legal Productivity: A Venture Opportunity
Market Analysis
Competition
Marketing & Sales
Operations
Management and Key Advisors
Financials
Future Growth

Start Up

Executive summary

Venture concept

LawTech is a new venture, which specializes in information technology consulting for legal offices. LawTech's services include evaluation and selection of appropriate software packages, system design, training, transition management, and follow-on support. LawTech's product lines include software systems and products created or customized to increase productivity in legal offices. LawTech makes law firms more profitable by increasing their productivity and reducing workflow inefficiencies. LawTech's primary market is midsize law firms of ten to sixty attorneys with other law firms forming secondary markets.

Legal productivity: a venture opportunity

A variety of newly emerging market pressures are forcing law firms to significantly improve their productivity in the practice of law, including significant forces from corporate clients to reduce the funds spent on legal activities, increasing competition among law firms for clients, and escalating personal costs. A variety of software products, as well as more effective office procedures, are available to help address these productivity pressures. Unfortunately, most midsized law firms lack the expertise and other skills needed to use these solutions effectively. LawTech's mission is to help midsized law firms address these problems.

Goals and strategies

LawTech's long-term objective is to be the leading provider of legal technology solutions to midsize law firms nationwide. During the first full year of operations, LawTech will primarily target the Atlanta, Georgia, and Savannah, Georgia metropolitan areas. During year two, LawTech will expand into other areas of Georgia. During years three and four, LawTech will begin expansion into the remaining Southeastern states. Extension outside the Southeast will begin in year five. Throughout this process of geographical expansion, LawTech will continue to expand its product line and consulting services to meet the needs of law firms.

Customer benefits and competitive advantages

LawTech provides its clients with two major benefits:

▶ Superior Knowledge of Legal Productivity Software and Systems: LawTech's personnel have spent over 2,000 hours evaluating over 45 different legal software packages tailored to the needs of law firms. LawTech not only knows which products are best for different types of law firms, it also knows which products work together and which do not.

▶ Efficient Systems Design and Installation: Because of its detailed knowledge of both the legal process and legal productivity software, LawTech can evaluate, select, and install new systems to enhance its clients' productivity rapidly and less expensively than the clients could do on their own.

Management team

All four members of the managerial team have experience with technology and the legal community. Robert Motyka, Esq., and W. Lamar Fields, Esq., have a combined 24+ years experience practicing law in Georgia. Charles Fowler has 16 years experience in technology implementation, most of which includes experience specializing in the legal field. Amanda Pullen has experience working with management in a midsized law firm and also has significant marketing research experience.

Financial information

The founders have provided all of the capital needed for LawTech's startup. Initial expansion throughout Georgia and the Southeast will be self-financed. During its first six months, LawTech generated $170,000 in sales, with profits of $20,000. By 2002, LawTech expects sales and net income to increase considerably as shown in Table 1:

(Table 1, not included here, shows the estimated Revenues, Cost of Services and Goods Sold, Gross Margins, Operating Expense, and Net Income for the period of 1998 through 2003.)

Company overview

Services and products

LawTech specializes in technology consulting services for law offices. At the start of the 21st Century, competition and customer pressures are forcing law offices to improve their processes and increase their efficiency. The use of information technology is one of the most effective ways to accomplish this goal. But most lawyers have not been well-trained in the use of such technology, and law firms often do not have internal management information systems (MIS) staff needed to effectively integrate such technology into the firms' legal practices. Moreover, while MIS consultants are increasing in number, few such individuals or firms have the skills needed to venture into the legal consulting and software services field.

LawTech is the exception to this rule. In fact, LawTech's only business is the provision of information technology consulting services to lawyers and law firms.

LawTech's product line is dynamic. Only the latest and best software products are featured. LawTech continuously seeks to improve the product mix by evaluating new legal technology products as they enter the market. The software systems that prove superior to the competition are added to our product line. Current products offered by LawTech provide law firms with the ability to manage time and documents effectively, and to improve efficiency.

Goals

LawTech's primary goal is to be the leading provider of cutting edge solutions designed to enhance the efficiency and productivity of today's modern legal offices, first in the Southeast market, and then nationwide. In addition to geographical expansion, LawTech will always strive to lead the legal technology industry by keeping current on the latest developments in technology and by providing its clients with the best services and software packages available in the market.

LawTech plans to expand by opening offices in all the major legal markets in the Southeast over the first five years of operations. After the regional expansion, LawTech will seek opportunities to expand its services and product line to the national market.

LawTech's business strategies are summarized in ***Exhibit 1***.

Exhibit 1: LawTech's Business Strategy

	Strategy Elements	1999	2000	2001	2002	2003+
SCOPE	Geographic	State of Georgia	Georgia, Alabama, Florida, South Carolina	Entire Southeastern US	Entire Southeastern US	Entire United States
	Products & Services	Expand Consulting & Software	Expand Consulting & Software	Expand Consulting & Software	Expand Consulting & Software	Expand Consulting & Software
	Customers	Mid-sized Law Firms	Mid-sized Law Firms	Mid-sized and Small Law Firms	Mid-sized, Small and Large Law Firms	Mid-sized, Small and Large Law Firms
BENEFITS AND SKILLS	Value Chain	Template and Forms Development	Template and Forms Development	Template and Forms Development	Some Program Integration	Some Program Integration
	Customer Benefits Offered	Software Program Evaluation	Software Program Evaluation	Software Program Evaluation	Software Program Evaluation	Software Program Evaluation
	Customer Benefits Offered	Software Training	Software Training	Software Training	Software Training	Software Training
	Customer Benefits Offered	Office Productivity Consulting	Office Productivity Consulting	Office Productivity Consulting	APICs Certification	APICs Certification

Legal productivity: a venture opportunity

New market conditions in the legal industry are forcing law firms to adopt more efficient practices. Most law firms, however, need assistance to run their offices efficiently while continuing to serve their clients. Technology solutions that are specifically tailored to the needs of law firms are a large part of the help required. Lawyers generally do not have the time to devote to research the software solutions available to their firms. LawTech offers both the technology consulting and an extensive line of legal software needed by law firms. In essence, LawTech is a "one stop shop" for the legal technology needs of the modern law firm.

Market forces facing law firms today

Pressures Limiting What Lawyers Can Charge —Beyond the traditional reliance on hourly fees, new attitudes about legal services and billing are beginning to invade the market. In his May 1995 article "Legal Technology Planning," Andrew Z. Adkins comments, **"...practicing law these days requires more efficiency than several years ago—clients are keeping a closer watch on their dollars."** In fact, specialized legal auditors have emerged specifically to audit the hours and billing practices of attorneys to ensure that clients are not "overcharged." These auditors have total power by contract to reduce or completely eliminate any legal fee the auditors believe to be excessive. As this environment evolves, **many industry experts predict that legal offices will increasingly switch to *value added billing*, or charge for a particular service based on the worth to the client rather than billable hours.** Whether a firm uses the conventional billing method or the fixed-fee policy, a firm's profitability is directly tied to the productivity and efficiency of each employee in an industry infamous for late hours and working weekends.

Focus on Efficiency —Because of this time-intensive environment, today's law firms need to continually search for ways to improve the overall productivity of personnel, systems, and processes. To remain competitive, many firms that relied only on typewriters and photocopiers 15 years ago have established technology committees and entire MIS departments. A list of common law office productivity problems is provided in *Exhibit 2*. An entire industry has emerged to provide tools for improving legal productivity; among these tools are legal software packages that enhance a variety of tasks from accounting and billing to case management. One natural problem, however, is that managing partners and office managers are often unable to devote the necessary—yet *unbillable*—time to pursue the technology and process development that would save time and money for the entire firm. *Exhibit 3* shows the significant amount of time and lost revenue a law firm incurs trying to select and install a new software package. *Exhibit 4* demonstrates the cost and billing pressures on law firms today.

Law firms rely heavily on multiple vendors for technical assistance. These firms are often forced to weigh the consequences between making an uninformed decision, and devoting unbillable time to research and lengthy vendor presentations. Rather than making this unappealing choice, law firms are willing to pay a premium for service representatives on whom they may rely for accurate and timely information, advice, and support.

Exhibit 2: Law Office Productivity Problems

- Turnaround on dictation is typically two days and every attorney wants his/her work expedited. Amendments, changes, and corrections are easier to make when the document is fresh in the attorney's mind. Faster dictation is needed.

- In the race to get work done, some tasks slip by unnoticed until too late. When multiple attorneys are working on the same project, it is difficult to keep track of who is doing what when.

- Law offices with large or shared staff often have personnel that are overburdened, while others have time to devote to an urgent project. Attorneys rarely have the time to devote to figure out what staff is and is not available to help.

- Most word processing programs are not designed specifically for law office use. Many law offices use word processing programs that do not have any of the time-saving functions useful to law firms.

- Many documents produced in a law firm are repetitive of old documents already in the computer database. The use of these documents to help draft new documents would save an enormous amount of time. The old documents, however, are difficult and sometimes impossible to find.

- Even relatively small cases produce thousands of pages of pleadings, depositions, research, and discovery documents. Multiply this by the dozens of cases each lawyer has active, and it becomes impossible to remember what documents contain what information and where the document is located.

- Time sheet preparation is a regular responsibility of everyone in a law firm. However, clients now require particular tasks to a certain description, limit the number of billable hours for tasks, and restrict the personnel who can do particular tasks. The rules are not uniform. Many attorneys lose large amounts of billable hours for their failure to follow the rules of a particular client.

- Most attorneys are not up-to-date on the latest technology for law firms. They also do not know the types of products available, and which products are the best for their law office. It would take hundreds of hours of research for a law firm to gather the information it needs to make an informed decision about what technology to purchase.

- Once a software purchase is made, no one in the office is capable of training the rest on how to use the technology. Indeed, no one is even capable of figuring out how to configure the software and change the hardware to fit the needs of the office. Further, office-wide technology changes require change management and technology project management skills that lawyers rarely possess.

Exhibit 3: The Costs to a Law Firm to Use an Internal Technology Committee of Four People to Evaluate Legal Software for a Specific Application

TASK	HOURS
• Research to find the software options available	10-15
• Research the software found to determine which packages to evaluate	10-20
• Obtain demonstration software for the selected packages	1
• Review the demonstration packages	6-20
• Discuss the results of the review of the demonstration packages	4-8
• Select three or four software packages for evaluation	2-4
• Evaluate the selected software	60-160
• Discuss results of evaluations	2-8
• Decide upon a preferred product	2-4

AVERAGE ~**175**

Personnel involved on a typical Technology Committee:
- Senior Associate   *billable at $200/hr*
- Paralegal   *billable at $75/hr*
- Secretary   *billable at $35/hr*
- Office Manager   *paid salary of $20/hr*

- *COST SO FAR   ~$14,000*

Still to be done:
- Obtain partners' approval
- Purchase of the software
- Compatibility testing on all of the law firm's systems
- Installation of the software
- Proper configuration of all the law firm's systems
- Training of the staff
- Training a staff member to perform technical support

Exhibit 4: Cost Pressures Facing Firms Today

Strong Downward Pressures on Billing Fees

- Billing Auditors
- Client Demands For Reasonable Bills
- Increased Competition (Specialized law firms)
- Movement to Value-Added Billing

Today's Law Firms

- Higher Salaries for Law School Graduates
- Increasing Complexity of Cases
- More Crowded Court Dockets

Strong Upward Pressures on Costs

LawTech's products

Law firms today, like most businesses, are turning increasingly to technology solutions to serve their clients more efficiently. Among these solutions are numerous software packages designed specifically for the legal environment. Some products are standard packages that have been customized to meet the specific needs of attorneys (for example, word processing programs that have legal vocabulary added), while others have been designed for the legal field from the ground up (such as a case management software package). A list of some of LawTech's technology solutions to today's law office productivity problems is shown in *Exhibit 5*. LawTech offers only the best products by keeping current on all these technologies, and the best way to make them work within law firms.

LawTech's services

LawTech offers all the assistance needed by law firms to implement a technology change. LawTech provides lawyers and law offices with a variety of services, from software evaluations and recommendations to change management. LawTech has already invested over 2,000 hours of testing and evaluating many of the software packages available on the market that are relevant to the legal industry. This intellectual capital includes not only basic information about the capabilities of each program, but also more obscure information, such as compatibility difficulties and other logistic matters that are often not readily revealed by the software manufacturers or vendors. This provides LawTech's clients with a time-saving advantage as LawTech provides process consulting and makes technology recommendations based on the specific needs of the law firm. LawTech also installs the software, configures and installs hardware, integrates the system, trains all personnel on the new technology, and helps the law firm to adapt to the change in technology. This service is key because it allows LawTech's clients to make most of the new technology and see the benefits of increased productivity and efficiency in that crucial place, the bottom line.

If LawTech does not have the expertise or current resources to handle a particular need, it finds a subcontractor to provide a solution, thereby continuing to provide the client with a consistent and reliable technology representative. Together, these services make LawTech the complete legal technology provider.

Market analysis

The legal field

The legal industry in the United States is as old as the country itself, and continues to grow steadily in the information age. According to the Georgia Bar Association Membership Department, there are 29,223 active members in Georgia, 11,020 of which practice in the Atlanta area.

The legal field is by nature time-driven. Revenues are traditionally based on hourly fees charged to the clients; the majority of costs are attributed to hourly rates for attorneys, legal assistants, and secretaries. Additionally, the salaries and performance rewards for individual attorneys within a firm are often at least partially based on the ratio of billable to non-billable hours per week.

Exhibit 5: LawTech's Software Product-Line

Need	Software	Supplier
Time Management	Time Matters® Amicus Attorney®	DATA.TXT Corporation Gavel & Gown Software, Inc.
Calendaring	Time Matters® Amicus Attorney	DATA.TXT Corporation Gavel & Gown Software, Inc.
Case Management	Time Matters® Amicus Attorney® Summation Blaze®	DATA.TXT Corporation Gavel & Gown Software, Inc. Summation Legal Technologies, Inc.
Client Management	Time Matters® Amicus Attorney®	DATA.TXT Corporation Gavel & Gown Software, Inc.
Document Management	Worldox 8® Amicus Attorney® Time Matters®	World Software Corporation Gavel & Gown Software, Inc. DATA.TXT Corporation
Time and Billing	Timeslips® TABS III	Sage U.S., Inc. Software Technology, Inc.
Accounting	TABS III Timeslips®	Software Technology, Inc. Sage U.S., Inc.
Word Processing	Word Perfect® 8 Legal Edition	Corel Corporation
Litigation Management	Summation Blaze®	Summation Legal Technologies, Inc.
Speech Recognition	Dragon Naturally Speaking® Legal Edition	Dragon Systems, Inc.
Links Between Products	The Pocket Docket ®	DATA.TXT Corporation

Target market

The primary market for LawTech's productivity services lies in mid-sized law firms, those with 10 to 60 attorneys. According to the Martindale-Hubbell Directory, these firms number around 100 in the city of Atlanta alone, not including the remainder of the metropolitan area and other populous areas in Georgia. These firms often have one or two personnel, possessing minimal training and knowledge, that act as internal technology "experts" or are part of a technology committee comprised of employees within the office. With a midsized law firm's limited resources, however, these employees often do not have the time or talent to pursue innovations that increase firm productivity. Often, the law firm's "technology experts" are too busy maintaining the firm's current systems, orienting new employees, trouble shooting, and purchasing basic equipment such as printers. In the case of the technology committee, the active attorneys and support staff within the firm may only pursue technology solutions in their "spare" time.

These technology experts within the midsized firm will provide a liaison between LawTech and the decision-makers at the firm. LawTech will work with these representatives to understand the firm's needs and work for a solution. Relationship marketing is crucial in this industry—attorneys work to build longstanding relationships of trust and reliability with their clients, and they expect the same from their vendors. LawTech will succeed in this environment by providing the firms with a reliable, consistent source for technology solutions and also by acting as a representative for any necessary subcontractors (such as networking companies). The target market will provide a stable and consistent client base for LawTech not only in Georgia but also as it expands to other areas.

Secondary markets

Very small firms—those with fewer than ten attorneys—are also numerous (there are 495 in the city of Atlanta alone), but they may be difficult to reach on a wide scale and have limited need for the type of service LawTech provides. Firms of more than 60 attorneys generally have an internal MIS (Management of Information Systems) department on whom these firms rely for many of the services LawTech offers. LawTech does consider, however, that the MIS departments of these large firms may be a valuable source of information regarding software tools and new technologies, as well as potential clients for occasional services and products,

Total market potential

Because reliable technology is becoming a matter of survival for many law firms, the market for LawTech's products and services is nearly as vast as the legal industry itself. Below are some figures summarizing the market for LawTech's objective areas:

Table 2 (not included here) shows the number of law firms in LawTech's target market areas (Georgia, Southeast, and Nationwide), the approximate number of attorneys in each area, and the dollar market for initial sales in each area.

This table demonstrates the tip of the iceberg concerning LawTech's market potential. The **Market for Initial Sales** figures are based upon a multiplier of $1,480 per attorney, as reflected in LawTech's 1998 sales invoices. The Number of Firms figures are based on a national law directory, Martindale-Hubbell (www.martindale.com). Please note that Martindale-Hubbell traditionally undercounts small law firms and therefore these figures may be conservative. However, this directory is very accurate with respect to the number of larger firms.

It is crucial to note that LawTech typically maintains an ongoing relationship with each of its customers, and that a law firm normally changes each aspect of its business gradually over time so that employees are not overwhelmed by too many software changes simultaneously. The 1998 sales also represent a "foot in the door" period, during which many of the customers simply purchased software and basic training services, and during which LawTech has been building the intellectual capital and expertise to provide the range of technology services that law firms require.

As time passes, more and more of LawTech's revenue will be generated by these additional services beyond the sale of software and training. As existing customers continue to upgrade, to move from one type of productivity improvement to another (for instance, from upgrading accounting and billing software to adding speech recognition software) and to train new employees and expand their offices, the per-attorney sales figure—and thus the total market potential—will increase dramatically. Because of the varying nature of the services LawTech provides, it is difficult to accurately predict how dramatic this increase will be; it is our estimation, however, that it could triple or more.

Fig. 1 (Not included) shows a map of the United States and the approximate number of attorneys in each state.

Exhibit 6 (Not included) shows the names of all of the law firms in Atlanta, Georgia, with between 11 and 25 lawyers, with between 25 and 50 lawyers, and with more than 51 lawyers.

Competition

LawTech's competition may be classified in three groups: direct competition, indirect competition, and potential future competition. The most significant points to remember about competition are:

- ▶ LawTech has few direct competitors.
- ▶ Most indirect competitors either specialize in either one software or product, rather than total solutions.
- ▶ The remaining indirect competitors do not provide solutions that are tailored to the legal community needs.

Direct competitors

Law office technology consulting is a very new field of operations. Thus there are no associations or other sources of information from which to get an exact total number of companies competing in this area. To get an approximation of the number of existing competitors LawTech might face, ten Web-search engines each covering between 40-60 percent of the Web were used. A list compiled from advertisements in legal publications and legal technology listservers validated this method, as all of the firms found this way, were already included on the list from the Web search. The result of the search showed that there is only one company in Georgia, and four in the rest of the Southeast, providing information technology consulting and sales specifically for law offices. In fact, only 19 such firms exist in the entire United States. *Exhibit 7* (not included) shows an overview of competitors and their locations.

Indirect competition

LawTech's indirect competitors include legal office software vendors, general management or productivity consultants, and information technology consultants. None of these, however, are able to provide the complete range of services that LawTech offers. *Table 3* below (not included) identifies types of services that LawTech's clients need which are provided by indirect competitors. Because of their lack of effective service coverage, LawTech has not found any of these types of firms to be effective competitors.

Substitutes

Most of the large law offices have internal information technology departments. Mainly, these employees are correcting problems with hardware, software, or users in the day-to-day business. They lack the time to conduct software evaluation, run problem analyses, and develop expertise comparable to that of LawTech.

Marketing and sales

Target customers

As previously mentioned, the target market for LawTech's services is the midsized law firm, of which there are around 100 within the Atlanta City limits. Of these 100 firms, LawTech plans to achieve solid client relationships with approximately 30 within the first full fiscal year (January to December, 1999). LawTech will begin by targeting those firms that specialize primarily in litigation, since this will utilize LawTech's current technology expertise and allow time for knowledge expansion into more specific practice areas, such as real estate or bankruptcy. Within the litigation area, LawTech will first focus on those firms with whom it has already established contacts.

Marketing strategy

The strategy for reaching our target market involves several steps. During the first year, LawTech is relying on current contacts in the legal field and word of mouth to reach law firms as it develops the business and expands sales and support staff. After the first year, LawTech anticipates using advertising in local trade journals, such as the Fulton County Daily Report and the Bar Association Newsletters (LawTech is already advertising in the Cobb County Bar Newsletter). LawTech also attends legal technology conferences, such as "LegalTech," an annual conference in Atlanta. LawTech hopes to use the company Web page to attract attorneys who are currently using the Internet and exploring either technology or general productivity enhancement tools. LawTech's goal is to build and maintain a strong and loyal client base, and focus on long-term relationship marketing rather than short-term mass marketing.

By demonstrating to each client the direct increase in long-term profitability, LawTech provides a simple cost/benefit analysis for its productivity services based on the particular needs of the client. LawTech will approach prospective clients with an inside understanding of the way that law offices operate; this advantage begins with two of the founding members of management, who have a combined 24 years experience practicing law, and will continue to be the focus of LawTech's expertise as we expand. Legal expertise gives LawTech an advantageous perspective from which to capitalize on strengths while eliminating inefficiencies. LawTech's process, systems, and change management consulting will increase a law office's productivity and profitability.

Pricing

The pricing of LawTech's services and products is designed to maintain the highest margins possible while remaining a justifiable expense to the client. Office audits are currently priced at $200 per man-hour and clients are given credit for the cost of the office audit toward the purchase of future product and services. Training and on-site support are priced at $100 per man-hour for one-on-one service. The per person training fee decreases incrementally as additional persons are simultaneously trained, either on site at the law firm or at the LawTech training facility. All software products are priced at the vendor-determined levels and are not otherwise available anywhere in the market at lower prices. This generally provides for an approximate 100% margin. LawTech intends to remain a high-margin service firm, putting productivity expertise at a premium in a time driven, high-profit industry.

Operations

Introduction

LawTech serves its clients in three unique ways: (1) By evaluating on a continuous basis new software programs developed for lawyers and law firms. The knowledge that it gains in this way becomes part of LawTech's intellectual capital. (2) By evaluating its clients' current systems and recommending new computer software and hardware. This is the typical consulting project that LawTech will engage in with a client. (3) By subcontracting or referring clients to other vendors on occasion. In the next three sections, each of these activities will be described in greater detail.

Evaluation of new software programs

LawTech has and continues to develop the knowledge base needed to service its customers. With over 24 years collective experience as practicing attorneys and 16 years of software marketing and sales experience, LawTech's founders understand the needs of the legal community and the technology products available to meet the needs of law firms. LawTech shall continue to build this knowledge base. All of the products offered by LawTech have been tested and chosen by LawTech because they are the best available on the market, and LawTech continuously evaluates new software and hardware products as they enter the market.

The software solutions available to law firms constantly change. LawTech uses its expertise to evaluate new software on the market, and our product line changes according to these software evaluations. The constant evaluation process allows LawTech to provide the best recommendations to its clients based on their individual needs and how well a particular technology meets those needs. The best of the new products are added to the product line, and LawTech personnel learn how to train new users on the product. There are times when competing products are in the product line simultaneously because the different products perform better in distinct client circumstances. A broad range of suppliers also helps LawTech maintain objectivity with regard to products in similar fields.

In addition, LawTech personnel learn the nuances of the software, such as incompatibilities with other programs and systems, how best to configure the hardware and run the software, and the most frequent problems new users have with the software. Armed with this information, LawTech offers its clients a specialized knowledge that few in the country can duplicate.

LawTech has evaluated over 45 different software products for law firms. The products are in the area of time management, calendarizing, case management, client management, document management, time and billing, accounting, word processing, litigation management, speech recognition, mortgage closing, and other software. In total, LawTech personnel have spent in excess of 2,000 hours evaluating software products for law firms prior to and since the formation of the company. Co-founder Charles Fowler holds the most intellectual capital at the present. Co-founders W. Lamar Fields, Esq., and Robert Motyka, Esq., however, are now doing the bulk of the new software evaluations. Six mortgage closing software packages are currently under review as well as new versions of competing speech technology software products.

Typical consulting project

LawTech's services and products are **tailored** to the legal community. Therefore, expertise in business processes in the legal field, along with a breadth of legal technology products, makes LawTech a natural choice to identify and meet a law firm's technology needs.

LawTech recommends products, installs software, configures hardware, trains the law firm personnel on the use of information technology (IT), and provides change management consulting. LawTech acts as the product manager for the law firms IT changes. As a project manager, LawTech evaluates the current technology in the law firm and identifies deficiencies, and helps the law firm establish a budget and time line for the project. When appropriate, LawTech assists the law firm in contract negotiations with other technology providers, oversees the other contractors working on the IT project for the law firm, and coordinates all the activities of the contractors. A typical consulting project is described in more detail in *Exhibit 8*.

Industry relationships

LawTech also has working relationships with other technology providers to support LawTech clients when needed. LawTech obtains other companies to do networking and any large-scale hardware installations. For instance, in the Atlanta area, LawTech contracts with LAN-TECH (one of only two local firms that specialize in law firm networking projects) to do the networking. In addition, when LawTech does not have a specialist trained in a particular software package, it contracts with a specialist to provide the software training.

Outside contractors, specifically networking companies, are eager to work with LawTech. Since networking companies operate at low margins (approximately 20 percent) they typically need high-volume projects to cover the cost of contacting customers and evaluating their needs. Operating as a subcontractor through LawTech, however, allows these companies to work on projects of varying sizes without many of the conventional cost outlays of finding and retaining customers. LawTech, leveraging the high margins on its services and software, acts as the marketing arm of the organization by contacting and maintaining communications with the client. LawTech

Exhibit 8: A Typical Consulting Project

Marketing effort

Law firms learn the products and services provided by LawTech through our advertisements, cold calls on law firms, and referrals. When technology issues come up, LawTech is the company that law firms already know can solve the problems.

Client contact

A typical client (for example, a law firm with 15 attorneys and 10 support staff) has a process problem with its accounting and billing system and calls LawTech. A LawTech employee schedules an appointment with the firm to do an office audit or an information technology (IT) analysis.

Office audit

Once at the firm, LawTech checks the following: the hardware in place (including printers, facsimiles, network lines, number of phone lines, etc.), the software being used for the firm's accounting and billing, time management and calendaring, and document management, and the compatibility of the use of speech recognition software. During the initial visit, LawTech also meets with key staff members at the law firm to discuss the uses and deficiencies of the current IT system. The discussions also focus upon describing how the law firm functions. The office audit provides LawTech with the information it needs to determine the underlying problems at the law firm and to work out the proper solution. The fee for the office audit is $200 per man-hour.

Discuss solutions with client and draft proposal

LawTech meets with a partner or the technology committee in the law firm about the preliminary findings and discusses a cost/benefit analysis that leads to a budget. Based on the discussion, LawTech puts together an offer that recommends hardware changes and software solutions for the law firm, itemizes product, installation, and training costs, and provides a timeline for the completion of the project. Often, evaluation or demonstration copies of software are provided to the firm.

Contract commitment

The proposal is changed as LawTech meets with the client to finalize project specifications. As part of the commitment to purchase, a pilot project of one or two computers is set up for the firm. LawTech requires a deposit of 50% of the price of the products at the time of order, with the remainder due at installation.

The project

A typical project contract for an accounting and billing system for a 15-attorney, 10-staff law firm is about $15,000, excluding hardware upgrades. The contract price includes the software, technology training, installation, and change management services. After the project, LawTech continues to provide on-site support and one-to-one training services to the law firm for a fee of $100 per man-hour. The price for training decreases incrementally for simultaneous training with each person added to the training session.

also evaluates the law firm's networking and hardware needs, eliminating much of this cost for the networking company and making these projects profitable.

Management and key advisors

In the management team, LawTech combines all the expertise necessary to attain its goals successfully. In addition to the traditional management qualities needed, the members of the management team account for LawTech's specific needs by adding almost 25 years experience in the area of litigation and more than 16 years experience in information technology. In the future, LawTech will adjust to changing needs by adding members to the management team or to the group of key advisors as needed. Key advisors to LawTech are listed in *Exhibit 9.*

LawTech's managerial team

Robert J. Motyka, Esq., *President and Chief Executive Officer.* Robert earned a Juris Doctorate in May, 1991. He worked in a two-attorney law firm in Athens, Georgia, from 1991 until 1996 focusing on small business law and litigation. He also spent a year with Womble, Carlyle, Sandridge & Rice, a national law firm with over 300 attorneys and 400 support staff where he provided litigation support services to a major corporate client. Robert has experience with the technology needs of both small and large law firms. Robert is a co-founder of LawTech and he established the company's office in Athens, Georgia.

Charles M. Fowler, *Chief Operating Officer and Technology Director.* Charles's professional background includes more than 16 years of software and hardware marketing and sales experience. He spent three years as the marketing director of a networking firm that specialized in law firm sales. Charles authors the "TechnoTalk" monthly column for the Cobb County Bar Association newsletter and is a well known expert in legal technology and speech recognition software. He manages the Atlanta office and directs LawTech's activities in north Georgia.

Amanda J. Pullen, *Marketing Manager.* Amanda has a rich background in the areas of public relations and market research. At Beaumont Products, Inc., a 25-employee company with its main operation in the retailing business, she planned and executed consumer surveys (with up to 400 participants) and conducted market research. Based on these surveys she wrote analyses for the president and vice president of marketing and drew conclusions about the consumers' buying habits. Amanda also ran analyses on the effectiveness of advertising in the different kinds of media and planned promotions based on this. From her work as assistant to managing counsel at Altman, Kritzer & Levick, P.C., a corporate law firm of over 60 attorneys, she has experience with the operations of law firms. Amanda will support LawTech in all marketing and promotion related areas.

W. Lamar Fields, Esq., *Legal Advisor and Chairman of the Board.* Willy is a recently practicing attorney with 18 years litigation experience. He currently serves as the Chairman of the Technology Committee of the Savannah Bar Association. He manages LawTech's Savannah office and directs activities in South Georgia.

Chief Financial Officer. We are aware that there is an urgent need for a Chief Financial Officer in our management team. We are currently seeking a person with a professional background in finance who is able to relate his expertise to a company dealing

Exhibit 9: The Board of Advisors

LawTech plans to use a talented selection of advisors from the business community to assist with its start-up activities. These advisors have experience that is crucial to LawTech's success and will provide assistance with strategy and other matters on an as-needed basis.

Doug Hood*, Financial Consultant*. Doug has received numerous small business advocacy awards, including 1991 Small Business Advocate of the Year for the state of Georgia. He is also a member of the Georgia SBA Advisory Council and recently served as its chairman. In 1996, he was appointed to the National SBA Advisory Council and he serves as the chairman of its Voice of America Small Business Committee. In 1998, Doug was named the SBA Financial Services Advocate of the Year for the state of Georgia and the Southeast region. This honor is awarded to individuals who assist small businesses in obtaining financing, either directly or through advocacy efforts.

Charles W. Hofer, Ph.D.*, Small Business Consultant*. Charles, Regents Professor of Strategy and Entrepreneurship at The University of Georgia, will serve LawTech as a business advisor. He gained several awards including the International Hall of Fame Entrepreneur Award. In 1998, the United States Association for Small Business and Entrepreneurship selected the University of Georgia's Ph.D. Program in Entrepreneurship Strategic Management (which Charles designed) as the winner of its National World Program Award for Excellence in Entrepreneurship Education.Charles will support LawTech in starting up the business and developing business strategies.

IT-consultant. We are currently seeking a well-known IT-specialist who also has extensive knowledge about the legal technology field. By adding to our current legal IT expertise, this consultant will help us more in the area of public relations and marketing than in the operation of the business. We expect that he will help establish the LawTech name in legal and technology publications by publishing articles written by himself and Charles Fowler. Moreover, he will help us to open doors with future clients through use of his name as one established in the legal and technology fields.

with IT-consulting services in the legal area. Until we have found the right person to support us in the financial area we will make extensive use of Doug Hood as our financial consultant.

Financials

Capital structure

Mr. Fields and Mr. Fowler provided the start-up capital of $15,000, each giving $7,500 for a 50 percent partnership in the company, and have subsequently increased the capital in recent months to finance the growth. As of December 31, 1998, invested capital stands at $50,000, with each founder owning 375 shares. In May 1999, Mr. Motyka will be vested with 150 shares, increasing the total number of shares to 1000. Similarly, Ms. Pullen will be vested in May 2000 by 100 shares of the company. This method will also be used for adding new partners in the future as needed. The projected ownership structure with respect to the number of shares each partner will own is as follows: *Table 4* (not included) shows the ownership structure as it is projected through 2003.

Financial projections

LawTech generated revenues of $175,000 and earned $20,000 in 1998, the first fiscal year of its operations. Since Robert Motyka, Esq., and Manda Pullen will start to work full time in the company in May 1999, revenues are expected to grow rapidly starting in June 1999. By 2003, both sales and profits will increase as shown in the following *Table 5*, Summary of Results of Operations (not included).

Investor returns

With net income reaching $20,000 in the first fiscal year and with the founders' total contribution of $50,000 to the capital as of December 31, 1998, the return on investment (ROI) has been 30 percent. As net income is expected to grow substantially by the year 2003, ROI for the initial partners will be high.

There are two main exit strategies for the investors. They are:

- **Adding new partners:** As has been explained in the capital structure, new partners will be added to the capital structure. Adding new partners will create attractive compensation packages to employees in addition to serving as an exit strategy for the existing investors.
- **Merging with existing companies:** As part of our future growth strategies, mergers will help LawTech expand in the national market, as well as provide investors with the ability to cash in their returns.

All services and products provide the company with a very high gross margin and since the company is planning to retain all of its earnings for the first few years, initial growth will be financed internally. As the future growth section of our business plan explains, growth potential in the national market is expensive, and an expansion in that respect may require funds surpassing the internal financial resources of the company. The company therefore would meet this need with outside financing as nationwide expansion continues.

Exhibit 10 and *Exhibit 11* include monthly financial statements for 1999, and *Exhibit 12* through *Exhibit 14* give yearly financial statements for the 1998-2003 period

Start Up

Exhibit 10: LawTech, LLC Monthly Cash Flow Statements for 1999

	Jan-99	Feb-99	Mar-99	Apr-99	May-99	Jun-99	Jul-99	Aug-99	Sep-99	Oct-99	Nov-99	Dec-99	1999 Total
C. F. From Operations	12,000	2,000	3,000	4,000	3,000	4,000	9,000	11,000	15,000	16,000	17,000	24,000	120,000
Net Income	4,000	6,000	7,000	8,000	10,000	15,000	16,000	18,000	18,000	20,000	20,000	16,000	155,000
Adjustments for Operating Activities													
Change in Acc. Rec.	8,000	(3,000)	(3,000)	(3,000)	(7,000)	(11,000)	(7,000)	(7,000)	(3,000)	(3,000)	(3,000)	7,000	(38,000)
Change in Inventory	2,000	(2,000)	(2,000)	(2,000)	(5,000)	(7,000)	(5,000)	(5,000)	(2,000)	(2,000)	(2,000)	5,000	(30,000)
Change in Acc. Pay.	(2,300)	2,300	2,300	2,300	5,300	7,300	4,400	4,400	2,400	2,400	2,400	(6,400)	29,000
Depreciation	300	300	300	300	300	300	400	400	400	400	400	400	4,000
Cash Flow From/(For) Investments	0	0	(2,000)	0	0	0	(5,000)	0	0	0	0	0	(7,000)
Purchases of Property & Equipment	0	0	(2,000)	0	0	0	(5,000)	0	0	0	0	0	(7,000)
Cash Flow from Financing Activities	0	0	0	10,000	0	0	10,000	0	0	10,000	0	0	30,000
Increase in Capital	0	0	0	10,000	0	0	10,000	0	0	10,000	0	0	30,000
Dividends Paid	0	0	0	0	0	0	0	0	0	0	0	0	0
Net Inc./(Dec.) in cash	12,000	2,000	1,000	14,000	3,000	4,000	14,000	11,000	15,000	26,000	17,000	24,000	143,000
Beg. Cash Balance	20,000	32,000	34,000	35,000	49,000	52,000	56,000	70,000	81,000	96,000	122,000	139,000	20,000
Ending Cash Balance	32,000	34,000	35,000	49,000	52,000	56,000	70,000	81,000	96,000	122,000	139,000	163,000	163,000

and shows projected cash flow for 1999. Exhibit 11 through Exhibit 14 showing sales and profit projections for future years are not included for reasons of confidentiality.

Future Growth

LawTech's primary short- to medium-term objective is to open and expand affiliate offices throughout the Southeast. During the first year of operations, the company aims to concentrate its activities in the state of Georgia; then from the second to the fifth years, to expand to surrounding states, such as Tennessee, South Carolina, Alabama, and Florida. Typically, only one or two offices will be established in any given state. The expansion will be fueled by our ability to attract qualified partners and employees. LawTech will recruit experienced attorneys with technological savvy to become partners to run other offices, and support staff with information technology experience. LawTech will use its technological expertise to create a knowledge base to support the knowledge transfer from experienced to new employees. Incentives will depend extensively on the use of and contribution to this knowledge base. After strengthening its position in the Southeast market, LawTech is planning national expansion.

There are two options for this national expansion, both of which will be used, but with a greater focus on the first:

- ▸ Leveraging local offices of clients that have national coverage: In cases where LawTech's local clients have operations in other parts of the nation, these law firms may provide LawTech with the ability to work with the other offices as well.

- ▸ Merging with or acquiring existing companies in related areas of expertise: Indirect competitors—for instance, developers and vendors of legal software solutions—that specialize in legal-specific technology and are likely to acquire the necessary legal-related knowledge are potential candidates for merger or acquisition.

Start Up

Our Customers Speak

LawTech evaluated our needs quickly, helped us put together a reasonable budget, obtained and supervised vendors for computer hardware, worked around our fluctuating business cycles, and delivered a completely new IT system on time and budget.
Marietta, Georgia

We had problems getting support from another vendor, so we called LawTech. LawTech responded quickly, and identified and solved our problems immediately. From now on, we are using LawTech.
Atlanta, Georgia

The software and hardware installed by LawTech freed me from the tyranny of the keyboard.
Marietta, Georgia

LawTech not only sold and sent us the software our firm needed, but they also customized the programs for our specific needs.
Sonoma, California

Using Dragon Naturally Speaking® installed by LawTech I can create and print 90 percent of my correspondence in 10 minutes or less. It used to take me one to two days using traditional dictation.
Marietta, Georgia

Appendix II

Sample Business Plan: Easy Shopper

The following business plan was developed as a course project in an M.B.A. class in entrepreneurship and new venture management, taught by Mr. James Doyle, lecturer at the William E. Simon Graduate School of Business Administration at the University of Rochester.

This is a very well written and well organized business plan that was prepared to achieve a greater understanding of starting an e-commerce business. It could begin as a small local business with good potential for growth.

The plan was prepared by:
Holly Clark Blanchard
Christopher Burns
Stephen Lai
Robert Turner

For questions please contact Mr. James Doyle, 315-331-7415.

Copyright © 1999 by Holly Clark Blanchard, Christopher Burns, Steven Lai, and Robert Turner and reprinted here with permission.
Please note that there may be omissions in the plan due to space limitations.

Table of Contents

Executive Summary
Business Description
Industry Analysis
Market Analysis
Marketing Plan
Competitive Analysis
Organization
Operations and Logistics
Exit Strategies
Funding Needs
Financial Plan
Appendix 1: *Pro Forma* **Cash Flow Year 1**
Appendix 2: *Pro Forma* **Income Statement Year 1**
Appendix 3: *Pro Forma* **Balance Sheet Year 1**

Executive Summary

Easy Shopper is a new business that aims to bring the variety available at supermarkets to students in college dormitories in the Western New York state area. Through use of the Internet and the World Wide Web, students will be able to survey our menu of offerings including nonperishable food, paper supplies, personal hygiene, and over the counter pharmaceuticals, and place their orders for same-day or next-day delivery.

This business opportunity capitalizes upon the remarkable growth of the Internet, where consumer sales through electronic commerce (e-commerce) are estimated to increase from $12.7 billion in 1997 to $22 billion in 1998. Leading the way are Amazon.com and Dell Computer, which have demonstrated that by minimizing inventory and providing greater consumer choice, Internet sales are a new road to profitability. Nonetheless, e-commerce retailers may experience many pitfalls such as inadequately defining and targeting a market to serve.

We have avoided this shortcoming by conducting extensive market research of the student population in Western New York State. Our research shows that there is a population of nearly 30,000 college students resident at the large campuses that can be easily served with a minimal number of trucks and drivers. Students indicated they have limited access to transportation due to time and cost constraints and that corner stores on campus offer an unacceptably limited selection of goods. We aim to satisfy this market by bringing consumer selections to the door.

Our marketing plan objective is to grow the market from our projected revenue of $2.4 million in 1999 to $5.3 million in 2003. We will provide small products which students use daily and can easily store in their dorm rooms. These will include nonperishable groceries (such as breads and soup), school supplies such as paper and pens, and personal hygiene and over-the-counter pharmaceutical products. Our pricing strategy is to match on-campus food vendors and bookstores, which we expect will yield a 20 percent gross margin over the comparable prices prevailing at supermarkets. We will base our promotional activities on conventional marketing techniques such as flyers and bulletin board advertisements, as well as on e-commerce techniques such as e-mail and catalogs that can be downloaded by the customer.

Since e-commerce is in its infancy and is susceptible to competition and replication, we believe that it is crucial that *Easy Shopper* gain a first mover advantage to quickly establish customer loyalty and brand equity. Without the benefit of large barriers to entry, *Easy Shopper* will need to develop unparalleled service as its competitive advantage. As such, we have developed our compensation and incentive schemes with this in mind. Since we are a new company, these schemes are free from encumbrances of existing organizational designs that will constrain potential competition from others such as supermarkets. We will retain operating staff experienced in information technology and delivery businesses, and our senior management will have stellar business credentials in their fields of expertise, such as an M.B.A.

Easy Shopper requires an initial injection of $220,000 equity financing. This will fund the development of the Web site and the computer system central to operations and working capital for the initial start up of the firm. Our financial projections are based on maintaining 20 percent gross margins and revenue growth from $2.4 million in 1999 to $5.3 million in 2003. Under this scenario, our *pro forma* cash flow statements indicate cumulative cash flow dropping to a value of $44,000, after completing our three month start-up phase in March 1999, and during which revenues are expected to be low, to a healthy $484,000 by the end of 2003. Our balance sheet assets will typically comprise cash and the value of our computer system. The value of our assets will drop from its initial value of $220,000 to $122,000 in March 1999 before rising to $484,000 by the end of 2003 when our computer system will be fully depreciated. At this time, cash reserves will be more than adequate to fund a replacement computer system. Our *pro forma* net income statements show a net loss of $65,000 initially, then rising to a profit of $12,000 in the year end 2000, followed by a string of profitable years ending with a profit of $143,000 in the year 2003. Quarterly profits will fluctuate, with the third quarter typically showing a loss due to seasonal variation in the revenue base.

We have conducted financial sensitivity analyses of the following scenarios: gross margins dropping to 15 percent, slower and faster revenue growth, reduced frequency of deliveries, and an additional 5 percent revenues from advertising. Under the slow-demand scenario, our net cash flow decreases significantly yet still remains positive. With the exception of the scenario of 15 percent gross margins, the other sensitivity analyses show improved results. The scenario of 15 percent gross margins, however, is severe, with net cumulative cash flows decreasing steadily and no net profits.

Our exit strategy is based upon seeking a partnership with a major retail supplier, such as Wal-Mart. This partnership will enable low-cost supplies for the business, and a large partner such as Wal-Mart could in turn fund this foray into e-commerce with little risk and investment. Clearly, the risk associated with the scenario of 15 percent gross margins is mitigated by this strategy. As well, this partnering would cater to the economies of scale in information technology available to major retailers, and provide a means for a clean break by the founders, who would not have to dissolve the business.

Start Up

Business Description

Easy Shopper was conceived to provide resident college-student customers in the Western New York State area the convenience of shopping for and ordering their essential food staples, personal hygiene, and paper supplies via the Internet or World Wide Web. Delivery to the dorm will be the primary means of distribution for those goods. Very simply, students will place their supply orders online, and we will then make daily deliveries to our customer's dorms.

The following chart shows a representative example of the range of goods we will offer in the start-up phases of *Easy Shopper*. We will use point-of-sale data to optimize the mix of products based on student preferences and profitability.

Snack foods	Beverages	Breads	Personal hygiene	Packaged meals	School/paper supplies
Chips	Brand name soft drinks	White	Shampoos	Macaroni & cheese	Notebooks
Snackwells™	Generic soda	Wheat	Soaps	Noodles	Binders
Crackers	Bottled water	Italian	Deodorant	Packaged rice	Pens
Popcorn	Hot chocolate	Pastries	Cotton balls	Soups	Pencils
Pretzels	Tea	Bagels	Q-tips		Batteries
Cookies	Gourmet coffee		Toothpaste		Disks
Candies	Juices		Tooth brushes		Video tapes
Nuts					Cassette tapes

In the initial phases, we would not carry any perishable items, such as fresh produce or fresh meats. We consider that such products truly require personal selection by customers, and that such items would introduce profound spoilage costs given their short freshness life. Additionally, we envision that including these goods would complicate our logistical operations. Specifically, we are concerned that refrigeration and storage of these goods would present costly challenges for a new company to overcome.

Our first target market is students who are computer literate, geographically concentrated, and who generally lack personal transportation. According to a recent survey of 100 University of Rochester students, 64 percent of students surveyed own computers while another 20 percent expect to purchase one soon. These students typically have easy Internet access at school facilities, which simplifies ordering goods over the Internet. Additionally, a large percentage (over 60 percent) of these students live in on-campus dormitories (in fact, only small portions of students in four-year colleges live outside the general vicinity of the college). Many of these students, such as those who are international and underclassmen, do not own cars. As such, they rely exclusively on friends and public transportation for their transportation needs. This can make shopping more time-consuming and difficult to schedule. Therefore, delivery of necessary and selected essential goods will better satisfy the daily needs of this group better than the on-campus convenience stores that provide only a limited selection of goods.

We will approach this student market in phases. First, we will target residential college students at campuses in Western New York. This is a region where this service should be particularly valuable given the absence of continuous public transportation and considerable distance between campuses and major retail shopping areas. After we have proven this business model in these markets, we will expand our business to other concentrated areas of universities. The next student populations we would target would have similar characteristics, including limited transportation services and significant access to computers. Areas under consideration include Boston and New York City.

The next wave of potential expansion would be targeting busy urban professionals (yuppies). The vast majority of these professionals own personal computers and are especially pressed for time. By using a home delivery service for their necessary goods, our company can save these customers time and effort. This is another population that has access to computers (either at home or at work), has a narrow variety of shops within walking distance, and has small neighborhood corner stores for competition. Premiums can be charged to this segment as *timesaving* is often more important than price sensitivity (as with students). Before expansion, our company will conduct further market research in this area to determine an optimal pricing policy and product mix.

Industry Analysis

Turning now to a discussion of the industry in which *Easy Shopper* would compete, a discussion of electronic commerce and Internet sales is particularly relevant.

E-commerce, the phrase used to describe the plethora of businesses using the Internet and home delivery as the primary means of transacting with customers, is rapidly growing. In fact, $12.7 billion in sales occurred via e-commerce in 1997 alone. Over 1998, sales are estimated to rise to $22 billion, a 73 percent increase. As the CEO of Netscape has noted, "We are witnessing the beginnings of the modern-day equivalent of a land grab, with businesses rushing to stake out their territory on the net." Many agree that the Internet will profoundly transform the way most businesses operate in the long-term as manufacturers and retailers become increasingly able to reach out directly to millions of consumers.

The Gartner Group Inc. has estimated that e-commerce sales will be approximately $40 billion in 1999. Further into the future, Forrester Research Inc. estimates that worldwide demand for e-commerce will reach $350 billion by 2002. *BusinessWeek* uses this data to estimate that e-commerce will increase the United States' gross domestic product by $10 billion to $20 billion annually by 2002. Even the US Department of Commerce estimates that Internet commerce will exceed $300 billion by 2002.

While Internet sales have been growing substantially, profits are often more ambiguous. E-commerce businesses starting today are paying millions of dollars in fees to major Internet providers and search engines (such as AOL, Excite, and Yahoo). These retailing companies pay these fees to Internet providers to post banners to attract users to e-commerce sites. Consequently, these companies (and not the small start-up firms) are absorbing many of the profits. In addition, retailers marketing to consumers are currently mass-marketing to *all* consumers. For example, the discount chain company Target sells "everything from hats to mouse pads to umbrellas." Many current e-commerce firms have not specified a target market and those companies are blindly trying to appeal to everyone. Profits will come when retailers narrow their consumer niches and cater to more limited sets of customers.

Consumers' fears of using credit cards on the Internet is another potential stumbling block that companies face. More popular sites (such as Amazon.com and Travelocity.com) use secured sites and browsers to overcome this problem. Other retailers guarantee that consumers will be reimbursed for any fraud occurring from transacting through their sites. In the regulatory environment, President Clinton supports these self-regulation steps against fraud. The government is working to make it easier for consumers to get redress if they do not get what they pay for. As a result of these issues, third parties (such as the Better Business Bureau) are approving consumer-friendly sites.

The most renowned Internet marketing story is Amazon.com, a company selling books and other entertainment products strictly through the Internet. This early experience has shown that selling goods over the Internet, such as books, has proven to be highly successful. According to *Dow Jones News Service*, in May 1998, Amazon.com's market value was $2.2 billion compared to the retail-store-based Barnes & Noble Inc. with a value of $2.4 billion. Amazon.com has successfully proven that the Internet is a viable and very successful means for distributing consumer goods. Furthermore, Dell Computer and Cisco Systems each sell several billions of dollars of computer products over the Internet and prove that conducting business over the Internet is profitable.

Easy Shopper plans to apply the "no inventory" strategy used successfully by Dell and avoid the pitfalls of the businesses mentioned above that rely on Internet providers. As discussed earlier, *Easy Shopper* will target only student populations. This focused target market will allow *Easy Shopper* to promote and advertise more effectively without using high-priced search engine banners to attract customers. The details are presented in the marketing plan section.

Market Analysis

Evaluation of Aggregate Market

Having provided a discussion of the Internet and electronic commerce industry, we now discuss the market in which *Easy Shopper* will compete. As mentioned in the business description, our primary target will be college students in dormitories at the larger campuses in Buffalo, Rochester, and Syracuse. In this area, our services should be particularly valuable because of the lack of continuous public transportation and the lack of close proximity of major retail shopping areas.

We based our evaluation of the aggregate revenue base for our service on estimates of the proportion of typical students' food and discretionary budgets available for spending on the type of goods provided by our service. This is based on estimating:

- The number of students who live in on-campus dorms or apartments, such as the population of the target market.
- The proportion of students *food* budgets that can be served and captured by our company.
- The proportion of students' *discretionary spending* budgets that can be served and captured by our company.

Using these guidelines, we calculated the revenue base for serving undergraduate students in Buffalo, Rochester, and Syracuse, New York, to range from a worst of $2.4M to a best of $5.3M.

Easy Shopper's Target Market - Undergraduate Population in Campus Residence—Rochester, New York, sits at the geographic epicenter of several university communities, each with reasonably large populations of undergraduate students. Student residences are generally apartment-style dwellings that house typically from 100 to 500 students. The proportion of students who live on or near campus is approximately 63 percent, based on data acquired for the University of Rochester and the University of Syracuse communities. We estimated the number living on-campus to be 29,482 students based on this 63 percent proportion and the respective undergraduate enrollments at those universities. This data is presented in Table 1 on the following page.

Initially, we have excluded students living in the dormitories at smaller college campuses in Buffalo, Rochester, and Syracuse, such as Nazareth and St. John Fisher colleges in the Rochester area. Including these students could increase the target market by up to 10 percent; however, given the relatively low volumes, we conclude that the incremental costs to serve these markets (such as drivers and trucks) may exceed the benefits. We would base plans to enter these markets upon further market analysis.

We excluded the population of first-year (freshman) and graduate students in on-campus residences from the total population estimate that can be served, since data concerning these student groups is less certain. However, from this perspective, our estimate of the target market's population is conservative since at least some portion of first-year and graduate students can be expected to patronize our offerings.

Proportion of Food Budget Available for Delivery Service—Resident students typically enroll in University-administered meal plans ranging from those that account for approximately one third of the student's food needs to those that can provide for nearly all of a student's food consumption, usually 19 meals a week. As an example, the U of R's Simon School of Business currently advises students to budget $2,862 per year for food; this amount equals the U of R's full 19-meal-per-week meal plan. For our analysis, we treat this value as the typical student food budget amount.

We estimated the total food budget available for food *other* than meal plans (such as restaurants and the *Easy Shopper* delivery service) as the difference between the nominal student food budget and the cost of the other meal plans, times the number of students on other plans. We estimated this amount to be $14.4 million, and the associated calculations are described in Appendix 1.

We expect that most of this amount would typically be spent at restaurants or bars near these universities and colleges. However, given the time demands placed on students, their penchant for snack food, and the poor variety of goods available at on-campus grocery stores, we expect that *Easy Shopper* could easily command a significant portion of this market. While arbitrary, we believe this proportion would range from a minimum of 10 percent to maximum of 20 percent and would yield a range of aggregate revenue for food products of between $1.5 and $3 million annually. We consider it reasonable to assume that *Easy Shopper* should be able to command at least 10 percent, or $1.5 million of this market, in the worst case.

Table 1: Estimated Number of Students in Campus Residence
Total Student Enrollment

School	First-year	Undergraduate	Graduate	Campus Residences
SUNY Buffalo	2724	13175	2956	yes
SUNY Brockport	874	5379	324	yes
SUNY Geneseo	1137	5127	47	yes
Rochester Institute of Technology	2022	8001	754	yes
Syracuse University	2617	10813	2225	yes
University of Rochester	896	4407	2323	yes
Total Student Population[1]	10270	46902	8629	
X proportion in residence (63 percent)				
= Target Market	N/A	29482	N/A	

Proportion of Discretionary Spending Budget Available for Delivery Service—The University of Rochester's William E. Simon School of Business Administration currently advises students to budget $1,644 per year to cover their discretionary expenses, such as clothing, transportation, toiletries, and cleaning supplies, among others. Since *Easy Shopper* will broaden the product offerings available on campus, a revenue base between 2 percent and 5 percent of the aggregate discretionary budget should be easily achievable. Given a population base of 29,482 students in the target market, this means our company would yield a range of aggregate revenue for discretionary products of between $0.9 and $2.3 million annually.

Local campus stores do not sell such products as toiletries, cleaning supplies, and over the counter pharmaceutical products. We believe *Easy Shopper* should be able to command at least 2 percent, or $0.9 million of this market, at worst, because we will offer these types of goods that typically command a portion of a students' expenses. However, because we expect major expenses such as clothing to consume a large portion of student's discretionary budgets, it is not reasonable for *Easy Shopper* to gain a large portion of this market.

Aggregate Revenue Base for Delivery Service—Aggregating the estimated revenue bases for food and discretionary products shows that *Easy Shopper* would yield a range of aggregate revenue for discretionary products between $2.4 and $5.3 million annually. Though arbitrary, we believe this worst case assumption is reasonable given the prevailing lack of breadth in on-campus store offerings, the demands on student time, and that these figures exclude likely revenues from students outside the target market, such as graduate students.

Market Characteristics

To gain a better perspective of the target market and its desire for our product offerings, we conducted an extensive campaign of direct market research. Among our key findings, we determined that one of the greatest barriers to an online ordering format is fear of credit card fraud. Beyond that point, our surveys demonstrated that many of the students surveyed are leery of making purchases of credence goods without first seeing them. Surprisingly, the students listed a variety of products they wished to see delivered in the free response section beyond even those we had contemplated. The results of our survey efforts are contained in Appendix 2.

The results indicate a sustainable demand for our product offerings and a noted dissatisfaction with current on-campus offerings. This makes us conclude that there is a strong demand for the products that we have chosen to offer. In a summary fashion, we learned the following highlights relevant to our business and business model:

General Trends - It is clear that the majority of students surveyed indeed are residential students. Roughly two-thirds of them currently owned a computer and, while 90 percent currently surf the Internet, only one third of respondents reported they currently make online purchases.

Roughly, two-thirds of those surveyed reported having a car on campus, a number likely explained by the fact that mostly upperclassmen were sampled. We suspect a correspondingly lower number for underclassmen. Students most often took either their own car or rode in someone else's when going to grocery shop.

Over 90 percent of those surveyed reported that they bought food at a grocery store, a number we again attribute to the majority of those with cars. Roughly three-quarters of students ate in the dining center. The majority of students reported eating meals in their dorms approximately one-quarter of the time. Purchases at the student commons restaurants and Campus Corner Grocery stores captured over half of those surveyed. Regarding where students purchased their school and paper supplies, grocery store, mass discounter, and the on-campus bookstore all received nearly the same response rate, between two-thirds and three-quarters of all respondents.

Service Preferences - Concerning current or contemplated purchases online, the hits were recreational books, textbooks, magazines, CDs, travel tickets, and clothing. Virtually no one currently ordered or had considered buying food or groceries online, and a slight percentage considered buying paper supplies online. The main concern toward online purchasing was consumers' fear of transmitting credit card information over the Internet. Students also strongly identified a preference for face-to-face dealings and the ability to try before purchase as obstacles to online purchasing. Other issues such as transaction hassle, delivery cost, and excess search time were identified, but were not as prevalent.

Students reported that the usual frequency with which they made grocery purchases was approximately every other week or so and reported spending between 30 minutes and an hour on each grocery-shopping excursion. Students reported that most likely they would buy from our service roughly monthly, with weekly being mentioned as a second choice, and the majority of students reported that they would likely buy between one and five items per order from our company.

Two-thirds to three-quarters of students reported making a major paper supplies purchase once a month or less often. The majority of students also reported being only sometimes preferential to particular brands when making paper supplies purchases. Our two surveys gave conflicting results about whether students are preferential in choosing brand names for their food purchases—the mean seems to be around "sometimes."

Concerning placing an order from our company for delivered goods, the two predominant methods reported were through our dedicated Web site, or over the telephone. Students reported with the greatest frequency that they would like to learn of our service through electronic means such as e-mail or our Web site, while on-campus flyers/posters were the second most popular choice for publicity.

Pricing - By over two-to-one, students reported that they did not budget their spending on paper supplies. The majority of students reported being "somewhat" concerned about price when buying paper supplies and indicated being nearly evenly split between paying the same or slightly less than bookstore prices for paper supplies our company would deliver to them, with a slight edge to being priced the same. However, students also reported that our prices should match a discounter's, such as Wal-Mart or Staples.

The results were basically evenly split between students who do and do not budget their periodic grocery and food purchases. Students reported that they would expect to pay the same or less, on average, for food from our company than they would from the on-campus corner store; however, roughly two-thirds of students reported they expected our prices would match the prices at a grocery store, such as Wegman's.

Marketing Plan

Having laid the foundation for *Easy Shopper* in the context of the industry and market analyses, this section is a more detailed discussion of our overall marketing plan.

Overall Marketing Strategy

Easy Shopper's objective is to provide time-limited and transportation-limited residential college students with a superior means to satisfy their basic grocery and paper or school supplies needs. We seek to provide a broader alternative to on-campus offerings and provide spatial convenience by virtue of on-campus delivery. Students will order products either by electronic (Internet e-commerce) or by telephonic means, and will pay for their orders either by secure electronic interchange or by calling in a credit card over the telephone. Our product selection includes grocery items, cleaning, and paper/stationery supplies, as well as personal hygiene and over the counter pharmaceuticals. Our pricing would match comparable on-campus offerings, admittedly higher than off-campus competitors. The relevant differentiator for our service is the delivery aspect and availability of one-stop, electronic ordering.

Customer Focus

Following is a brief description of our target customers.

Location - Our target customers are *residential* college students. These students are housed on-campus in dormitories or other university-supplied housing, and are relatively centralized/localized, providing relatively concentrated markets of target customers.

Market Segment - We wish to limit our targeting efforts to on-campus students, primarily those without cars, who are not very price-sensitive, and those for whom *convenience* is a *critical* issue. We wish to provide these students with the products they need at competitive prices, in a way that minimizes the time spent "shopping" for those goods.

Market Growth - We expect that the popularity among students of *Easy Shopper* will rise over time on those campuses we serve. However, the size of the target markets is not growing very quickly; rather, college students are in a steady, but slow, state of growth. One way to expand the reach of our marketing efforts would be to target also those residential students who do own cars; those who are not price sensitive present an opportunity for us to provide a significant convenience advantage; however, those who *are* price sensitive would be a more challenging conquest.

A further market extension would be to reach out to non-residential students who do not own cars, as they too would appreciate the convenience of delivered daily necessities. With this option, we trade off easier delivery with a greater geographical dispersion for deliveries. That is, by delivering to off-campus students, we can deliver literally to their doors, though we would have to cover greater distances driving from one student's home to another, which will increase our costs, although not by significant amounts as they will most likely live near campus.

Consumer attitudes and buying habits - As previously mentioned in Market Characteristics, college students value several attributes with regards to their purchases of both grocery products and paper supplies, to varying degrees. These include:

- Price (relative).
- Brand.
- Spatial convenience.
- Time convenience.
- Variety in offerings.

Regarding grocery purchases, our market research indicates that most students made their purchases on a biweekly basis, and generally spent between half an hour and an hour doing that shopping. Our results also indicated that students often take either their own car or get a ride in someone else's to get to a grocery store. Most students reported that they did indeed shop at least occasionally at grocery stores, a strong indication that their needs were not adequately served through on-campus offerings. Students reported an occasional preference for brand names in food purchases, and half of students do budget grocery and food purchases on a periodic basis.

Regarding paper supplies purchases, our market research indicates that most students made their purchases once a month or less often. Most students reported that their purchases were made at grocery stores, at mass discounters such as Wal-Mart, or at the campus bookstore. Students reported an occasional preference for brand names in paper supplies, but only a third or so budgeted such purchases. Price was indicated to be "somewhat" of a concern regarding such purchases, likely because of the relatively infrequent purchase of those items.

Needs of market - As identified in our primary research results, residential college students need a means to quickly and conveniently shop for their periodic grocery and paper supplies purchases. Time is a real issue for college students, and many simply do not have the time, because of classes and extracurricular activities, to shop for all the products they desire at large stores, especially given the time it takes to get to such stores. Additionally, many students do not even have a car of their own, which makes the prospect of getting out to a large grocery or office supplies or mass discounter that much more of a logistical challenge.

Our research identified a profitable opportunity to provide "one-stop shopping" to students for these types of goods. Also, given the prevalence both of on-campus computers with Internet access, and the majority of students who have computers of their own in their dorms, an electronic means for browsing and ordering is clearly a quantum leap in convenience.

Industry pricing - Our research has identified that prices at the local campus store are approximately 15 to 23 percent higher than they are at the nearest major supermarket.

Principal Marketing Elements

Our principal marketing elements analysis with respect to our company's offerings is as follows:

Products - For all of the products we will offer, the intent is to provide small products which students use usually on a daily basis, and can easily store in their dorm rooms or other such accommodations. Please note that in all cases, the products listed are examples, and are not exhaustive lists.

As we envision it, we would offer the following types of grocery goods that do not require refrigeration:

- **Snack foods:** Potato or corn chips, dips, Snackwells™ brand snacks, crackers, popcorn, pretzels, cookies, candies, and nuts.
- **Beverages:** Coke and other branded sodas, generic sodas, bottled waters, hot chocolate mixes, teas, instant and gourmet coffees beans, and juice.
- **Packaged meals:** Macaroni and cheese, ramen noodles and soup mixes, and canned soups.
- **Regular staples:** breads, cereals, pastries, doughnuts, bagels, rolls, peanut butter, jams and jellies, sauces and condiments, and canned goods, such as tuna or fruit.

A particular issue with regard to food is the question of refrigeration. Informal results suggest that at least half of all on-campus students have access to refrigerators, whether that is a personal compact refrigerator in a dorm room, a shared apartment refrigerator, or a refrigerator shared on a dorm floor. This result suggests that a case could be made for delivering such goods to students; however, the issue under consideration is that doing so provides a substantial increase in carrying and holding/storage costs for our company, complicating those areas and delivery.

We are considering, based upon the increased costs for refrigerated storage and delivery, the following types of refrigerated foods:

- **Prepackaged foods:** salads, sandwiches, frozen pizza, toaster oven goods, microwave meals (TV dinners), and lunch meats.
- **Other:** juices, milk, butter, cheese, ice cream, frozen yogurt, yogurt, cottage cheese, salad dressing, and mayonnaise.

Note that we would not carry such items as fresh produce or fresh meats. We consider that such products truly require personal selection by customers, and that these items would introduce profound spoilage issues into our business, given their short freshness life.

Our market research indicated a strong demand for the following items, which we will carry:

- **Personal hygiene/ toiletries/ health and beauty aids:** shampoos, conditioners, toothpaste, toothbrushes, dental floss, cotton balls, shaving equipment, soaps, deodorants, mouthwash, pain-killers, antihistamines, bandages, and feminine products.
- **Other:** laundry detergents, fabric softeners, and bleach.

Turning now to the paper supplies aspect of our business, we intend to offer the following products:

- Pens, pencils, notebooks, filler paper, three-ring binders, white-out, notepads, rulers, disks, cassette tapes, video tapes, batteries, highlighters, calendars, scissors, staplers, folders, paper by the ream, and transparencies.

Pricing - Very simply, our pricing strategy is to match on-campus food vendors such as the U of R Corner Store, and on-campus paper supplies vendors such as the U of R bookstore. However, our prices, given our cost structure, and given that we will be delivering our wares to students on campus, will be above those prevailing at either grocery stores or mass discounters. These prices would yield approximately a 20 percent gross margin over the prices prevailing at supermarkets.

Since our market research indicates that students would likely order in small quantities, at least at first, we do not envision any sort of price discounting to encourage larger purchases. Finally, we wish to service students frequently, with a changing variety of ordered goods on each purchase occasion.

Advertising and Promotion - Our marketing research indicated that students welcomed the possibility of an online promotion of our service. They indicated that both e-mail or Web site publicity was acceptable, and we would supplement those activities with a more traditional means, such as flyers and posters posted up on college campuses. These posters and flyers would both raise awareness for our company and our service and offer an initial glimpse of the sorts of products we will offer.

The main cataloging function will be handled in a few ways. Firstly, in keeping with the electronic nature of this business, we will make an online catalog that can be browsed via the World Wide Web. Students will be able to select certain categories (such as paper supplies), and will then enter subcategories, and finally browse individual products with the option to either place an item in a virtual "shopping basket" and later on a printable order form/order record.

We will also offer a downloadable (PDF-format) version of our entire product catalog on our Web site, so students can either browse it offline or print it for themselves. With this, we will ask students for their e-mail addresses, so that we can send them periodic e-mail with new items and alert them to download a new version of the catalog. As an alternative, we will offer students a printed version of the catalog for a nominal fee to cover our internal printing costs.

We will provide a means for "security" to assure that only college students view our site, so that we do not risk getting orders from nonstudents who we cannot profitably serve due to distribution and delivery logistics. Though we will initially target our efforts to a limited number of university communities, we will allow our Web site to operate in an information-gathering capacity to help identify additional strong prospective markets. An example might be a smaller liberal-arts college, such as St. John Fisher College in Rochester, New York.

Concerning promotional vehicles, we envision the following, which are primarily awareness-building and public relations vehicles:

- Word of mouth—this may be the most critical component.
- Visibility of our delivery vehicles and personnel on-campuses.
- Placement on university computing public-domain areas, with an icon on computer desktops that brings students to our company's Web site and catalog.
- We would offer, in exchange for placements on-campus, a "donation" to the participating universities for computer upgrades in a dollar amount which is a percentage (say one percent) of that university's student orders.
- A yearly, company-sponsored scholarship for students.
- Sponsorships and/or advertising at university sporting events or social events.
- A discount to student "volunteers" who would distribute our flyers or catalogs to other students.
- "Frequent buyer points"—In this scheme, consumer purchases would be aggregated over a period, say two semesters. If the purchases exceeded a predefined threshold, the student would be awarded a voucher for perhaps $20 of purchases.
- Ad placement in campus student newspapers.

Distribution - As mentioned above, students could browse through a catalog of products either online through our Web site, offline, in a downloaded format, or in a hard copy. With regards to ordering, we would offer the following options:

- Submit an order online, through our Web site.
- Submit an order via e-mail.
- Submit an order over the phone.

With regard to payment, our market research indicated a strong resistance to transmitting credit card information electronically for fear of fraud, even though this is the quickest method. As a result, we would offer the following methods for payment:

- Pay by credit card through our secured Web site, at the time of ordering.
- Call our company to give a credit card number after having placed an order either electronically or over the phone.

Please note that our delivery component focuses on local delivery, rather than long distance delivery. The center of operation would be located in Rochester within reasonable distance of major shopping centers and sources of supplies, and within one hour's drive of the college campuses served. It is intended to provide daily delivery service to each campus at scheduled times in the late afternoon and early evening. We discuss the delivery details in the operations section of the business plan.

Competitive Analysis

Competitive Advantage

With minimal investment and large distribution opportunities, there are often few barriers to e-commerce competition. Priceline.com has revamped this theory by patenting their software, which is intricately intertwined with their business design. No longer do companies need to distinguish company technology from business design for patents. *Easy Shopper* will use this new business development to patent our retailing and student-centered design. While barriers to entry are low for our business concept, patents provide a protected barrier. In the worst case scenario, we will be able to collect licensing fees from our competitors.

In addition, we will offer premium service to maintain a competitive advantage. This will rest upon our ability to offer a wide variety of products coupled with reliable delivery to a highly-focused market. Cost advantages include our plan not to hold inventory and the bonus flexibility designed into our organizational architecture. Finally, compared to free-standing stores, we can convey our product line to customers with computer technology relatively easily.

Identification of competing companies

We face competition from the following sources, in the Rochester, New York U of R market:

Food and groceries:
- On-campus convenience stores (Corner Store).
- On-campus dining centers (Douglass Dining Center, or even Blimpie Subs).
- Off-campus convenience stores (7-Eleven).
- Off-campus grocery stores (Wegman's, Tops).
- Off-campus mass discounters (Wal-Mart).

Paper supplies:
- On-campus bookstore.
- Off-campus mass discounters.
- Off-campus office supplies stores.

Though competition for sales from all of these sources will always be present, we consider that our company offers a unique means for providing a broad selection of products to students at reasonable prices and with unbeatable spatial convenience. Currently none of the competitors listed above offers a similar service. On-campus competitors offer relative spatial convenience in exchange for high prices, and off-campus competitors offer lower price at the cost of spatial convenience.

Size, trends, and shares of market of each competitor

Mass discounters are well-established, as are grocery stores. On-campus offerings are also well established, but are currently the only options for residential students without cars (or without friends with cars). Given their target markets and current sales, grocery stores and mass discounters will not view our company as a threat, and we expect no reaction from them. Residential college students make up a relatively small component of those competitors' total sales. The campus stores and bookstores may however have a more pronounced reaction, which could range from lowering prices, to more determined retaliations.

Our strategy is to price toward the higher of these two groups of competitors, such as the campus corner stores, and to offer a service which neither group currently does and which both would seemingly find unprofitable given their current markets.

Customers' perceptions of competitors

From our market research, students find the on-campus offerings to be generally overpriced, offering very limited selection and variety, and students tend to shop there only out of necessity. Students find off-campus offerings to have better selection and better prices, but they also involve time and transportation costs in getting to those stores.

Comparison of competitive features

We aim to offer delivery service with a wide variety of goods and prices comparable to on-campus stores.

These competitive features are summarized in the table below:

	Price	*Variety*	*Service*	*Proximity*
Easy Shopper	High	Wider	Delivery	Closest
On-campus	High	Limited	Self-service	Close
Grocery stores	Lower	Wide; includes perishables	Self-service	Far
Mass discounter	Lowest	Widest	Self-service	Far
Office superstores	Lowest	Widest	Self-service	Far

Easy Shopper Strengths and Weaknesses

Based on the above competitor analysis, we conclude that Easy Shopper has the following SWOT analysis.

Strengths:
- We can provide a currently unserved target market with products they seek but cannot buy, because of lack of time or lack of transportation.
- Given our relative youth, we are sensitive to the concerns and needs of students, and can better serve them.
- We are starting fresh, and can tailor a system to specifically and efficiently meet the needs of our customers, rather than having to adapt a system used for different channels to this particular market.
- The prevalence of Internet shopping and e-commerce is in a rapid growth phase.
- Virtually all college students have access to computers that access the Internet.

Weaknesses:
- Our business idea is as yet untested.
- We are dependent on college students for business, which can be a fickle market.

- We face the inherent seasonality of the academic calendar.
- We may face challenges to avoid incurring costs in the warehousing function.

Opportunities:
- As mentioned above, we have the opportunity to serve students who live off-campus, but who may not have cars of their own, and do not have the time to get out to larger stores for groceries or other supplies. The issue to consider is the added distribution (delivery) costs.
- We also have the opportunity to gain greater sales and/or a larger market through the inclusion of refrigerated goods in our product mix. However, we have to balance the cost of adding refrigerated storage in every step of our process.
- We have the opportunity to enlarge the delivery trucks to be more of a "travelling storefront" than is currently contemplated. This may result in larger spontaneous sales; however, issues are raised with regard to drivers handling cash and transactions, and drivers' time being split between handling walk-up purchases and giving students their orders made in advance.

Threats:
- Seasonality. The greatest issue we face is the seasonal schedule of colleges. That is, the majority of students are in session only from September to June (or an academic calendar very close to these dates). As a result, our sales would fall dramatically during those interim summer months, and we would need to either pursue other customers during that time, or greatly contain our costs.
- The next issue is that our company's service could be easily copied by a local grocer such as Wegman's, or a national mass discounter such as Wal-Mart. Our suspicion is that these firms consider residential student populations to be too small a target market to bother with; we would have to hope they would continue to feel that way. Our patents will help serve as additional incentive to stay away from our business design.
- Delivering directly to student rooms may be difficult for security reasons and might turn into a logistical nightmare, as we become dependent on students to come to our drivers to claim their orders. If a student misses his order pickup, timely follow-up could be costly.

Business and economic conditions

Since the goods we plan to sell are staple products to a stable market, i.e., university students in residence, our services are considered relatively insulated from economic cycles.

Social factors - Many people enjoy the "fun" of grocery shopping or shopping at other larger stores, as they can browse through many products and compare items side-by-side. Among students, there seems to be a resistance to providing credit card information online, but we can circumvent this shortcoming by offering an alternative means for transmitting such information to us, i.e., over the phone, and by publicizing a secured Web site.

The limited-time and lack-of-transportation issues are the greatest obstacles to being able to shop as a recreational activity. However, the need for daily necessities does not diminish in the face of time constraints. Therefore we will position our company as being able to provide a shopping and browsing experience in real time, that can be done in the comfort (or convenience) of one's dorm or computer center, and that will bring needed products directly to the students.

Legal constraints - We may face problems with reselling the goods, especially if we buy from Wal-Mart or BJ's, to the extent their products available for sale are labeled as not being for resale.

Key success factors - One of the key success factors for our company will be generating orders/sales. To accomplish this task, we must:
- Generate high levels of awareness as quickly as possible.
- Maintain a profitable margin.
- Deliver impeccable service.
- Provide hassle-free ordering and payment services.
- Keep it simple, especially for online browsing/ordering.

Organization

Business Form

Easy Shopper will be a corporation. Shareholders will then have limited personal liability from the business's debts and obligations (except those prohibited by statute such as payroll taxes). Limited personal liability is important for deliveries and the products sold in our business (the driver could get into an accident and subsequently launch a suit against *Easy Shopper* or a consumer could receive a faulty good). The corporation form will not provide any tax benefits to the shareholders (except that taxes can be deferred on capital stock appreciation). The limited liability and flexibility in capital structure offset the potential for double taxation on earnings and dividends, as well as the higher cost of maintaining a corporation. Finally, the ability to transfer shares of ownership with ease is also critical to the development of *Easy Shopper*.

Management

CEO/President: Holly Clark Blanchard - Ms. Blanchard joins the firm with several years of financial experience and a finely developed interest in technology. As a CPA, Ms. Blanchard has Big Five accounting experience where she explored the financial workings of multiple middle-market companies and Fortune 500 experience where she was able to participate in a critical business spin-off. More recently, Ms. Blanchard has invested in her technology knowledge and recently consulted for American Management Systems, Inc., one of the top twenty largest technology consulting firms. As an M.B.A. graduating this June, Ms. Blanchard is still close to the student community and will help provide close customer analysis. Finally, the Kauffman Center has recognized Ms. Blanchard as a potential up and coming entrepreneur with a recent award. Ms. Blanchard will work part-time at the company at this time.

Chief Financial Officer: Stephen Lai – Mr. Lai joins the firm with several years of financial experience. Mr. Lai is familiar with the equity markets and funding responsibilities. Graduating from the William E. Simon Graduate School of Business at the University of Rochester, Mr. Lai has studied and applied all of the latest financial techniques and market analysis. Since one of his previous experiences is with a brokerage house, Mr. Lai will be able to converse fluently with investor priorities. Mr. Lai will be working part-time at this time.

Chief Marketing Officer: Christopher Burns – Mr. Burns is a rising star coming straight out of the M.B.A. community at the Simon school. After completing his undergraduate degree, Mr. Burns progressed rapidly and directly to his M.B.A. Mr. Burns's marketing experience comes from Oldsmobile. During his tenure in brand management there, Mr. Burns learned new marketing methodologies, as well as applied research, to move continuously with customers. Mr. Burns will be responsible for all marketing plans and for spearheading new target markets based on his expert knowledge in marketing research. Another of Mr. Burns's great strengths is his closeness to the student customers since he has just spent six continuous years as one of the target market. Mr. Burns will be working part-time.

Chief Operations Officer: Robert Turner – Mr. Turner brings a wealth of technical business consulting, project management, and general management knowledge from which to run the daily operations. He has 16 years of experience in technological fields leveraging his bachelor's degree in electrical engineering. Mr. Turner is also graduating with an M.B.A. from the Simon School where he has pursued a general program while focusing in finance. He is familiar with the inner workings of e-commerce and has a finely tuned interest and skill base using the Internet. Mr. Turner will be the backbone of the business's operations. For this he will draw upon the wealth of his international and technological experience. In addition, Mr. Turner will be instrumental in assisting Mr. Burns to explore the urban target markets based on his previous experiences with this customer base.

Board of Directors - Easy Shopper will retain a board of directors comprising the following personnel

- Ms. Holly Blanchard.
- Mr. Robert Turner.
- A person having senior management experience in the operation of a large delivery business.
- A person having extensive senior management experience in the operation of a grocery business, in particular, evaluation of the product line.

Easy Shopper Organizational Chart

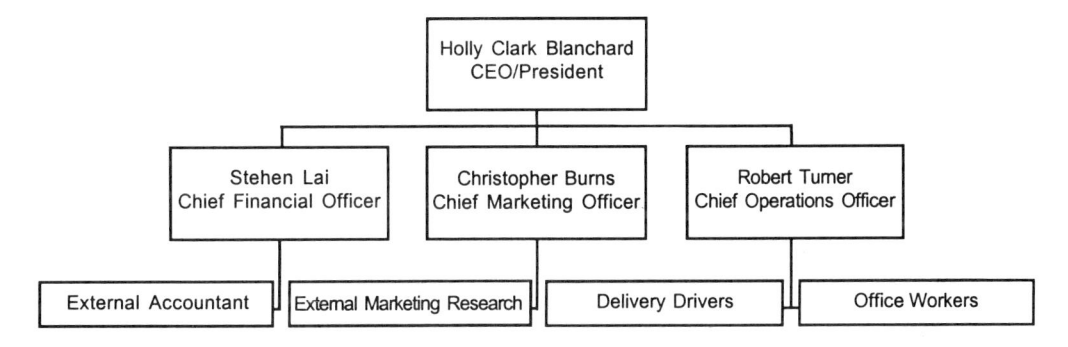

```
                    Holly Clark Blanchard
                       CEO/President
                             |
        ┌────────────────────┼────────────────────┐
    Stehen Lai        Christopher Burns       Robert Turner
Chief Financial Officer  Chief Marketing Officer  Chief Operations Officer
        |                    |                    |           |
External Accountant  External Marketing Research  Delivery Drivers  Office Workers
```

Organizational Architecture

Decision Rights - At the outset, *Easy Shopper* will run as a highly centralized company. The company's officers will jointly oversee the Web site development and product selection, with Mr. Turner having primary responsibility. We will not emphasize decentralization even in expansion as we can centrally manage *Easy Shopper's* Internet storefront effectively. Little specific knowledge beyond the market research that Mr. Burns will obtain will be necessary to expand *Easy Shopper's* target markets. Decision rights will be focused on each officer's expertise. Each officer will have two votes in their area of expertise.

Performance Measurement - Performance will be measured through business growth and profits. Officers will be evaluated on a firm-modified Economic Value Added (EVA®) approach called return on investor capital. Tracking all business decisions using return on investor capital, *Easy Shopper* will ensure that the company undertakes only profitable ventures. The nuances of accounting losses and reporting rules are not necessarily in line with long-term company growth or development; therefore, all business decisions will be based on investor capital return. Preliminary investor return on capital adjustments includes calculations to adjust for the cost of leasing and branding activities. For example, Web development is an expense according to generally accepted accounting principles; however, officers and employees will not face penalty in the first year for this multi-year investment. Therefore, return on investor capital is a better performance measurement since it reflects positive economic profits and does not encourage detrimental business decisions based merely on accounting figures. Finally, this performance measurement will communicate our financial expertise and commitment to our investors.

The officers will evaluate employees based on quality of service delivered. For example, drivers will be evaluated on percentages of repeat business and receive bonuses for repeat customers. All employees will also have quantitative and subjective goals that they agree to meet per quarter. Bonuses will be paid quarterly if employees meet these goals.

Incentive Structure - Incentives and performance bonuses will be a critical element to this business. First, for employees, *Easy Shopper* will pay wages higher than market wages to attract the best people with strong customer service aptitudes. Higher wages will attract driven and talented employees because we will attract a larger pool of workers to choose from. In addition, workers will be paid bonuses based on company performance. Large potential bonuses will provide incentives for employee creativity and perseverance. Employees will be empowered to make suggestions to improve business markets or operations. Hierarchy will not be stressed, but good ideas will be rewarded. The performance bonuses will help reward exceptional employees, while the stockholders also gain from these benefits as bonuses are funded through improved performance.

The four company officers will be the first company owners. Only common shares will be issued at this time. The officers will have equal shares of *Easy Shopper*. In addition, the officers will be paid a bonus collectively equal to 35 percent of EVA® for each year once the company starts to break even. The balance of earnings will be invested back into the company. This organization's strength will be that the management team has significant ownership and will act in the best interest of the company. As funding is needed, the officers are prepared to give up significant shares of the business to finance its growth. After common shares are exchanged to other parties, ownership will remain equal among the officers. An equal share in the business will ensure that the officers facilitate teamwork and work toward the best actions for growth.

Employee Promotion and Development - As *Easy Shopper* grows, the number of employees will also increase. The company will strive, however, to stay "lean, mean and nimble." These attributes are necessary for our small company to compete with giant, well-funded competitors. As growth permits, technical employees will be added to enhance and further develop our E-commerce site. Drivers and clerks will also be needed to ensure proper ordering, delivery, and payment processing. Technology will be used to enhance the ability of these employees to produce superior outputs. For example, *Easy Shopper* will have automated financial statements that integrate with the ordering and payable systems. Employees will be promoted at their own rate. Only officers will manage other employees; however, employees will be promoted in duties and title. For example, drivers will move up in pay scale as they earn the following titles: assistant, associate, and driver expert. Employees will be encouraged to seek out the officers for additional training needs and business knowledge.

Operations and Logistics

Easy Shopper's operations begin with the ordering process whereby customers will place their orders via the Internet. The orders will then reside in a database such that they can be aggregated and then sorted to facilitate purchasing. Data entry by *Easy Shopper* will be minimal because the customers will typically undertake this task. Upon completion of purchasing, the goods will then be sorted and packaged according to required delivery location and receiving customer. Finally, orders will be delivered to our customers during a prescribed time window late in the day to minimize conflict with students' class times.

Ordering

Customers will be allowed to place their orders via the Internet, e-mail, telephone, and facsimile. Customers placing orders via the Internet will begin the order process at the *Easy Shopper* Web site's homepage. Here, existing customers will choose to log into the site to commence ordering, while new customers will set up an 'account' with particulars including name, address, telephone, and customer profile. Once the profile has been completed, these customers will be granted a log in name and asked to provide their own unique password for subsequent identification and order confirmation.

We envision the ordering process to be similar to Amazon.com's, where customers use a "shopping basket" to collect their choices prior to order confirmation and payment options. Customers will make selections from a variety of menus itemizing goods in the various categories being offered, such as snack foods, beverages, and personal hygiene. These menus will be based on general trends of customer preferences, their associated ease of delivery, and trends of profitability observed over the course of providing the service.

To ease the ordering process, catalogs may be downloaded from our Web site so customers may more easily identify items they are looking for, or so previous orders can be retrieved to identify routine purchases. Suggestion forms will be provided so customers may request that certain items be added to the catalogs or make requests for special delivery. Special delivery requests will be subject to a review of pricing and feasibility of service before confirmation.

Once the selection process is complete, our customers will submit their orders for verification, and the Web site will automatically respond with a list of the respective items and prices and delivery date. If the customer is not satisfied with the selections made, he or she may return to the selection process, or if satisfied, he or she may proceed to confirm the order and payment. At this stage, our customers will submit credit card information for payment. We intend to handle all payments at the ordering stage to minimize accounts receivable and bad debts. Once the confirmation process and payment processes are completed, the customer will be presented with an acknowledgement form listing the items ordered and payment status.

Purchasing

Customers' orders that are received prior to office opening will be aggregated via the computer database and then sorted by school (region), residence, and customer. Operations personnel will then pick up ordering lists in the morning and proceed to purchase the goods at selected stores such as Wal-Mart, BJ's, or Top's. Operations personnel will work in teams during the purchasing operation to realize any economies and efficiencies of teamwork. After completion of the purchasing exercise we expect that some degree of sorting will be required to assemble the individual delivery packages.

Inventory Management

We intend that all purchases will be delivered to customers on the day of purchase. Therefore, *Easy Shopper* will not maintain inventory. Space will be reserved at the office site to facilitate any sorting operations required after purchasing. To minimize the logistical problems, we will choose a location for the *Easy Shopper* offices near the epicenter and in close proximity to the major suppliers from which *Easy Shopper* will purchase its supplies.

Sorting

Through use of the analytical tools available in the database package forming the "back-end" of the *Easy Shopper* Web site, we expect that lists can be developed such that the actual goods comprising individual orders can be sorted to some extent during the actual purchasing operation. However, given the overall variances among the orders we do not expect it to be feasible to complete the entire sorting process during the purchasing operation. Therefore, some sorting will be required at the office to finalize the delivery packages and ensure orders are packaged according to customer and residence location. This activity will occur upon completion of the purchasing operation and prior to actual delivery.

The reliability of the sorting process is key to ensuring final customer satisfaction. Accordingly, the design of appropriate incentive compensation will be critical to ensure delivery and that purchasing personnel avoid any mix-ups of individual orders during the sorting process. Administrative personnel will be involved to provide independent and ad-hoc checks of orders to ensure a minimum statistical level of conformance. Once this is completed Operations personnel will proceed to deliver the goods to customers.

Delivery

Information from the University of Rochester indicates that delivery directly to students living in campus residences is difficult due to security constraints. Therefore, delivery of goods will occur by having the delivery vehicles park in front of residences at scheduled times of day within a period referred to as the delivery window. Delivery of goods to a particular campus is planned to be daily and delivery personnel will be equipped with cellular phones to allow them to be in contact with customers to advise delivery status or revisions to the schedule if need be.

We will schedule the delivery window for late afternoons to early evenings to maximize the likelihood of students not being in class. Thus, the delivery period should nominally be longer than the duration of one class period (approximately 90 minutes) plus time before and after to allow reasonable access to the delivery vehicles. Since there are typically several residences (approx. five to 10) within a campus area, a delivery schedule that allows approximately five to 10 minutes at each site, twice within the delivery window, should be sufficient to ensure reasonable access to goods. Customers will be appraised of the delivery schedule at their residence upon confirming their order at the Internet site.

Reliability of the delivery schedules is considered key to achieving customer satisfaction. Accordingly, the design of appropriate incentive compensation will be critical to ensure delivery personnel provide a reliable delivery service. Delivery personnel will be not expected to handle payments (cash or credit card) since it is intended that all payments be handled upon ordering. Delivery personnel will be rotated among the target schools to ensure travel time is balanced.

Exit Strategies

Easy Shopper will seek a partnership with a major retail supplier, such as Wal-Mart. This partnership will enable low-cost supplies for the business, and Wal-Mart could in turn fund this experiment in e-commerce with little risk and investment. Wal-Mart could be charged consulting fees throughout the development process, or the officers are willing to give Wal-Mart a sixty percent share of ownership. To exit, the owners could sell out to the retailing partner or sell the business design to another competitor. Other interested buyers may include high-tech consulting companies looking to experiment with e-commerce. For example, a recent precedent is the joint venture between Bank of Montreal and American Management Systems, Inc. designed to fund banking e-commerce.

Funding Needs

After carefully analyzing *Easy Shopper's* cash flows for five years, we found that the minimum initial business investment is about $130,000. To compensate for any unforeseeable or hidden costs, we conservatively added another 70 percent to the capital requirement. Thus, *Easy Shopper* will need $220,000 to start the business.

Of the $220,000 capital required, $100,000 will be evenly contributed by the four co-founders. This will prove to potential investors that the entrepreneurs are committed to the company. The rest of the capital requirement, $120,000, will be raised through private wealthy investors, "angels." The minimum investment size from private investors should be at least $20,000 because *Easy Shopper* prefers to have fewer shareholders in the beginning stages of the company.

Another alternative for the $120,000 funding will be venture capitalists. There might be a challenge to obtain funds from venture capitalists since the founders do not have any prior experience starting a business. Also, the return on investment will not reach 25 percent until 2001. However, smaller venture capitalists might look favorably on *Easy Shopper* because the company has a high probability of achieving break-even during the first half of 2000. Moreover, *Easy Shopper* should be able to achieve over $2 million in revenue during the first year of operation. Finally, *Easy Shopper* will not raise funds through the capital market since it does not have enough annual revenue to qualify for listing on the stock exchanges.

Financial Plan

Financial Highlights

Using e-commerce to reach student populations in the Rochester area is financially viable. Cash flows to cover the initial investment will be earned in 2000 (the second year of operations). Cumulative cash flow thrown off by the business will be $484,535 after five years of operation. We estimate earning net profits beginning in 1999 and continuing into the foreseeable future. *Easy Shopper* will achieve break-even in the first half of year 2000. The break-even point will be reached at approximately the $3 million revenue level. This assumes that gross profit margins will stay at 20 percent.

The following table provides financial and ratio highlights:

Financial Data Equity Flows	Return on Flows	Cumulative Cash	Net Cash	Asset Turnover (000s)	Net Sales
1999	-.43%	$91,942	$91,942	15.67	$2,216
2001	31%	$219,281	$94,598	16.08	$3,887
2003	30%	$484,536	$154,249	10.97	$5,317

Complete *pro forma* financial statements for Year 1 are presented in Appendices 1-3. Sensitivity analysis on critical assumptions is also demonstrated in the following Sensitivity Analysis section.

Sensitivity Analysis

There are four main drivers for cash flows and profitability. These include demand, gross margins, advertising revenues, and frequency of deliveries. The following analysis discusses what happens to cash flows and profitability if different scenarios surrounding these factors occur.

Demand - On the one hand, demand can increase slower than we have forecasted in the *pro forma* financial statements. Slower demand forecasts are shown in the table below for when demand only increases to the average potential of $3.9 million as discussed in the Market Analysis Section, and then steadies at this number (never to reach the upper potential of $5.3 million). On the other hand, demand can increase significantly faster than is estimated in the formal *pro forma* financial statements for *Easy Shopper*. Results are also shown in the table on the next page.

The effects due to different demand rate of changes are as follows:

Option	Cumulative Cash Flows (excluding financing)	Total Sales (in 000s)	Return on Equity for 2003	Asset Turnover
Original Projections	$264,535	$19,334	30%	10.97
Slower Demand Increases	$107,331	$17,158	12%	11.81
Faster Demand Increases	$2,144,953	$74,906	61%	16.35

Gross Margins - *Easy Shopper* financial statements are also driven by gross margins. We expect to achieve twenty percent gross margins based on two critical assumptions. First, the margin difference between the University of Rochester corner store and the local Wegmans is fifteen to twenty-three percent. As discussed in the Marketing Plan, *Easy Shopper* will be priced between these two entities. Furthermore, *Easy Shopper* purchases will be made according to lowest available prices (which are not necessarily at Wegmans) which will lower our cost structure from Wegmans' retail prices. While *Easy Shopper* does not expect eroded gross margins, the following analysis assumes that gross margins decrease to fifteen percent. If margins decrease, the following significant changes occur in the forecasted *pro forma* statements:

- Capital need increases to approximately $436,000, a significant increase over twenty percent margins.
- Net cash flow decreases so significantly that *Easy Shopper* does not turn positive cash flows in the first five years.
- Cash and retained earnings both decrease sharply in the balance sheets.
- There are no profits under this scenario.

Significant financial highlights for this scenario are shown below, as benchmarked against the *Easy Shopper pro forma* statements. For detailed financial statements, see Appendix 3. Due to the severity of this scenario, other strategies besides our original assumptions would need to be deployed. Potential options include reducing delivery frequency and/or entering strategic partnerships to ensure a lower cost structure.

Option	Cumulative Cash Flows (excluding financing)	Total Sales (in 000s)	Return on Equity for 2003	Asset Turnover
Original Projections	$264,535	$19,334	30%	10.97
15 percent Gross Margins	-$502,606	$19,334	5%	-18.82

Cumulative cash flows for this scenario are shown in the following graph:

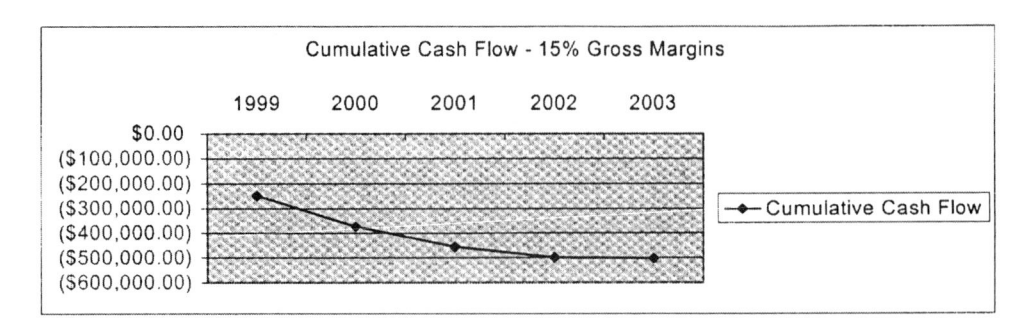

Cumulative Cash Flow - 15% Gross Margins

Advertising Revenues - Many e-commerce businesses make significant revenues through advertising revenues. In addition, wholesale providers pay retailers (such as Wal-Mart and Wegmans) shelf space to display their product. Advertising revenue is not included in the original *Easy Shopper* projections because amounts and probability to obtain sponsors were both difficult to predict. The following scenario assumes that advertising revenues could be gained that are equal to five percent of sales. This yields the following changes to the financial statements:

- Capital needed decreases drastically to only $55,000.
- Net cash flow increases significantly, and *Easy Shopper* turns positive cash flow by 2000.
- Both cash and retained earnings increase in the balance sheets.
- Profits are earned every year.

Significant financial highlights for this scenario are shown below, as benchmarked against the *Easy Shopper pro forma* statements. For detailed financial statements, see Appendix 3.

Option	Cumulative Cash Flows (excluding financing)	Total Sales (in 000s)	Return on Equity for 2003	Asset Turnover
Original Projections	$264,535	$19,334	30%	10.97
5% Ad Revenues	$815,557	$19,334	29%	5.13

Cumulative cash flows for this scenario are shown in the following graph:

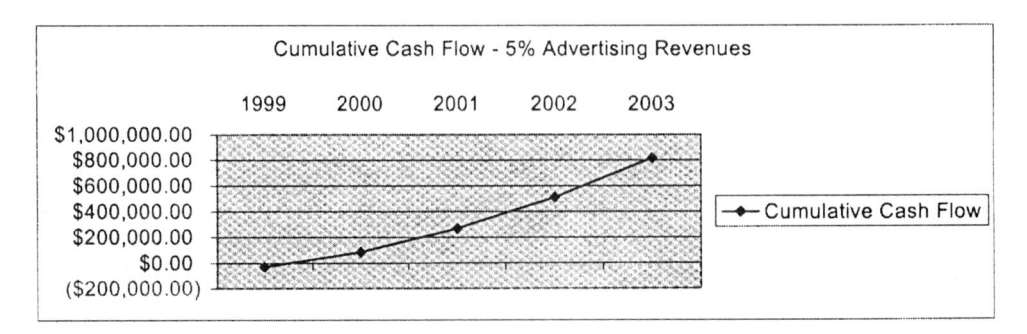

Cumulative Cash Flow - 5% Advertising Revenues

Sample Business Plan: Easy Shopper

Reduced Delivery Frequency – Demand or market experience may show that delivery frequency can be reduced. The number of drivers and trucks would be halved in this scenario. These changes yield the following changes to the financial statements:
- Capital needed would decrease to $26,744.
- Net cash flow increases significantly, and is only negative in 1999.
- The cash and retained earnings balances both increase in the balance sheets.
- This scenario earns profits every year.

Significant financial highlights for this scenario are shown below, as benchmarked against the *Easy Shopper pro forma* statements. For detailed financial statements, see Appendix 3.

Option	Cumulative Cash Flows (excluding financing)	Total Sales (in 000s)	Return on Equity for 2003	Asset Turnover
Original Projections	$264,535	$19,334	30%	10.97
Reduced Delivery Frequency	$660,100	$19,334	26%	6.04

Cumulative cash flows for this scenario are shown in the following graph:

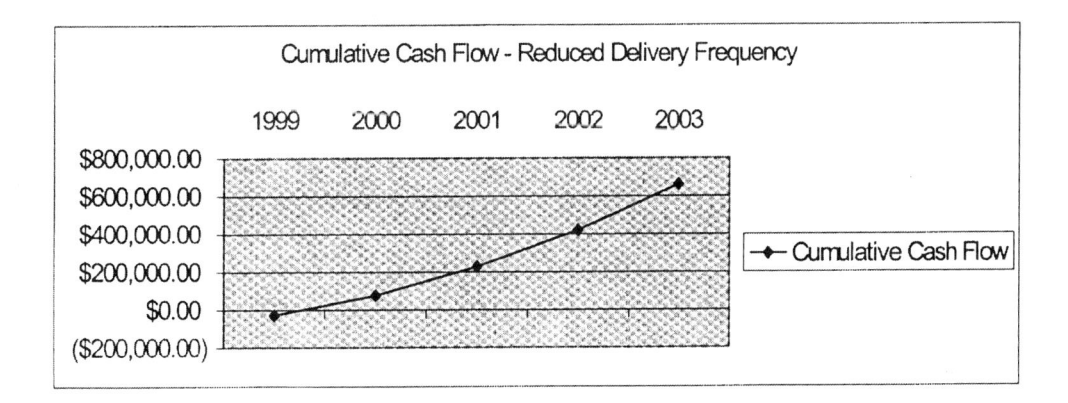

Appendix 1: *Pro forma* Cash Flows Year 1

Easy Shopper
1999 Cash Flow
(Figures in Thousands)

	Jan-99	Feb-99	Mar-99	Apr-99	May-99	Jun-99	Jul-99	Aug-99	Sep-99	Oct-99	Nov-99	Dec-99
Receipts												
Net Product Sales	$0	$101	$201	$326	$326	$137	$97	$97	$326	$326	$326	$157
Equity Financing	$220	$0	$0	$0	$0	$0	$0	$0	$0	$0	$0	$0
Cash Inflow	$220	$101	$201	$326	$326	$137	$97	$97	$326	$326	$326	$157
Expenditures (All Cash)												
Purchased Goods	$0	$80	$160	$260	$260	$109	$77	$77	$260	$260	$260	$125
Fulfillment operations	$26	$26	$26	$26	$26	$8	$4	$4	$26	$26	$26	$9
General and administrative	$23	$23	$23	$23	$23	$23	$23	$23	$23	$23	$23	$23
Marketing and selling	$2	$2	$2	$2	$2	$0	$0	$0	$2	$2	$2	$1
System development and maintenance	$83	$1	$1	$1	$1	$1	$1	$1	$1	$1	$1	$1
Taxes	$0	$0	$0	$0	$0	$0	$0	$0	$0	$0	$0	$0
Cash Outflow	$134	$132	$212	$312	$312	$141	$105	$105	$312	$312	$312	$159
Net Cash Flow	$86	-$31	-$11	$14	$14	-$4	-$8	-$8	$14	$14	$14	-$2
Cumulative Cash Flow	$86	$55	$44	$58	$72	$68	$60	$52	$66	$80	$94	$92

Appendix 2: Pro forma Income Statement Year 1

Easy Shopper
1999 Income Statement
(Figures in Thousands)

	First Quarter	Second Quarter	Third Quarter	Fourth Quarter
Revenues:				
Net product sales	201	137	326	157
Total revenues	201	137	326	157
Costs and expenses:				
Cost of goods sold	160	109	260	125
Fulfillment operations	26	8	26	9
General and administrative	23	23	23	23
Marketing and selling	2	0	2	1
System development and maintenance	1	1	1	1
Depreciation and amortization	2	2	2	2
Total costs and expenses	214	143	314	161
Operating Income	-13	-6	12	-4
Estimated Taxes (43%)	0	0	0	0
Net Profit	-13	-6	12	-4

Appendix 3: *Pro forma* Balance Sheet Year 1

Easy Shopper
1999 Balance Sheet
(Figures in Thousands)

Assets	First Quarter	Second Quarter	Third Quarter	Fourth Quarter
Current assets:				
Cash and cash equivalents	$44	$68	$66	$92
Receivables	$0	$0	$0	$0
Other current assets	$0	$0	$0	$0
Total current assets	$44	$68	$66	$92
Property and equipment:				
Computer equipment and software	$83	$83	$83	$83
Accumulated depreciation	$5	$10	$15	$20
Net property and equipment	$78	$73	$68	$63
Total assets	**$122**	**$141**	**$134**	**$154**

Liabilities and Stockholders' Equity Current Liabilities

	First Quarter	Second Quarter	Third Quarter	Fourth Quarter
Liabilities:				
Accounts payable	$0	$0	$0	$0
Accrued compensation	$0	$0	$0	$0
Other accrued liabilities	$0	$0	$0	$0
Total liabilities	$0	$0	$0	$0
Owners' equity:				
Retained Earnings	($98)	($79)	($86)	($66)
Common Stock at par value(200,000 shares @ $0.01)	$2	$2	$2	$2
Paid-in capital	$218	$218	$218	$218
Total Owners' equity	$122	$141	$134	$154
Total liabilities and stockholders' equity	**$122**	**$141**	**$134**	**$154**

About the Author

Bill Stolze is a graduate of Polytechnic University of New York, MIT, and Rochester Institute of Technology, with degrees in Electrical Engineering, Industrial Management, and Professional Photography. He began his career as a design engineer at RCA Laboratories. Following this he was an engineering manager and marketing manager with the Electronics Division of General Dynamics.

In 1961, with three associates, he founded RF Communications. In eight years as an independent company, RF became a world leader in long-range radio communications. When it merged with Harris Corp in 1969, RF had about 800 employees, had sold equipment in more than 100 countries, and was listed on the American Stock Exchange. As an independent company RF had only one loss quarter—its first quarter in business.

After spending 10 years with Harris as vice president and group executive, he launched a private consulting practice. He has been an investor, advisor, and consultant to numerous new ventures and is the founder of the Rochester Venture Capital Group.

For about ten years, he taught entrepreneurship and new venture management in the M.B.A. Programs at the University of Rochester and RIT. Bill is also the author of *Start Up Finance, An Entrepreneur's Guide To Financing A New or Growing Business*.

His awards include: the RCA Laboratories Research Award "for the development and presentation of television receiver circuitry widely used by the industry," the Rochester Small Business Council's "Small Businessperson of the Year," the Rochester Engineering Society's "Engineer of the Year Award," the Rochester Chamber of Commerce's "Civic Award For High Technology," the "1995 Entrepreneur of the Year Award in Upstate New York" in the category of "Supporter of Entrepreneurs" (in a program sponsored by Ernst & Young, Merrill Lynch and *Inc.* magazine), and Distinguished Alumnus and Fellow of the Institute of Polytechnic University of New York.

Stolze is married, has six children and eight grand children. His hobbies include reading, sailing, photography, and playing with his grandchildren. As he gets older, he is inclined to reverse this order.

Index

A

Acquisitions
  benefits, 166
  difficulties, 167-168
  Gannett's philosophy of, 169-171
  seller's role in, 170-171
Active reasons, 17-18
Amazon.com, 127
America Online (AOL), 76
Apple Computer, 45, 55, 59-60, 63, 116, 160, 200
Ash, Mary Kay, 187
AT&T, 44
Atari, 60
Autodesk, Inc., 200

B

Bankers
  benefits of, 32-33
  problems with, 33-34
  working with, 142, 144-145
Bushnell, Nolan, 60
Business plan(s),
  examples of, 228-280
  financial plans key part of, 92
  how lenders review, 89
  outline of, 90-93
  using professional writer, 93-95
    benefits of, 94

Business, start-up
  as a team, 32-34
  decisions involved, 13-14
  franchises, 64-65
  how to and why, 15
  reasons to, 16-18
  reward and risk, 23-24
  strategies, 43-52
  timing, 30-31
  value of, 126-127

C

Calyx & Corolla, 72-73
Capital,
  insufficient, 217
  raising enough, 100-102
  raising too much, 101-102
  venture, 104
    funds, 103
Carlson, Nancy, 187
Cash flow,
  ensuring adequate, 100-102
  Homemaker's Theory of, 96-99
  loans to increase, 108-112
  projecting, 97-98
C-corporation, 84
Claiborne, Liz, 54
Coca-Cola, 37, 66
Compaq, 45, 55, 148

Computers, entrepreneurial uses of
  hardware, 223-224
  networks, 224
  software, 220-223
Copyrights, 162, 164

D

Death traps, entrepreneurial, 216-219
Digital Equipment Corp. (DEC), 45, 115
Direct mail,
  Direct Marking Association, 73
  examples, 72-73
  sales, 71-73
  using mailing lists, 72
Distinctive competence, theory of, 37-39
Domino's Pizza, 46

E

E-mail, 77, 224
  spamming, 77
Empire State Development Corporation, 140
Entrepreneur(s),
  "cashing chips," 202-204
  death traps of, 216-219
  educational level of, 22
  qualities of successful, 19-21
  retired, 27-29
  risk-taking, 21, 23-24, 26
  stepping aside, 200-201
  successful, 25
  what makes an, 19-22
Exit strategies, 202-204
Exley, Charles, 167-168
Exporting, 172-177

F

Fads,
  as opposed to trends, 59-61
  examples of, 60-61
Federal Express, 57-58, 73

Federal Trade Commission, 65
Financing,
  governmental, 137-141
  looking for, 103-107
  scams in, 107
  where to look for, 105-107
Firing,
  legal process, 150
  less painful, 150-151
Forbes magazine, 25
Forms of business organization, 83-85
Franchise(s),
  as a startup, 64
  multilevel marketing, 80-82
  selling through, 71

G

Gannett, 168, 169-171
Goal setting, 86-87
Going public, 132-136
Golisano, Tom, 46-47, 205-209, 210
Government funding, 137-141
  state programs, 140-141
  Web sites, 138-139

H

Hard work, 20
Help,
  books, tapes, and videos, 179
  business incubators, 180-181
  college courses, 179-180
  entrepreneurial magazines, 181
  for women, 188-189
  general business publications, 182
  Internet, the, 178-179
  networking, 182
  other entrepreneurs, 178
  professional associations for small
    businesses, 182-183
  Service Corps of Retired Executives
    (SCORE), 181
  Small Business Administration
    (SBA), 180

Index

small business councils, 181
small business seminars, 181
Small Business Development Centers (SBDCs), 180
venture capital clubs, 182
Hiring,
  contract employees, 149-150
  former employees, 148
  salary policy, 148-149
  unions, 149
Holiday Inn, 64, 81
Home offices, 187-188
Homemaker's Theory of Cash Flow, 96-99

I

In Search of Excellence, 225
Initial Public Offerings (IPOs), 103
Infomercials, 73
Innovation,
  additional help from, 131
  corporate, 123-125
    intrapreneurship, 124
    external ventures, 124-126
  informal, 117-120
  in operation, 44-47
  institutional, 120, 128-131
International market, 172-177
  Internet as, 60-61
  risks involved in, 175-177
Internet, 51, 76-79, 178-179, 224
  access to, 76-77
  e-mail, 77
  promoting business on, 78
  selling over, 78-79
  Web sites, 77-78, 138-139
Intuit, 48-49
Investors,
  taking on, 113
  importance of control with, 115-116
  venture, 119-127

J

Jobs, Steve, 200-201
Jolt Cola, 37-38, 119

K

Kinko's, Inc., 210-215
Kodak, 27, 38, 116, 119

L

Land's End, 72
Large firms,
  benefits of, 40
  financial resources, 40
Lawyers
  working with, 142, 145-146
Leadership, 20
Lillian Vernon, 73
Limited Liability Corporation (L.L.C.), 84-85
Joint venture, 85
Limited partnership, 84
Liquidity, achieving, 202-204
Loans,
  impotance of business plan in, 109-111

M

Mannix, Valerie, 190-195, 210
Marketing, same as selling, 68-69
Markets,
  Internet, 51
  niche, 49-50
  zig-zag, 62
Mary Kay Cosmetics, 80, 102, 187
McCorkindale, Douglas, 168, 169-171
Mentoring, 158-159
Mercury Print Productions, 190-195
Microlytics, 124-125
Motivation, 19-20

Multilevel marketing, 80
  criticism of, 81
National Technical Information System (NTIS), 137

N

NCR, 167-168
New York Business Development Corporation (NYBDC), 140
Nonconformity, 20

O

Operating "lean and mean," 160-161, 167
Orfalea, Paul, 210-215
Ormec Systems, 119

P

Partnership, 83-84
  problems in, 216-217
Patents, 162-164
Paychex, Inc., 46-47, 62-63, 205-209
Performance appraisals, 152-154
  forms, 155-157
Peter Principle, 35-36
Pizza Time Theater, 60
Pricing,
  for value, 66
  for benefits, 67
Product/Market Matrix, 53-55
Product/Market Zig-Zag, 62-63, 65
Professional associations for small businesses, 182-183
Public accountants, working with, 142-144
Publicity, 73-74

R

R&D Limited Partnerships, 117
Rapp, C.J., 119

Reasons
  active, 17-18
  importance of control, 115-116
  reactive, 16-17
  to start business, 16-18
Retirement, 27-29
Rewards and risks, 23-24
Rich, how to become, 25-26
Risk-taking, 21, 23-24, 26
  reduction in, 32-33

S

Safety First, Inc., 60
Sales,
  companies failing due to lack of, 75
  direct, 69
  direct mail, 71-73
  high-level, 69
  infomercials, 73
  Internet, 71, 78-79
  publicity, 73-74
  same as marketing, 68-69
  through advertising, 71
  through intermediaries, 69-70
  through resale, 70-71
Scully, John, 200
Securities and Exchange Commission (SEC), 118, 132, 134-135, 209
  Regulation SB, 135
Service Corps of Retired Executives (SCORE), 181
Setting goals, 86-87
Small Business Association (SBA), 77, 112, 120, 139-140, 180
  7(a) loan guarantee, 139-140
Small Business Development Centers (SBDCs), 180, 188
Small Business Innovation Research Program (SBIR), 138-139
Small Business Investment Companies (SBIC), 117

Small Business Technology Transfer Program (STTR), 139
Small companies
 strengths, 40-42
Small Company Offering Registration (SCOR), 135
Sole proprietorship, 83
Sony, 60
Southwest Airlines, 49-50
Start-up strategies, 43-52
 customer accommodation, 47
 market selection, 48-51
 operational innovation, 44-47
 selecting a product/service, 44
Staying private, 132-136
Stereotyping, 19
 gender, 21-22, 184-195
"Stolze's Law," 35-36
Street smarts, 20-21
Subchapter S corporation, 84
Successful entrepreneurs
 qualities of, 19-21
Supply-side Strategy, 56-58

T

Trade secrets, 162, 164-165
Trademarks, 162, 164
Trend(s), as opposed to fads, 59-61
Trivial Pursuit, 101
Turnaround management, 196-199

U

U.S. Postal Service, 57
Unions, problems with, 149

V

Venture capital funds, 103, 120

W

Walker, John, 200
Woman Entrepreneurs, 184-195

X

Xerox, 27-28, 38, 44, 56-57, 63, 124-125, 168